W9-COS-929

CAMBRIDGE GREEK AND LATIN CLASSICS

GENERAL EDITORS

E. J. KENNEY
Emeritus Kennedy Professor of Latin, University of Cambridge
AND
P. E. EASTERLING
Regius Professor of Greek, University of Cambridge

CICERO

SELECT LETTERS

EDITED BY

D. R. SHACKLETON BAILEY

*Emeritus Pope Professor of the Latin
Language and Literature Emeritus
Harvard University*

PUBLISHED BY THE PRESS SYNDICATE OF THE UNIVERSITY OF CAMBRIDGE
The Pitt Building, Trumpington Street, Cambridge, United Kingdom

CAMBRIDGE UNIVERSITY PRESS
The Edinburgh Building, Cambridge CB2 2RU, UK   http://www.cup.cam.ac.uk
40 West 20th Street, New York, NY 10011–4211, USA   http://www.cup.org
10 Stamford Road, Oakleigh, Melbourne 3166, Australia
Ruiz de Alarcón 13, 28014 Madrid, Spain

First published 1980
Reprinted 1990, 1992, 1995, 1998, 2000

Library of Congress Cataloguing in Publication Data
Cicero, Marcus Tullius.
Select letters.

(Cambridge Greek and Latin classics)

Bibliography p.
Includes indexes.

1. Cicero, Marcus Tullius - Correspondence.
2. Authors, Latin - Correspondence. I. Bailey, David Roy Shackleton.

PA6297.A23   1979   876'.01   78-67430

ISBN 0 521 22492 6 hardback
ISBN 0 521 29524 6 paperback

Transferred to digital printing 2002

CONTENTS

[v]

PREFACE

The letters in this selection have been chosen partly as revelatory of Cicero's personality or otherwise intrinsically interesting, partly to give an impression of the variety of the correspondence and to illustrate the main types of letter to be found in it. Though some of my choices are historically important, it has not been my aim to present a conspectus of historical source-material. I have judged it best to exclude (with one small exception) letters not written by Cicero, interesting and valuable though some of these are.

In conformity with the purposes of the series, its editors, Professor Kenney and Mrs Easterling, suggested numerous additions and amplifications in the original draft of my notes. Practically all these suggestions I have gratefully adopted.

June 1978   D.R.S.B.

BIBLIOGRAPHICAL NOTE

A full list of relevant publications might fill a volume larger than this. Here are a few noteworthy items.

Critical texts: (i) *Ad Atticum*: Oxford Classical Text ed. W. S. Watt (I–VIII, 1965) and D. R. Shackleton Bailey (IX–XVI, 1961). *Cicero's letters to Atticus* (with commentary and translation), ed. D. R. Shackleton Bailey (Cambridge Classical Texts and Commentaries, 7 vols., 1965–70). (ii) *Ad familiares*: ed. D. R. Shackleton Bailey (with commentary) in the same series (2 vols., 1977). The Oxford Text by L. C. Purser (1901) is poorly edited and of course far out of date. The editions of H. Sjögren (Teubner, 1925) and U. Moricca (Paravia, 1950) are preferable, but with many deficiencies. (iii) *Ad Quintum fratrem, Ad M. Brutum, Fragmenta*: Oxford Classical Text ed. W. S. Watt (1958).

Commentaries: See above. The commentary of Tyrrell and Purser (Dublin, 7 vols., 1904–33), containing the whole correspondence, is a work of very indifferent scholarship, now hopelessly antiquated. The earlier volumes of the unfinished Budé edition (1950) by L.-A. Constans have some good notes and introductions. On the historical side W. W. How's *Cicero, select letters* (Oxford, 1925, based on an earlier selection by A. Watson) was admirable in its day.

Translations: A translation of the entire correspondence by D. R. Shackleton Bailey (including the already published translation of the letters to Atticus) appeared in the Penguin Classics series in 1978. Of earlier English translations the least unsatisfactory is by E. S. Shuckburgh (London, 1899–1900).

Biographies: Three more in English have appeared in the current decade: D. Stockton, *Cicero: a political biography* (Oxford, 1971); D. R. Shackleton Bailey, *Cicero* (Classical life and letters series, London, 1971; based on the correspondence); E. Rawson, *Cicero: a portrait* (London, 1975). Gaston Boissier's *Cicéron et ses amis* (1865; Engl. tr. 1897) remains unsurpassed as a charming and sympathetic presentation.

Historical background: As a general survey, T. Rice Holmes, *The Roman Republic* (3 vols., 1923), can still be recommended, along with the relevant chapters of the *Cambridge ancient history* (vol. IX, Cambridge, 1932). Mommsen's *History of Rome*, being a work of genius, can never become obsolete and the same is true of R. Syme's *Roman revolution* (Oxford, 1939). A great deal in the history of this period is actively controversial, producing an unabated flow of books and articles. Anything by E. Badian and P. A. Brunt is sure to be of high scholarly quality; much of their output is addressed to specialists. Though sometimes tendentious in argument and not free from errors of detail E. S. Gruen's massive and challenging *Last generation of the Roman Republic* (Univ. of California Press, 1972) calls for mention even in so brief a list as this. For penetrating political analysis the work of Christian Meier, especially *Res publica amissa* (Wiesbaden, 1966) and *Caesars Bürgerkrieg* (1964; reprinted in *Entstehung des Begriffs Demokratie* (Frankfurt am Main, 1970)), stands alone. Unfortunately his difficult German has not yet been translated. J. Carcopino's venomous and totally untrustworthy *Secrets de la correspondance de Cicéron* (2 vols., 1947), translated into English almost as badly as it deserved in 1951, is noticed here only by way of warning.

INTRODUCTION

1. CICERO

Thanks to the survival of many of his private letters more is known of Cicero in later life than of any other personality in Greco-Roman antiquity. The same applies to the period which they cover, the last twenty years of the Roman republic. Conversely, much of Cicero's correspondence will not be properly understood without some knowledge of his personal life and its historical background. Innumerable accounts of both have been written in greater or less detail. Here they can be sketched only very briefly.

M. Tullius Cicero was a native of Arpinum (Arpino), an ancient Volscian township in the hills about seventy miles east of Rome, which had received Roman citizenship early in the second century.[1] His date of birth was 3 January 106. The family was old, wealthy, and locally prominent, with an estate near the town which Cicero inherited in due course. He was the eldest son. A second, Quintus, followed about two years later. There were no daughters. Not much is known of the parents. M. Cicero senior was something of an invalid with bookish tastes; references to him in his son's works are few and colourless, and there are none at all to his wife Helvia. But she is described elsewhere as well-born and well-behaved, and a random reminiscence in a letter of Q. Cicero presents her as a strict and careful housewife. When the future orator was about ten, the family residence was moved to Rome, where his father owned a house in a fashionable neighbourhood (Carinae). Like many leading members of the Italian communities (*domi nobiles*), the elder Cicero had friendly relations with Roman aristocrats. There was also a family link between the Ciceros and the great general C. Marius, for the Marii too came from Arpinum. The great Marius seems to have had little to do personally with these rather distant relatives, but his marriage connexions with members of the nobility may have been helpful. The orator L. Licinius Crassus, whose daughter had married the general's son, took a close interest in the two young Ciceros and their

---

[1] Dates are B.C. unless otherwise stated.

two cousins, the sons of his friend Aculeo, an eminent jurist. Crassus died when young M. Cicero was fifteen.

Naturally the boys were given the best possible schooling and Marcus was an outstanding student. Among his schoolfellows some will have borne historic names and played their part along with him in history to come. T. Pomponius (later Atticus), however, was, like Cicero, of merely equestrian family, though old and Roman. With him, his senior by three years, Cicero formed a friendship which lasted the rest of his life. Pomponius was also a close friend of Cicero's relative, the younger C. Marius, and of his future rival in oratory, Q. Hortensius.

The times were badly out of joint. The political institutions of the old Roman city-state were poorly adjusted to the government of a large empire. During nearly three decades prior to Cicero's birth, the Senate, the effective governing body, had been battered in political storms, its authority challenged by ambitious popular leaders. Marius' career ushered in a new epoch, in which the loyalty of Roman armies could centre on their commanders, and a successful general could coerce the home authorities. From 91 to 89 B.C. Italy was ravaged by the struggle between Rome and her revolted Italian allies, in which Cicero had his first taste of military service as a recruit of seventeen – not to be experienced again until nearly forty years later, when the chances of politics put him in command of an army in Asia Minor. The Social War was hardly won when the Consul, L. Cornelius Sulla, countered the manoeuvres of his political opponents by marching his army on Rome and putting their leaders to death or flight. But Sulla soon left for the East to fight the formidable King Mithridates of Pontus, and mice in Rome began to play. After much violence, power came into the hands of old Marius, back from refuge in Africa, and one of the Consuls of 87, L. Cornelius Cinna. The ensuing massacre of leading senators and friends of Sulla, some of them friends and patrons of Cicero, outdid anything of the kind previously seen in Rome. Marius soon died, but his associates remained in control for another five years.

Cicero always refers to this régime with contempt and aversion, notwithstanding his own family connexion with the Marii. Hortensius, only a few years his senior, was already making his reputation in the law-courts, but Cicero held back. He seems to have spent much time writing poetry, which in its day had a considerable vogue. Most of it has disappeared, and what is left is of little interest apart from advances in verse technique which may or may not be due to Cicero.

Sulla returned in 83 with a victorious army at his back. Once again fighting raged up and down the peninsula, Cicero taking no part, though his sympathies were on the winning side. A new Marian blood-bath in Rome carried off another patron, the great jurist and Pontifex Maximus, Q. Mucius Scaevola. Established as Dictator, Sulla wreaked a vengeance which was remembered with horror for centuries to come. But he re-established the Senate's control, and in the eyes of many people, Cicero included, 'restored the republic'.

Cicero now began to emerge as an advocate of exceptional talent. He made his name in 81, as defending counsel for a victim of one of the Dictator's minions, in the extant speech *Pro Roscio Amerino*. The victim had powerful friends among Sulla's supporters, and the Dictator does not seem to have taken offence. Cicero's departure from Rome in 79 for a three-year sojourn in Athens and the Greek East was probably due to health and other personal motives. He had previously married a rich and well-connected wife, Terentia. Their daughter Tullia may have been born soon afterwards. A son, another M. Cicero, came many years later.

On his return in 76 Cicero found a changed Rome. Sulla had withdrawn into voluntary retirement, soon followed by death, and the aristocratically orientated constitution was working fairly smoothly. Cicero resumed forensic practice, but also started to climb the political ladder. He was a 'new man', with no senators among his forbears, and of municipal origin, so that his enemies in Rome could call him a 'foreigner' (*peregrinus*). But he had money, connexions, and talent. Such a young man could reasonably hope to get as far as the praetorship, even under the post-Sullan régime. The consulship might seem out of reach, but Cicero's ambitious drive was equal to the attempt. He traversed the lower offices of Quaestor (service in Sicily), Plebeian Aedile, and Praetor without misadventure, holding each at the earliest legal age and scoring excellently at the polls. At the same time he overtook Hortensius as the foremost speaker of the day, a day when public speaking was a key to celebrity and political success, often editing and publishing his speeches soon after delivery (most of them forensic, but at least one political). His social gifts and his services in court, for which the law forbade him to take any monetary payment, brought him the friends his career needed. Roman candidates for political office did not require a party or a programme. Normally they simply offered themselves on the strength of past services to the community, their own or their ancestors'. Success, apart from actual bribery, which was not uncommon, would mainly depend on personal and hereditary influence (*gratia*). While he was on his way up the ladder, Cicero's political thought will have been focused on how to get to the top. As a 'new man' he had to face aristocratic prejudice, on which he made some bitter comments in his prosecution of Verres in 70. Subsequently, though, he took a more conciliatory line. Atticus, whose sister Pomponia had married Q. Cicero, had intimate friends among the nobility. In 64 he came back from Greece to Rome to assist in his friend's campaign for the consulship. Cicero was triumphantly elected. His two principal competitors were two noblemen of bad character. One of them was also elected, the other, Catiline (L. Sergius Catilina), looked dangerous to leading conservatives, and they preferred Cicero.

Catiline was to be responsible for Cicero's most spectacular success. After another rejection at the hustings, he and his associates, many of them like himself in desperate financial straits, plotted to take over Rome by a *coup de main*, to be combined with insurrections elsewhere. Cicero kept himself informed by spies. When the time was ripe, he denounced Catiline in the Senate and called on him to leave the city, which he did. Shortly afterwards, five of the leading conspirators were arrested on Cicero's instructions, with incriminating documents. After a contentious debate, the Senate decreed their execution, which was carried out under Cicero's orders (5 December 63). Catiline and his band of insurgents were destroyed in battle some months later.

Cicero could be relied upon to make the most of his achievement. But the marks of honour and massive demonstrations of gratitude which he received were no sham. Conservatives in the Senate and solid citizens in general (the 'optimates', the *boni*) fêted him as their rescuer from real peril. His prestige stood at a peak which it was not to regain until the end of his career twenty years later. On the other hand, Catilinarian sympathizers were numerous, and it was a bad sign that the executions were openly denounced as an unlawful exercise of arbitrary power by one of the new Tribunes, none other than Pompey's brother-in-law, Q. Metellus Nepos.

Pompey the Great (Cn. Pompeius Magnus), Rome's greatest living soldier until Caesar matched him, was born the same year as Cicero. After a series of military successes, first as Sulla's lieutenant, then against Marians and native insurrectionaries in Spain and a slave revolt in south Italy, he became Consul in 70 in contravention of legal rules as to preliminary offices, from which he was specially dispensed. In 67 a popular assembly gave him sweeping powers to cope with the intolerable nuisance of piracy in the Mediterranean: the nuisance was abated with swift efficiency. The following year he was appointed in the same manner and with Cicero's oratorical support to an overall command in the East, where Mithridates was still on the rampage. Four years brought total victory and an administrative reorganization of the whole area. At the end of 62 Pompey returned to Italy with his army, which to the Senate's relief and perhaps surprise he promptly disbanded.

The conservative leader M. Porcius Cato and his allies distrusted Pompey and resented his brilliantly unconventional career. Relieved from the threat of military force, they chose to block his reasonable demands: land-grants for his discharged soldiers and ratification of his dispositions in the East. In frustration Pompey turned to the popular leader C. Julius Caesar. Together with M. Licinius Crassus, an enormously wealthy nobleman with an independent following, they formed a coalition which dominated the political scene for years to come. It is often known as the First Triumvirate, though, unlike the Second Triumvirate in 43, it had no official status. Cicero was invited to join, but though he strongly disapproved of Cato's tactics, he refused.

Caesar was elected Consul for 59 and pushed through a legislative programme in defiance of constitutional obstruction by an ultra-conservative colleague. Pompey, of course, got what he wanted and Caesar got a five-year command in the two provinces of Gaul, one on each side of the Alps. For Cicero these developments spelled disaster. Two years previously he had made a dangerous enemy in P. Clodius Pulcher, a scion of one of Rome's greatest families who attained to political importance by unscrupulous demagogy and the organization of gangs to terrorize the streets and Forum. Since Cicero continued to reject overtures from Caesar, Clodius was enabled to become Tribune, an office for which as a patrician he was constitutionally ineligible, and in March 58, just before Caesar's departure for the north, he succeeded in driving Cicero out of Rome. Pompey, Cicero's supposed friend, had given his word that no harm would come to him, but at the crisis he refused to interfere, and his satellite, the Consul A. Gabinius, collaborated with Clodius. A formal banishment followed.

Unnerved and desperate, Cicero retired to Greece. Eighteen months later he was back again in triumph. Pompey had quarrelled with Clodius and engineered the recall. But Cicero's morale had received a shock from which it never quite recovered.

Caesar's command was renewed for another five years when Pompey and Crassus held the consulship together for the second time in 55. He used it to add the whole of modern France north of the old Roman province and modern Belgium to the empire. Rome during these years was often in turmoil. Street riots and clashes between Clodius' gangs and those of his no less redoubtable adversary Milo held up elections, so that three out of four consecutive years (55–52) started without curule magistrates. At the beginning of 52, however, Clodius was killed in a scuffle with Milo, and Pompey, created Sole Consul (an unprecedented title), restored order with a firm hand.

After his return in the autumn of 56 Cicero had hoped to play a significant role by exploiting differences which had arisen within the ruling coalition. But these were ironed out at the conference of Luca in 56, and Cicero received a sharp warning from Pompey to drop activities against Caesar's interests. He took it to heart, and in late May or June 56 delivered a speech in the Senate (*De provinciis consularibus*) containing a glowing panegyric of Caesar's victories. Writing to Atticus he called it his 'palinode'.[1] After that he lay low politically, devoting his energies to the courts, domestic and social life, and literature; two of his most important and original treatises, *De oratore* and *De re publica*, belong to this period. Some of his forensic clients were old enemies like Gabinius, whose cases he took under pressure from the 'Triumvirs', or at any rate from Pompey. In pursuance of this new course he established warmly amicable relations with Caesar, who appointed Quintus as one of his lieutenants in Gaul.

The later fifties produced a new configuration. Pompey's laurels

[1] See Letter 13.

were fading, and his partner's spectacular achievements inevitably made him jealous. Crassus might have constituted a buffer, but in 54 he went off to Syria to make war on the Parthians and perished the following year in one of the worst military disasters in Roman history. Also in 54 died Caesar's daughter and Pompey's much loved wife, Julia. Pompey's election as Sole Consul was the result of a rapprochement with Cato and his other old adversaries in the Senate, in which Caesar could not but see a threat to himself. Thus in 52–50 a new civil war was in the making.

Cicero does not seem to have been much involved in these developments. In 51 he reluctantly left to govern a province, having previously avoided such assignments. The province was Cilicia, then comprising the entire southern coast of Asia Minor and a large part of the interior. His term was limited to one year (not including the journeys) and, unlike most Roman governors, he was genuinely anxious not to have it extended. But he was at pains to earn the reputation of an upright and conscientious Proconsul, receiving a public testimonial to that effect from Cato, who took a special interest in promoting better administration in the provinces. With the assistance of his brother and other experienced officers he even gained some military successes against the refractory highlanders of Taurus and Amanus, which won him the title of Imperator from his troops and a Thanksgiving (*supplicatio*) from the Senate. But for the outbreak of war he would infallibly have been granted a Triumph in due course. But by the time he got back to Italy in November 50 the war clouds were thickly gathered. The matters ostensibly at issue, Caesar's right to stand for the consulship *in absentia* and the terminal date of his command, were of less importance than mutual distrust and confidence of victory on both sides. When Cicero arrived outside Rome at the beginning of the new year, he did everything in his power for peace, but on 11 January Caesar and his troops crossed the river Rubicon, the boundary of his province, to invade the homeland. A week later Pompey, the Consuls, and many others, including Cicero, fled from Rome.

By mid March the war in Italy was over. Part of the republican armies had been captured by Caesar, the rest crossed the Adriatic with Pompey, the Consuls, and a large part of the Senate. Cicero was not with them. He had spent the previous two months on his coastal estates south of Rome in a fever of indecision, whether to join Pompey if he evacuated Italy or to take no part on either side. But finally in June he too left for Greece with his brother and their sons, and by the beginning of 48 he was in Pompey's camp in Epirus. Apparently he was not offered any employment suitable to his rank and his principal contribution to the republican cause consisted in sarcastic comments on the army and leadership.

This phase came to an end with Caesar's victory at Pharsalia in August. Cicero had been absent from the battle through indisposition and promptly accepted its verdict. By November he was back in Italy by Caesar's invitation, conveyed in a letter from Cicero's son-in-law Dolabella, but this did not extend to his return to Rome. He therefore remained at Brundisium in poor health and distress of mind. Aggravating factors were fears lest the republicans, now staging a revival in Africa, might win after all and a bitter quarrel with his brother and nephew, who had remained in Greece. Meanwhile Caesar was held up in the East by problems in Egypt and Asia Minor. On his return to Italy in September 47 almost his first act was to meet Cicero and give him the permission he wanted in the most gracious fashion.

Once again in his house on the Palatine, which he had not seen for over four years, Cicero could resume his old life, with some major differences. Caesar did not enlist his services, as he did those of certain other prominent ex-republicans, and there was no scope for him in the Senate. His voice was no longer heard in the courts, for the *causes célèbres* with political overtones in which he had been accustomed to shine, trials for provincial misgovernment, lèse-majesté, electoral malpractice, or violence, belonged to the past. Domestic ties had snapped. The friendship with Atticus held firm, but the quarrel with Quintus was patched up only superficially. Relations with Terentia had been cool for a long while past, mainly as it seems because her husband believed she had been cheating him financially, and ended in divorce in 46. Cicero promptly remarried, choosing a young ward of his own with a large fortune, but a second divorce followed within a few months. Early in 45 he lost his idolized daughter – his son, a rather commonplace young man, meant comparatively little to him. To offset these curtailments there were society and literary work. Many of Caesar's principal followers were old friends of Cicero and glad to have him at their dinner-tables. And this was his most active period of authorship. Most of it was on philosophy, a subject to which he had given much study, at least in early life, and which gained a new meaning for him in these melancholy times. Original ideas he did not profess to have, but by making the crabbed and abstruse Greek of the Stoics and other Hellenistic schools available in elegantly written Latin adaptations he contributed something of permanent importance to the culture of western Europe.

Caesar meanwhile had had his work largely cut out suppressing resurgent republicans in Africa (47–46), and then in Spain (46–45), where they had combined with a mutinous army of his own. Six months after his final return to Rome he was assassinated by a band of conspirators led by two close friends of Cicero, M. Junius Brutus and C. Cassius Longinus, both ex-republicans whom he had pardoned and promoted. Cicero had not been admitted to the plot, but heartily rejoiced, notwithstanding Caesar's generous treatment of himself: as a despot Caesar had forfeited the right to live, and his régime had thrown Cicero's career into eclipse. But the results proved disappointing. Caesar's surviving colleague in the consulship, Mark Antony, soon showed unconstitutional tendencies as well as unexpected vigour and address. The 'liberators' were forced out of Rome by mob violence, and Cicero retired to the country in disgust. In July he set out for Athens, where his son was completing his education, but got no further than Syracuse. Turned back to Italy by contrary winds, a false report of a reconciliation between Antony and the 'liberators' made him give up the journey altogether, and on the last day of August he re-entered Rome. In answer to a summons by Antony to attend the Senate on 1 September he sent his excuses, but on the 2nd in Antony's absence he delivered the first of his fourteen 'Philippics'. The title was taken by Cicero himself, at first as a joke, from Demosthenes' speeches against Philip of Macedonia.

In restrained language, for he and Antony were still nominally friends, he protested against the Consul's high-handed conduct during the previous three months. Antony replied violently on 19 September, repudiating the friendship. There were no further consequences for the time being, but the opposition was now in the open. By the end of the year all eyes were turned on the town of Mutina (Modena) in

Cisalpine Gaul, where Antony was besieging another leading
assassin, D. Brutus, whom he intended to dispossess of the province
assigned him by Caesar. Against Antony were two republican armies
outside the town under the Consul A. Hirtius and Caesar's nineteen-
year-old great-nephew C. Julius Caesar Octavianus, adopted son
and heir under Caesar's will. He had come to Italy from Macedonia
in April to take up his inheritance and soon rivalled Antony as a focus
for the loyalty of Caesar's veterans. In Rome Cicero had asserted
leadership of the anti-Antonian Senate in another speech on 20
December (Third Philippic), in the course of which, as in other
speeches later on, he expressed full confidence in this young man.
As for the 'liberators', M. Brutus and Cassius, they had left for the
East in the autumn and within six months had managed to take over
the entire empire east of the Adriatic in the interest of the republic.
The West, Italy and the islands apart, was controlled by four
governors, all followers of Caesar and appointed by him: M. Aemilius
Lepidus (Narbonese Gaul and Hither Spain), L. Munatius Plancus
(Gallia Comata, i.e. northern Gaul), C. Asinius Pollio (Further
Spain), Q. Cornificius (Africa). All four professed loyalty to the
Senate, but none, except perhaps Cornificius, could be relied upon
at a pinch.

At Mutina the republicans were strengthened in April by the
arrival of the other Consul, Pansa, with a large force of recent levies.
Antony was soundly defeated in two bloody engagements, and forced
to raise the siege and hurry off westward with the remnants of his
army. But both Consuls lost their lives, and the armies under their
command refused to serve under Caesar's assassin, D. Brutus, so that
Octavian found himself in command of the entire relief force. If he
had cooperated with Decimus, Antony would probably have been
finished, but, as was soon to become plain, Caesar's heir had other
ideas. Belatedly pursued by Decimus, Antony was able to join up
with three legions under his lieutenant Ventidius and crossed the
Alps into Lepidus' province. Lepidus promptly made common cause
with him, coerced, as he claimed, by his own troops who refused to
fight their comrades. Plancus still held out for the republic, and was
presently joined by Decimus, his designated colleague in the consulship of 42. But in August or September Plancus and Pollio, who had
marched up from Spain, went over to the opposition. Decimus'

army deserted. He managed to escape to north-east Italy, but was there captured and killed by brigands.

In Italy Octavian had grasped his opportunity. When the Senate refused his demand for one of the vacant consulships (outrageous at his age), he marched south and occupied the capital without bloodshed. After his election on 19 August, he met Antony and Lepidus on an island in a river near Bologna and a common front was established. The three were made 'Triumvirs for the constitution of the republic' and divided the western half of the empire between them. One of their first proceedings was to institute proscriptions on the Sullan model, partly, especially on Antony's side, for revenge, partly to raise money. Cicero was among the first victims. An effort to escape by sea failed, and he was killed at his Formian villa on 7 December. His brother and nephew met with similar fates, but his son, who was overseas with M. Brutus, survived to become Consul by favour of Octavian twelve years later.

In 42 the republic went down to final defeat at Philippi. In 31 monarchy was established when Octavian, soon to be Augustus, defeated Antony at Actium.

Even an outline shows Cicero as a complex man in a complex and dangerous environment: 'In his various phases he became what circumstances made him, sometimes paltry, sometimes almost heroic. His ambition was rooted in insufficiency. Carrying all his life a set of traditional ideas which he never consciously questioned, he seldom ignored his code, but was easily swayed and perplexed by side issues and more or less unacknowledged personal inducements. His agile mind moved on the surface of things, victim of their complexity. Always the advocate, he saw from ever-shifting angles, and what he saw he rarely analysed. Often confused himself, he perplexes us. He failed to realize that self-praise can defeat its end. Alongside the image of the wise and dauntless patriot which he tried to project into posterity has arisen the counter-image of a windbag, a wiseacre, a humbug, a spiteful, vain-glorious egotist. And that is not because, as some of his admirers have urged, the survival of his private correspondence has placed him at a disadvantage. His published speeches bewray him to a generation intolerant of his kind of cliché. The flabbiness, pomposity, and essential fatuity of Ciceronian rhetoric at its too frequent worst does him more damage than any epistolary "secrets". No other antique personality has inspired such venomous dislike. His modern enemies both hate and despise him...The living Cicero was hated by some, but not despised. His gifts, matching the times, were too conspicuous. And many opponents were disarmed; Mommsen himself might have capitulated to a dinner-party at Tusculum.'[1]

2. THE LETTERS

Letters in Cicero's day were generally written on sheets of papyrus with a reed pen (*calamus*), which like the papyrus usually came from Egypt, and ink (*atramentum*). Wooden tablets with a wax coating (*codicilli*) were used for short, informal notes. Rolled up, sealed, and addressed, the letter was despatched, often in a package along with others, by a bearer who happened to be going to the right destination or by a special courier (*tabellarius*); some of Cicero's slaves were regularly so employed. Or it might be possible to use the couriers with which the great tax-farming companies in Rome kept in regular contact with their agents in the provinces. For greater security couriers were often sent in pairs. Another safeguard was to send duplicate copies of important letters separately. Once or twice we find Cicero writing in Greek or using pseudonyms against the danger that a confidential letter might find unauthorized readers.

Friends usually wrote to one another in their own hand rather than use an amanuensis, though when the friendship became as close as that between Cicero and Atticus ultimately did this courtesy could be dispensed with. The letter was headed with the writer's name followed by that of the addressee: e.g. CICERO PLANCO. Normally s. D. (*salutem dicit*) or the like came between. Often the names appeared in a fuller form and titles might be added even in more or less informal correspondence: e.g. M. CICERO S.D. D. BRVTO IMP. COS. DESIG. The letters to Atticus are regularly headed CICERO ATTICO S(AL)., but since Cicero does not address Atticus by his cognomen in the body of a letter until 50, these headings are presumed to be spurious. Some letters end with *vale*(*te*) and/or the date and place of origin, but this was not a rule.

Romans of this epoch, those of the upper class at least, necessarily

---

[1] From my *Cicero*, pp. 279f.

tended to be frequent letter-writers. A man of position would have friends and clients all over Italy, his family home might be in an Italian township, he might himself spend much time in country houses, receiving public and domestic news from correspondents in Rome. All over the empire administrative and business activities required constant communication with the capital. Persons employed in them or travelling for their own pleasure and improvement needed to keep in touch with their families and friends.

No doubt people often preserved the letters they received and kept copies of their own, as Cicero did. We hear, for instance, of letters in verse sent from Corinth to Rome in 146 by the brother of the Roman commander-in-chief, Mummius Achaicus, and handed down in the family.[1] Occasionally collections seem to have been published, as Cato the Censor's to his son or some by Cornelia, mother of the Gracchi. But almost the sole survivors from the classical period are in the Ciceronian corpus. Except for some official or semi-official documents and some studied compositions which were probably intended for wider circulation, this consists of genuine day-to-day letters intended only for the recipient, some of them highly confidential. That distinguishes them from 'literary' letters, written for publication, or at any rate with publication in mind, and edited by their authors (Horace, Seneca, Pliny the Younger). They number over nine hundred, including about ninety by writers other than Cicero. The manuscripts present them in two large collections and two small ones, as follows:

1. Letters to Atticus. In sixteen 'books' (libri), dating from 68 to 44 (but with only eleven letters prior to 61). The sequence was intended to be chronological, but whoever edited them (not Cicero; see below) made many errors in this respect which modern research has often been able to put right. Atticus' letters are unfortunately not included, though we know that Cicero kept them. Hence many obscurities.

T. Pomponius Atticus is known chiefly from the correspondence and from a biographical sketch by his and Cicero's younger friend, Cornelius Nepos. He was born in 109 of an old and well-to-do non-senatorial Roman family. After his father's death he left Rome, then under Cinna's régime, and settled in Athens, where he lived for the

[1] *Att.* 13.6.4.

next twenty years. He came to regard this cultural centre as a second *patria*, whence his acquired cognomen, 'the Athenian'. The remainder of his long life (he died in 32) was passed mostly at his house on the Quirinal or two modest properties close by, except for frequent and lengthy visits to a large estate near the town of Buthrotum in Epirus, opposite Corcyra (Corfù). His time was occupied in the management of a large fortune, literary and antiquarian interests (he wrote the history of several great Roman families and a chronicle of Rome) and endless services to friends, of whom Cicero and Hortensius were especially close. Favouring the doctrines of Epicurus, he kept out of public affairs. Cicero called him a political animal (*natura* πολι-τικός),[1] and he was on familiar terms with many leading figures, particularly Cato and his circle; but he does not seem to have wished to influence public events even from behind the scenes, content with the role of benevolent spectator. Through the convulsions of the first century Atticus preserved himself, his money, and his friendships in opposing camps.

His relations with Cicero passed beyond friendship when, probably in 68, Q. Cicero married Atticus' sister Pomponia. M. Cicero is said to have made the match, which turned out unhappily, though divorce was staved off for over twenty years. But friction between the principals seldom affected the good understanding between their respective brothers. Atticus was Cicero's confidant and adviser in public and domestic concerns. When the advice was clear, which it occasionally was not, it was sometimes taken. More important perhaps was his supervision of Cicero's financial affairs and a variety of other practical good offices, including the dissemination of Cicero's literary works by means of a large staff of copyists. Nothing indicates that there was any financial arrangement between them. Atticus did not need money. It was enough that he could call on Cicero's influence when convenient. Intimacy with such a man carried rewards not to be expressed in sesterces.[2]

The style of the letters to Atticus is generally very informal, and they mostly disregard the rhythmical clausulae of Cicero's literary prose.[3]

---

[1] *Att.* 4.6.1.
[2] The introduction to my edition of the Letters to Atticus surveys their relationship in detail (1 3–59).
[3] On these see R. G. M. Nisbet's edition of *In Pisonem* (1961), pp. xvii–xx.

Some are brief notes in a sort of verbal shorthand, freely omitting words which the reader could be expected to supply for himself ('ellipse'). Along with most of the letters to Quintus and some of those to 'friends' they represent for us the colloquial Latin of the educated. Greek, in which both correspondents prided themselves on their fluency, is plentifully scattered both in the form of Homeric and other literary quotations and in words and phrases from the contemporary language; so too in the letters to Quintus and some to 'friends'. Cicero's attitude to the Greeks, it may be remarked, was complex, though probably not unusual in Romans of his type. He revered the earlier Greek philosophers, Plato above all, and admired the classical literature, though prone to make exaggerated patriotic claims on behalf of older Latin writers and the resourcefulness of the Latin language. For the generality of contemporary Greeks, which term was often used to comprise the Greek-speaking inhabitants of Western Asia, he had little but contempt. Unlike some other Romans of the time, he had no more than a perfunctory interest in Greek art, preferring painting to sculpture.

2. Letters to 'friends' (*Epistulae ad familiares*). Also in sixteen 'books', but not originally a single corpus (see below). The arrangement is mainly by correspondents or subject matter, not by date, except within particular groups, and the several 'books' show varying degrees of internal cohesion.[1] The earliest datable letter is of January 62, the latest of July 43. Most of the extant letters addressed to Cicero are in this collection. The 'friends' are a numerous and diverse company – great nobles, governors and generals, Varro the polymath, old cronies like M. Marius and Papirius Paetus, younger protégés like the lawyer Trebatius Testa. Cicero's domestic circle is represented by the fourteenth 'book', consisting of letters to his wife, and the sixteenth, of letters to or concerning his freedman, confidential secretary, and literary assistant, Tiro. Most of the figures prominent in the history of the period are included. The subjects are no less various, including two despatches to the Senate from Cilicia, letters of condolence, and letters of introduction, at which last Cicero was considered a past master (the thirteenth 'book' consists entirely of such). Style naturally

[1] On this see the introduction to my edition (Shackleton Bailey (*Fam.*), i 20–3).

varies with correspondent and occasion, often as elaborate (and rhythmical) as in Cicero's published works, sometimes business-like, sometimes familiar and jocular.

3. The earlier of the two smaller collections consists of letters to Quintus (*Ad Quintum fratrem*) in three 'books'. They extend from 59 to 54. One very long letter (i.i), really a tract and evidently designed for circulation, was addressed to him as Proconsul in Asia and might be entitled 'Advice to a governor'. The rest are private. Most belong to the years following M. Cicero's return from exile, when the brothers were on the best of terms. Marcus had a genuine, if slightly patronizing affection for his junior, and did not suspect until years later that Quintus, a moody character, all the time harboured ambivalent feelings towards himself.[1]

4. Twenty-six letters between Cicero and M. Brutus belong to the spring and summer of 43 at the height of the struggle with Mark Antony, while Brutus was in Macedonia.

Two other documents are sometimes included. In a treatise epistolary only in form known as *Commentariolum petitionis* Quintus advises his brother on how to conduct his campaign for the consulship. Its authenticity is in some doubt. A letter purporting to be from Cicero to Octavian in late 43 is undoubtedly spurious.

In antiquity the fund of Ciceronian letters will have been more than twice as large. Scattered references reveal the existence of now lost collections of correspondence with Pompey, Caesar, Octavian, M. Cicero the younger, and a number of others.

Cicero kept copies of many of his own letters, and shortly before his death planned to publish a carefully edited selection.[2] Fortunately, he never found the time. The letters to Atticus were preserved by their recipient. Cornelius Nepos tells us that after Cicero's death friends were allowed to read them, and adds the well-known, if not entirely well-judged, comment that anyone who did would have little need for a connected history of the period.[3] The date and

---

[1] Biographers and commentators have missed most of the clues; see *Cicero*, ch. 19.   [2] See Shackleton Bailey (*Att.*), I 59f.
[3] *Vit. Att.* 16.2-4.

circumstances of their publication are controversial, but the formerly paramount theory that this happened in Nero's reign, after Asconius wrote his commentaries on Cicero's speeches (in which the letters are not mentioned), remains in my opinion the most probable.[1] The rest of the correspondence seems to have been published piecemeal during the Augustan period, and there are strong indications that Tiro, who survived his former master for nearly forty years and devoted himself to his memory, was responsible.[2] The origin of the arrangement in sixteen 'books' is unknown, except that it must be later than the grammarian Nonius Marcellus (beginning of fourth century A.D.), whose citations show that he had no knowledge of it. The title *Epistulae familiares*, later *ad familiares* or *ad diversos*, first occurs in manuscripts of the Renaissance period.

All the correspondence seems to have been produced with a minimum of editorial interference. In one letter (*Att.* 13.9.1) a scandalous story about young Quintus has been removed, presumably by Atticus himself, but that is an isolated case.

Twentieth-century scholarship has greatly improved the text of the correspondence, as well as its interpretation, but many problems remain. In the first half of *Ad familiares* a manuscript of the ninth or tenth century, Mediceus 49.9, is virtually our only authority, whereas in the later books other manuscripts deriving from a different ancestor are important. In the rest of the correspondence the extant manuscripts are all late and very corrupt, though they are supplemented at times by more or less reliable reports of earlier and better ones now lost. The situation varies from one part of the collection to another; it is worst in the last four books of *Ad Atticum*. The details are set out in the introductions to my editions. In this selection it has seemed sufficient to record such departures from the manuscript tradition, variant readings, and conjectures not adopted in the text as seem to call for notice. The text follows my editions of the two main collections. In the letters to Quintus W. S. Watt's Oxford Text is followed with a few variations.

---

[1] See Shackleton Bailey (*Att.*), I 59f.
[2] See id. (*Fam.*) I. 23ff.

THE LETTERS

Scr. Romae m. Nov. an. 68

CICERO ATTICO SAL.

Quantum dolorem acceperim et quanto fructu sim privatus et **1**
forensi et domestico Luci, fratris nostri, morte in primis pro
nostra consuetudine tu existimare potes. nam mihi omnia
quae iucunda ex humanitate alterius et moribus homini
accidere possunt ex illo accidebant. qua re non dubito quin **5**
tibi quoque id molestum sit, cum et meo dolore moveare et
ipse omni virtute officioque ornatissimum tuique et sua sponte
et meo sermone amantem adfinem amicumque amiseris.

Quod ad me scribis de sorore tua, testis erit tibi ipsa quantae **2**
mihi curae fuerit ut Quinti fratris animus in eam esset is qui
esse deberet. quem cum esse offensiorem arbitrarer, eas litteras
ad eum misi quibus et placarem ut fratrem et monerem ut
minorem et obiurgarem ut errantem. itaque ex iis quae postea **5**
saepe ab eo ad me scripta sunt confido ita esse omnia ut et
oporteat et velimus.

De litterarum missione, sine causa abs te accusor. numquam **3**
enim a Pomponia nostra certior sum factus esse cui dare litteras
possem; porro autem neque mihi accidit ut haberem qui in
Epirum proficisceretur nequedum te Athenis esse audiebamus.
de Acutiliano autem negotio, quod mihi mandaras, ut primum **4**
a tuo digressu Romam veni, confeceram; sed accidit ut et
contentione nihil opus esset et ut ego, qui in te satis consili
statuerim esse, mallem Peducaeum tibi consilium per litteras
quam me dare. etenim cum multos dies aures meas Acutilio **5**
dedissem, cuius sermonis genus tibi notum esse arbitror, non
mihi grave duxi scribere ad te de illius querimoniis, cum eas
audire, quod erat subodiosum, leve putassem. sed abs te ipso
qui me accusas unas mihi scito litteras redditas esse, cum

10 et oti ad scribendum plus et facultatem dandi maiorem habueris.

5   Quod scribis etiam si cuius animus in te esset offensior a me recolligi oportere, teneo quid dicas neque id neglexi; sed est miro quodam modo adfectus. ego autem quae dicenda fuerunt de te non praeterii; quid autem contendendum esset ex tua
5 putabam voluntate me statuere oportere. quam si ad me perscripseris, intelleges me neque diligentiorem esse voluisse quam tu esses neque neglegentiorem fore quam tu velis.

6   De Tadiana re, mecum Tadius locutus est te ita scripsisse, nihil esse iam quod laboraretur, quoniam hereditas usu capta esset. id mirabamur te ignorare, de tutela legitima, in qua dicitur esse puella, nihil usu capi posse.

7   Epiroticam emptionem gaudeo tibi placere. quae tibi mandavi et quae tu intelleges convenire nostro Tusculano velim, ut scribis, cures, quod sine molestia tua facere poteris. nam nos ex omnibus molestiis et laboribus uno illo in loco
5 conquiescimus.

8   Quintum fratrem cottidie exspectamus. Terentia magnos articulorum dolores habet. et te et sororem tuam et matrem maxime diligit salutemque tibi plurimam adscribit et Tulliola, deliciae nostrae. cura ut valeas et nos ames et tibi persuadeas
5 te a me fraterne amari.

LETTER 2 (*Att.* 1.11)

Scr. Romae m. Sext. an. 67

CICERO ATTICO SAL.

1 Et mea sponte faciebam antea et post duabus epistulis tuis perdiligenter in eandem rationem scriptis magno opere sum commotus. eo accedebat hortator adsiduus Sallustius, ut agerem quam diligentissime cum Lucceio de vestra vetere

1 5.2 teneo *add. Orelli*

gratia reconcilianda. sed cum omnia fecissem, non modo eam 5
voluntatem eius quae fuerat erga te recuperare non potui
verum ne causam quidem elicere immutatae voluntatis.
tametsi iactat ille quidem illud suum arbitrium et ea quae iam
tum cum aderas offendere eius animum intellegebam, tamen
habet quiddam profecto quod magis in animo eius insederit, 10
quod neque epistulae tuae neque nostra legatio tam potest
facile delere quam tu praesens non modo oratione sed tuo
vultu illo familiari tolles, si modo tanti putaris; id quod, si me
audies et si humanitati tuae constare voles, certe putabis. ac ne
illud mirere, cur, cum ego antea significarem tibi per litteras 15
me sperare illum in nostra potestate fore, nunc idem videar
diffidere, incredibile est quanto mihi videatur illius voluntas
obstinatior et in hac iracundia obfirmatior. sed haec aut sana-
buntur cum veneris aut ei molesta erunt in utro culpa erit.

Quod in epistula tua scriptum erat me iam te arbitrari 2
designatum esse, scito nihil tam exercitum esse nunc Romae
quam candidatos omnibus iniquitatibus nec quando futura
sint comitia sciri. verum haec audies de Philadelpho.

Tu velim quae nostrae Academiae parasti quam primum 3
mittas. mire quam illius loci non modo usus sed etiam cogitatio
delectat. libros vero tuos cave cuiquam tradas; nobis eos,
quem ad modum scribis, conserva. summum me eorum
studium tenet, sicut odium iam ceterarum rerum; quas tu 5
incredibile est quam brevi tempore quanto deteriores offensurus
sis quam reliquisti.

2 1.18 affirmatior *codd.*   2.1 me iam te *ego* (te iam me *Lambinus*): me
iam *codd.*

LETTER 3 (*Att.* 1.2)

Scr. Romae m. Quint. an. 65

CICERO ATTICO SAL.

1 L. Iulio Caesare C. Marcio Figulo consulibus filiolo me auctum scito, salva Terentia. abs te iam diu nihil litterarum. ego de meis ad te rationibus scripsi antea diligenter. hoc tempore Catilinam, competitorem nostrum, defendere cogita-
5 mus. iudices habemus quos volumus, summa accusatoris voluntate. spero, si absolutus erit, coniunctiorem illum nobis fore in ratione petitionis; sin aliter acciderit, humaniter feremus.

2 Tuo adventu nobis opus est maturo. nam prorsus summa hominum est opinio tuos familiares, nobiles homines, adversarios honori nostro fore. ad eorum voluntatem mihi conciliandam maximo te mihi usui fore video. qua re Ianuario ineunte, ut
5 constituisti, cura ut Romae sis.

LETTER 4 (*Fam.* 5.1)

Scr. in Gallia Cisalpina c. prid. Id. Ian. an. 62

Q. METELLVS Q.F. CELER PRO COS. S.D.
M. TVLLIO CICERONI

1 Si vales, bene est.

Existimaram pro mutuo inter nos animo et pro reconciliata gratia nec absentem umquam me abs te ludibrio laesum iri nec Metellum fratrem ob dictum capite ac fortunis per te oppug-

---

3 1.2 iam *Boot*: etiam *codd.*   **4** 1.1 benest *M(ediceus 49.9)*   **3** absentem umquam me abs te *ego*: absente *M*: absentem me a te *Wesenberg*: abs te me *Kleyn*: me abs te *Maixner*

natum iri. quem si parum pudor ipsius defendebat, debebat 5
vel familiae nostrae dignitas vel meum studium erga vos
remque publicam satis sublevare. nunc video illum circumventum, me desertum, a quibus minime conveniebat.

Itaque in luctu et squalore sum, qui provinciae, qui 2
exercitui praesum, qui bellum gero. quae quoniam nec
ratione nec maiorum nostrum clementia administrastis, non
erit mirandum si vos paenitebit. te tam mobili in me meosque
esse animo non sperabam. me interea nec domesticus dolor 5
nec cuiusquam iniuria ab re publica abducet.

LETTER 5 *(Fam. 5.2)*

Scr. Romae med. m. Ian. an. 62

M. TVLLIVS M.F. CICERO Q. METELLO Q.F.
CELERI PRO COS. S.D.

Si tu exercitusque valetis, bene est.   1
   Scribis ad me te existimasse pro mutuo inter nos animo et
pro reconciliata gratia numquam te a me ludibrio laesum iri.
quod cuius modi sit satis intellegere non possum; sed tamen
suspicor ad te esse adlatum me in senatu, cum disputarem 5
permultos esse qui rem publicam a me conservatam dolerent,
dixisse a te propinquos tuos, quibus negare non potuisses,
impetrasse ut ea quae statuisses tibi in senatu de mea laude
esse dicenda reticeres. quod cum dicerem, illud adiunxi, mihi
tecum ita dispertitum officium fuisse in rei publicae salute 10
retinenda ut ego urbem a domesticis insidiis et ab intestino
scelere, tu Italiam et ab armatis hostibus et ab occulta
coniuratione defenderes, atque hanc nostram tanti et tam
praeclari muneris societatem a tuis propinquis labefactatam,
qui, cum tu a me rebus amplissimis atque honorificentissimis 15

2.5 speraram *Wesenberg*   5 1.1 benest *M*

ornatus esses, timuissent ne quae mihi pars abs te voluntatis mutuae tribueretur.

2   Hoc in sermone cum a me exponeretur quae mea exspectatio fuisset orationis tuae quantoque in errore versatus essem, visa est oratio non iniucunda, et mediocris quidam est risus consecutus, non in te sed magis in errorem meum et quod me abs
5   te cupisse laudari aperte atque ingenue confitebar. iam hoc non potest in te non honorifice esse dictum, me in clarissimis meis atque amplissimis rebus tamen aliquod testimonium tuae vocis habere voluisse.

3   Quod autem ita scribis, 'pro mutuo inter nos animo', quid tu existimes esse in amicitia mutuum, nescio; equidem hoc arbitror, cum par voluntas accipitur et redditur. ego si hoc dicam, me tua causa praetermisisse provinciam, tibi ipse levior
5   videar esse; meae enim rationes ita tulerunt, atque eius mei consili maiorem in dies singulos fructum voluptatemque capio. illud dico, me, ut primum in contione provinciam deposuerim, statim quem ad modum eam tibi traderem cogitare coepisse. nihil dico de sortitione vestra; tantum te suspicari volo, nihil
10   in ea re per collegam meum me insciente esse factum. recordare cetera, quam cito senatum illo die facta sortitione coegerim, quam multa de te verba fecerim, cum tu ipse mihi dixisti orationem meam non solum in te honorificam sed etiam in
4   collegas tuos contumeliosam fuisse. iam illud senatus consultum quod eo die factum est ea praescriptione est ut, dum id exstabit, officium meum in te obscurum esse non possit. postea vero quam profectus es, velim recordere quae ego de te in senatu
5   egerim, quae in contionibus dixerim, quas ad te litteras miserim. quae cum omnia collegeris, tu ipse velim iudices satisne videatur his omnibus rebus tuus adventus, cum proxime Romam venisti, mutue respondisse.

5   Quod scribis de reconciliata gratia, non intellego cur reconciliatam esse dicas quae numquam imminuta est.

2.5 iam] nam *Wesenberg*   3.4 tibi ipsi *nescio quis*: mihi ipse *Lange*
5.1 gratia (*i.e.* gr̄ā) *Mendelssohn*: nostra (*i.e.* nr̄ā) *M*: gratia nostra *vel* n- g- *alii*

Quod scribis non oportuisse Metellum, fratrem tuum, ob **6**
dictum a me oppugnari, primum hoc velim existimes, animum
mihi istum tuum vehementer probari et fraternam plenam
humanitatis ac pietatis voluntatem; deinde, si qua ego in re
fratri tuo rei publicae causa restiterim, ut mihi ignoscas (tam **5**
enim sum amicus rei publicae quam qui maxime); si vero
meam salutem contra illius impetum in me crudelissimum
defenderim, satis habeas nihil me etiam tecum de tui fratris
iniuria conqueri. quem ego cum comperissem omnem sui
tribunatus conatum in meam perniciem parare atque meditari, **10**
egi cum Claudia, uxore tua, et cum vestra sorore Mucia, cuius
erga me studium pro Cn. Pompei necessitudine multis in rebus
perspexeram, ut eum ab illa iniuria deterrerent. atqui ille, **7**
quod te audisse certo scio, prid. Kal. Ian., qua iniuria nemo
umquam in ullo magistratu improbissimus civis adfectus est, ea
me consulem adfecit, cum rem publicam conservassem, atque
abeuntem magistratu contionis habendae potestate privavit. **5**
cuius iniuria mihi tamen honori summo fuit; nam cum ille
mihi nihil nisi ut iurarem permitteret, magna voce iuravi
verissimum pulcherrimumque ius iurandum, quod populus
idem magna voce me vere iurasse iuravit.

Hac accepta tam insigni iniuria tamen illo ipso die misi ad **8**
Metellum communes amicos qui agerent cum eo ut de illa
mente desisteret. quibus ille respondit sibi non esse integrum;
etenim paulo ante in contione dixerat ei qui in alios animum
advertisset indicta causa dicendi ipsi potestatem fieri non **5**
oportere. hominem gravem et civem egregium, qui, qua poena
senatus consensu bonorum omnium eos adfecerat qui urbem
incendere et magistratus ac senatum trucidare, bellum maximum conflare voluissent, eadem dignum iudicaret eum qui
curiam caede, urbem incendiis, Italiam bello liberasset! itaque **10**
ego Metello, fratri tuo, praesenti restiti. nam in senatu Kal. Ian.
sic cum eo de re publica disputavi ut sentiret sibi cum viro

7.1 atque *M*   2 scio *om.* (*in fine paginae*) *M*   3 ullo *ego*: animo *M*: aliquo
vel minimo *vel* infimo *alii*

forti et constanti esse pugnandum. a. d. III Non. Ian. cum agere
coepisset, tertio quoque verbo orationis suae me appellabat,
15 mihi minabatur, neque illi quicquam deliberatius fuit quam
me, quacumque ratione posset, non iudicio neque disceptatione
sed vi atque impressione evertere. huius ego temeritati si
virtute atque animo non restitissem, quis esset qui me in
consulatu non casu potius existimaret quam consilio fortem
20 fuisse?

9   Haec si tu Metellum cogitare de me nescisti, debes existimare te maximis de rebus a fratre esse celatum; sin autem
aliquid impertivit tibi sui consili, lenis a te et facilis existimari
debeo qui nihil tecum de his ipsis rebus expostulem. et si intel-
5 legis non me dicto Metelli, ut scribis, sed consilio eius animo-
que in me inimicissimo esse commotum, cognosce nunc
humanitatem meam, si humanitas appellanda est in acerbis-
sima iniuria remissio animi ac dissolutio. nulla est a me umquam sententia dicta in fratrem tuum; quotienscumque
10 aliquid est actum, sedens iis adsensi qui mihi lenissime sentire
visi sunt. addam illud etiam, quod iam ego curare non debui
sed tamen fieri non moleste tuli atque etiam ut ita fieret pro
mea parte adiuvi, ut senati consulto meus inimicus, quia tuus
frater erat, sublevaretur.

10   Qua re non ego oppugnavi fratrem tuum, sed fratri tuo
repugnavi; nec in te, ut scribis, animo fui mobili, sed ita
stabili ut in mea erga te voluntate etiam desertus ab officiis tuis
permanerem. atque hoc ipso tempore tibi paene minitanti
5 nobis per litteras hoc rescribo atque respondeo: ego dolori tuo
non solum ignosco sed summam etiam laudem tribuo (meus
enim me sensus, quanta vis fraterni sit amoris, admonet); a te
peto ut tu quoque aequum te iudicem dolori meo praebeas; si
acerbe, si crudeliter, si sine causa sum a tuis oppugnatus, ut
10 statuas mihi non modo non cedendum sed etiam tuo atque
exercitus tui auxilio in eius modi causa utendum fuisse.

Ego te mihi semper amicum esse volui, me ut tibi amicis-
simum esse intellegeres laboravi. maneo in voluntate et, quoad

voles tu, permanebo, citiusque amore tui fratrem tuum odisse
desinam quam illius odio quicquam de nostra benevolentia 15
detraham.

LETTER 6 (*Att.* 1.13)

Scr. Romae vi Kal. Febr. an. 61

CICERO ATTICO SAL.

Accepi tuas tres iam epistulas, unam a M. Cornelio quam a Tribus **1**
ei Tabernis, ut opinor, dedisti, alteram quam mihi Canusinus
tuus hospes reddidit, tertiam quam, ut scribis, iam ora soluta
de phaselo dedisti; quae fuerunt omnes, ut rhetorum pueri
loquuntur, cum humanitatis sparsae sale tum insignes amoris 5
notis. quibus epistulis sum equidem abs te lacessitus ad
rescribendum, sed idcirco sum tardior quod non invenio
fidelem tabellarium. quotus enim quisque est qui epistulam
paulo graviorem ferre possit nisi eam perlectione relevarit?
accedit eo quod mihi non, ut quisque in Epirum proficiscitur, 10
ita ad te proficisci videtur. ego enim te arbitror caesis apud
Amaltheam tuam victumeis statim esse ad Sicyonem oppu-
gnandum profectum, neque tamen id ipsum certum habeo,
quando ad Antonium proficiscare aut quid in Epiro temporis
ponas. ita neque Achaicis hominibus neque Epiroticis paulo 15
liberiores litteras committere audeo.

Sunt autem post discessum a me tuum res dignae litteris **2**
nostris, sed non committendae eius modi periculo ut aut
interire aut aperiri aut intercipi possint. primum igitur scito
primum me non esse rogatum sententiam praepositumque esse
nobis pacificatorem Allobrogum, idque admurmurante senatu 5
neque me invito esse factum. sum enim et ab observando
homine perverso liber et ad dignitatem in re publica retinen-

---

6 1.3 iam ora *Dahlman* (ora iam *Casaubon*): anc(h)ora *codd.*   **4** ut
rhetorum pueri *Madvig*: rhetorum pure *codd.*   11 ita...videtur *addidi*
exempli causa

dam contra illius voluntatem solutus, et ille secundus in
dicendo locus habet auctoritatem paene principis, voluntatem
10 non nimis devinctam beneficio consulis. tertius est Catulus,
quartus, si etiam hoc quaeris, Hortensius. consul autem ipse
parvo animo et pravo tamen, cavillator genere illo moroso quod
etiam sine dicacitate ridetur, facie magis quam facetiis
ridiculus, nihil agens in re publica, seiunctus ab optimatibus,
15 a quo nihil speres boni rei publicae quia non vult, nihil metuas
mali quia non audet. eius autem collega et in me perhonorificus
3 et partium studiosus ac defensor bonarum. qui nunc leviter
inter se dissident, sed vereor ne hoc quod infectum est serpat
longius. credo enim te audisse, cum apud Caesarem pro
populo fieret, venisse eo muliebri vestitu virum, idque sacrifi-
5 cium cum virgines instaurassent, mentionem a Q. Cornificio
in senatu factam (is fuit princeps, ne tu forte aliquem nostrum
putes); postea rem ex senatus consulto ad virgines atque
pontifices relatam idque ab iis nefas esse decretum; deinde ex
senatus consulto consules rogationem promulgasse; uxori
10 Caesarem nuntium remisisse. in hac causa Piso amicitia P.
Clodi ductus operam dat ut ea rogatio quam ipse fert, et fert
ex senatus consulto et de religione, antiquetur. Messalla
vehementer adhuc agit et severe. boni viri precibus Clodi
removentur a causa, operae comparantur. nosmet ipsi, qui
15 Lycurgei a principio fuissemus, cottidie demitigamur. instat
et urget Cato. quid multa? vereor ne haec †iniecta† a bonis,
defensa ab improbis magnorum rei publicae malorum causa
sit.
4   Tuus autem ille amicus (scin quem dicam? de quo tu ad me
scripsisti, postea quam non auderet reprehendere laudare
coepisse) nos, ut ostendit, admodum diligit, amplectitur, amat,
aperte laudat, occulte, sed ita ut perspicuum sit, invidet. nihil
5 come, nihil simplex, nihil ἐν τοῖς πολιτικοῖς illustre, nihil
honestum, nihil forte, nihil liberum. sed haec ad te scribam
alias subtilius. nam neque adhuc mihi satis nota sunt et huic

2.14 in] cum *codd.*   3.13 et *add. Lambini margo*   3.16 iniecta] *vide comm.*

terrae filio nescio cui committere epistulam tantis de rebus
non audeo.

Provincias praetores nondum sortiti sunt. res eodem est loci 5
quo reliquisti. τοποθεσίαν quam postulas Miseni et Puteolorum
includam orationi meae. 'a. d. III Non. Dec.' mendose fuisse
animadverteram. quae laudas ex orationibus, mihi crede,
valde mihi placebant, sed non audebam antea dicere. nunc 5
vero, quod a te probata sunt, multo mihi 'Αττικώτερα videntur.
in illam orationem Metellinam addidi quaedam. liber tibi
mittetur, quoniam te amor nostri φιλορήτορα reddidit.

Novi tibi quidnam scribam? quid? etiam. Messalla consul 6
Autronianam domum emit HS ⌐cxxxiiii⌐. 'quid id ad me?'
inquis. tantum, quod ea emptione et nos bene emisse iudicati
sumus et homines intellegere coeperunt licere amicorum
facultatibus in emendo ad dignitatem aliquam pervenire. 5
Teucris illa lentum negotium est, sed tamen est in spe. tu ista
confice. a nobis liberiorem epistulam exspecta.

VI Kal. Febr. M. Messalla M. Pisone coss.

LETTER 7 (Att. 2.14)

Scr. in Formiano c. v Kal. Mai. an. 59

CICERO ATTICO SAL.

Quantam tu mihi moves exspectationem de sermone Bibuli, 1
quantum de colloquio Βοώπιδος, quantam etiam de illo delicato
convivio! proinde ita fac venias ut ad sitientes aures. quamquam nihil est iam quod magis timendum nobis putem quam
ne ille noster Sampsiceramus, cum se omnium sermonibus 5
sentiet vapulare et cum has actiones εὐανατρέπτους videbit,
ruere incipiat. ego autem usque eo sum enervatus ut hoc otio
quo nunc tabescimus malim ἐντυραννεῖσθαι quam cum optima
spe dimicare.

7 1.3 ut add. Vdalbinus

2   De pangendo quod me crebro adhortaris, fieri nihil potest.
basilicam habeo, non villam, frequentia Formianorum †ad
quam partem basilicae tribum Aemiliam†. sed omitto vulgus;
post horam quartam molesti ceteri non sunt. C. Arrius proxi-
5 mus est vicinus, immo ille quidem iam contubernalis, qui
etiam se idcirco Romam ire negat ut hic mecum totos dies
philosophetur. ecce ex altera parte Sebosus, ille Catuli
familiaris. quo me vertam? statim mehercule Arpinum irem,
ni te in Formiano commodissime exspectari viderem, dumtaxat
10 ad prid. Non. Mai. vide enim quibus hominibus aures sint
deditae meae. occasionem mirificam, si qui nunc, dum hi apud
me sunt, emere de me fundum Formianum velit! et tamen illud
probe, 'magnum quid adgrediamur et multae cogitationis
atque oti'. sed tamen satis fiet a nobis neque parcetur labori.

LETTER 8 (*Att.* 3.3)

Scr. in itinere c. ix Kal. Apr., ut vid., an. 58

CICERO ATTICO SAL.

Vtinam illum diem videam cum tibi agam gratias quod me
vivere coegisti! adhuc quidem valde me paenitet. sed te oro ut
ad me Vibonem statim venias, quo ego multis de causis converti iter meum. sed eo si veneris, de toto itinere ac fuga mea
5 consilium capere potero. si id non feceris, mirabor; sed confido
te esse facturum.

2.13 probem *codd.*

LETTER 9 (*Fam.* 14.2)

Scr. Thessalonicae iii Non. Oct. an. 58

TVLLIVS S.D. TERENTIAE SVAE ET TVLLIOLAE
ET CICERONI SVIS

Noli putare me ad quemquam longiores epistulas scribere, **1**
nisi si quis ad me plura scripsit, cui puto rescribi oportere. nec
enim habeo quid scribam nec hoc tempore quicquam difficilius
facio. ad te vero et ad nostram Tulliolam non queo sine
plurimis lacrimis scribere. vos enim video esse miserrimas, 5
quas ego beatissimas semper esse volui idque praestare debui,
et, nisi tam timidi fuissemus, praestitissem.

Pisonem nostrum merito eius amo plurimum. eum, ut potui, **2**
per litteras cohortatus sum gratiasque egi, ut debui. in novis
tribunis pl. intellego spem te habere. id erit firmum, si Pompei
voluntas erit; sed Crassum tamen metuo.

A te quidem omnia fieri fortissime et amantissime video, 5
nec miror, sed maereo casum eius modi ut tantis tuis miseriis
meae miseriae subleventur. nam ad me P. Valerius, homo
officiosus, scripsit, id quod ego maximo cum fletu legi, quem
ad modum a Vestae ad Tabulam Valeriam ducta esses. hem,
mea lux, meum desiderium, unde omnes opem petere solebant, 10
te nunc, mea Terentia, sic vexari, sic iacere in lacrimis et
sordibus, idque fieri mea culpa, qui ceteros servavi ut nos
periremus!

Quod de domo scribis, hoc est de area, ego vero tum denique **3**
mihi videbor restitutus si illa nobis erit restituta. verum haec
non sunt in nostra manu; illud doleo, quae impensa facienda est,
in eius partem te miseram et despoliatam venire. quod si conficitur negotium, omnia consequemur; sin eadem nos fortuna 5
premet, etiamne reliquias tuas miseras proicies? obsecro te,
mea vita, quod ad sumptum attinet, sine alios, qui possunt si

9 2.6 casum ⟨esse⟩ *Ernesti*

modo volunt, sustinere; et valetudinem istam infirmam, si me
amas, noli vexare. nam mihi ante oculos dies noctesque versaris.
10 omnes labores te excipere video; timeo ut sustineas, sed video
in te esse omnia. quare, ut id quod speras et quod agis con-
sequamur, servi valetudini.

4   Ego ad quos scribam nescio, nisi ad eos qui ad me scribunt
aut ad eos de quibus ad me vos aliquid scribitis. longius,
quoniam ita vobis placet, non discedam; sed velim quam
saepissime litteras mittatis, praesertim si quid est firmius quod
5 speremus.

Valete, mea desideria, valete.

D. a. d. III Non. Oct. Thessalonica.

LETTER 10 (*Att.* 3.13)

Scr. Thessalonicae Non. Sext. an. 58

CICERO ATTICO SAL.

1 Quod ad te scripseram me in Epiro futurum, postea quam
extenuari spem nostram et evanescere vidi, mutavi consilium
nec me Thessalonica commovi, ubi esse statueram quoad
aliquid ad me de eo scriberes quod proximis litteris scripseras,
5 fore uti secundum comitia aliquid de nobis in senatu ageretur;
id tibi Pompeium dixisse. qua de re quoniam comitia habita
sunt tuque nihil ad me scribis, proinde habebo ac si scripsisses
nihil esse, meque temporis non longinqui spe ductum esse non
moleste feram. quem autem motum te videre scripseras qui
10 nobis utilis fore videretur, eum nuntiant qui veniunt nullum
fore. in tribunis pl. designatis reliqua spes est. quam si ex-
spectaro, non erit quod putes me causae meae, voluntati
meorum defuisse.

2   Quod me saepe accusas cur hunc meum casum tam graviter
feram, debes ignoscere, cum ita me adflictum videas ut

10 1.8 non *post* esse (*alterum*) *add. Tyrrell*

neminem umquam nec videris nec audieris. nam quod scribis
te audire me etiam mentis errore ex dolore adfici, mihi vero
mens integra est. atque utinam tam in periculo fuisset, cum 5
ego iis quibus meam salutem carissimam esse arbitrabar,
inimicissimis crudelissimisque usus sum! qui ut me paulum
inclinari timore viderunt, sic impulerunt ut omni suo scelere et
perfidia abuterentur ad exitium meum.

Nunc quoniam iam est Cyzicum nobis eundum, quo rarius 10
ad me litterae perferentur, hoc velim diligentius omnia quae
putaris me scire opus esse perscribas. Quintum, fratrem meum,
fac diligas. quem ego miser si incolumem relinquo, non me
totum perisse arbitror.

Data Non. Sext.   15

LETTER 11 (*Att.* 4.3)

Scr. Romae viii Kal. Dec. an. 57

CICERO ATTICO SAL.

Avere te certo scio cum scire quid hic agatur tum ea a me scire, 1
non quo certiora sint ea quae in oculis omnium geruntur si a
me scribuntur quam cum ab aliis aut scribuntur tibi aut
nuntiantur, sed velim perspicias ex meis litteris quo animo ea
feram quae geruntur et qui sit hoc tempore aut mentis meae 5
sensus aut omnino vitae status.

Armatis hominibus a. d. III Non. Nov. expulsi sunt fabri de 2
area nostra, disturbata porticus Catuli, quae ex senatus consulto consulum locatione reficiebatur et ad tectum paene
pervenerat, Quinti fratris domus primo fracta coniectu lapidum
ex area nostra, deinde inflammata iussu Clodi inspectante 5
urbe coniectis ignibus, magna querela et gemitu non dicam
bonorum, qui nescio an nulli sint, sed plane hominum omnium.

2.11 perferuntur *codd.*   11 1.3 scribuntur (*Wesenberg*)...scribuntur]
scribantur...scribantur *codd.*   2.7 nulli *Lambinus*: ulli *codd.*

ille vel ante demens ruere, post hunc vero furorem nihil nisi
· caedem inimicorum cogitare, vicatim ambire, servis aperte
10 spem libertatis ostendere. etenim antea, cum iudicium nolebat,
habebat ille quidem difficilem manifestamque causam, sed
tamen causam; poterat infitiari, poterat in alios derivare,
poterat etiam aliquid iure factum defendere: post has ruinas,
incendia, rapinas desertus a suis vix iam †Decimum† dissigna-
15 torem, vix Gellium retinet, servorum consiliis utitur; videt,
si omnes quos vult palam occiderit, nihilo suam causam
difficiliorem quam adhuc sit in iudicio futuram.

3   Itaque a. d. III Id. Nov., cum Sacra via descenderem,
insecutus est me cum suis. clamor, lapides, fustes, gladii; et
haec improvisa omnia. discessi in vestibulum Tetti Damionis.
qui erant mecum facile operas aditu prohibuerunt. ipse occidi
5 potuit; sed ego diaeta curare incipio, chirurgiae taedet.
ille omnium vocibus cum se non ad iudicium sed ad supplicium praesens trudi videret, omnes Catilinas Acidinos
postea reddidit. nam Milonis domum, eam quae est in
Cermalo, prid. Id. Nov. expugnare et incendere ita conatus
10 est ut palam hora quinta cum scutis homines eductis gladiis,
alios cum accensis facibus adduxerit. ipse domum P. Sullae pro
castris sibi ad eam impugnationem sumpserat. tum ex Anniana
Milonis domo Q. Flaccus eduxit viros acres; occidit homines
ex omni latrocinio Clodiano notissimos, ipsum cupivit, sed ille
15 †ex interiorem aedium Sulla se in†. senatus postridie Id. domi
Clodius. egregius Marcellinus, omnes acres. Metellus calumnia
dicendi tempus exemit adiuvante Appio, etiam hercule familiari tuo, de cuius constantia vitae tuae verissimae litterae.
Sestius furere. ille postea, si comitia sua non fierent, urbi
20 minari. Milo proposita Marcellini sententia, quam ille de

2.8 vel ante demens *ego* (demens *Pius*): uehemens *codd.*   14–15 dissignatorem *Vetter*: designatorem *codd.*   3.3 vestibulum Tetti(i) *Victorius*: uestibulo M. tetii *vel sim. codd. plerique*   5 diaeta curare *Cobet*: dia et accurari *codd. plerique*   7 trudi] uideri *codd.*   8–9 eam...Cermalo *Turnebus*: meamque ceramio *codd.*   10 deductis *codd.*   13 agris *codd.*   15 senatus *Manutius*: senatu *codd.*   20 Milo *add. Tyrrell (post* proscripsit *R. Klotz)*

scripto ita dixerat ut totam nostram causam areae, incendio-
rum, periculi mei iudicio complecteretur eaque omnia comitiis
anteferret, proscripsit se per omnes dies comitiales de caelo
servaturum. contiones turbulentae Metelli, temerariae Appi, **4**
furiosissimae Publi; haec tamen summa, nisi Milo in campo
obnuntiasset, comitia futura.

A. d. xii Kal. Dec. Milo ante mediam noctem cum manu
magna in campum venit. Clodius, cum haberet fugitivorum **5**
delectas copias, in campum ire non est ausus. Milo permansit
ad meridiem mirifica hominum laetitia, summa cum gloria.
contentio fratrum trium turpis, fracta vis, contemptus furor.
Metellus tamen postulat ut sibi postero die in foro obnuntietur;
nihil esse quod in campum nocte veniretur; se hora prima in **10**
comitio fore. itaque a. d. xi Kal. [Ian.] in comitium Milo de
nocte venit. Metellus cum prima luce furtim in campum
itineribus †prope† deviis currebat; adsequitur inter lucos
hominem Milo, obnuntiat. ille se recipit magno et turpi Q.
Flacci convicio. a. d. x Kal. nundinae. contio biduo nulla. **15**

A. d. viiii Kal. haec ego scribebam hora noctis nona. Milo **5**
campum iam tenebat. Marcellus candidatus ita stertebat ut ego
vicinus audirem. Clodi vestibulum vacuum sane mihi nuntiabatur: pauci pannosi sine lanterna. meo consilio omnia illi
fieri querebantur, ignari quantum in illo heroë esset animi, **5**
quantum etiam consili. miranda virtus est. nova quaedam
divina mitto, sed haec summa est: comitia fore non arbitror,
reum Publium, nisi ante occisus erit, fore a Milone puto, si se in
turba ei iam obtulerit occisum iri ab ipso Milone video. non
dubitat facere, prae se fert; casum illum nostrum non extime- **10**
scit. numquam enim cuiusquam invidi et perfidi consilio est
usurus nec inerti nobilitati crediturus.

Nos animo dumtaxat vigemus, etiam magis quam cum **6**

4. 11 Ian. *removit Corradus*   5. 1 xiiii *vel* viii *codd. plerique*   4 paucis *codd.*
sine alanterna(m) *vel sim. codd.*   meo consilio *Manutius*: eo conscio *codd.*
7 mittite *codd.*   8–9 se in turba ei *R. Klotz, duce Baiter*: se uti turb(a)e iam
vel sentitur hanc iam (*vel* ue(h)iam) *codd.*   12 usurus *R. Klotz*: usus *codd.*
nobilitati *ego*: nobili *codd.*

florebamus; re familiari comminuti sumus. Quinti fratris
tamen liberalitati pro facultatibus nostris, ne omnino exhaustus
essem, illo recusante subsidiis amicorum respondemus. quid
5 consili de omni nostro statu capiamus te absente nescimus.
qua re adpropera.

LETTER 12 (*Q.fr.* 2.4)

Scr. Romae med. m. Mart. an. 56

MARCVS QVINTO FRATRI SALVTEM

1 Sestius noster absolutus est a. d. 11 Id. Mart. et, quod vehementer interfuit rei publicae, nullam videri in eius modi causa
dissensionem esse, omnibus sententiis absolutus est. illud quod
tibi curae saepe esse intellexeram, ne cui iniquo relinqueremus
5 vituperandi locum qui nos ingratos esse diceret nisi illius
perversitatem quibusdam in rebus quam humanissime ferre-
mus, scito hoc nos in eo iudicio consecutos esse, ut omnium
gratissimi iudicaremur; nam defendendo moroso homini
cumulatissime satis fecimus et, id quod ille maxime cupiebat,
10 Vatinium, a quo palam oppugnabatur, arbitratu nostro
concidimus dis hominibusque plaudentibus. quin etiam Paulus
noster, cum testis productus esset in Sestium, confirmavit se
nomen Vatini delaturum si Macer Licinius cunctaretur, et
Macer ab Sesti subselliis surrexit ac se illi non defuturum
15 adfirmavit. quid quaeris? homo petulans et audax [Vatinius]
valde peturbatus debilitatusque discessit.

2   Quintus filius tuus, puer optimus, eruditur egregie; hoc
nunc magis animum adverto, quod Tyrannio docet apud me.
domus utriusque nostrum aedificatur strenue; redemptori tuo
dimidium pecuniae curavi; spero nos ante hiemem con-
5 tubernales fore. de nostra Tullia, tui mehercule amantissima,

12 1.8 homine *codd.*   15 Vatinius *removit Baiter*   2.1 filius *removit*
Manutius

spero cum Crassipede nos confecisse; sed dies erant duo qui
post Latinas habentur religiosi (ceterum confectum erat
Latiar), et erat exiturus.

LETTER 13 (*Att. 4.5*)

Scr. Antii ex. m. Iun. an. 56

CICERO ATTICO SAL.

Ain tu? an me existimas ab ullo malle mea legi probarique **1**
quam a te? cur igitur cuiquam misi prius? urgebar ab eo ad
quem misi et non habebam exempla duo. quin etiam (iam
dudum enim circumrodo quod devorandum est) subturpicula
mihi videbatur esse παλινῳδία. sed valeant recta, vera, honesta **5**
consilia. non est credibile quae sit perfidia in istis principibus,
ut volunt esse et ut essent si quicquam haberent fidei. senseram,
noram inductus, relictus, proiectus ab iis. tamen hoc eram
animo ut cum iis in re publica consentirem. iidem erant qui **10**
fuerant. vix aliquando te auctore resipivi.

Dices ea te suasisse quae facerem, non etiam ut scriberem. **2**
ego mehercule mihi necessitatem volui imponere huius novae
coniunctionis ne qua mihi liceret relabi ad illos qui etiam tum
cum misereri mei debent non desinunt invidere. sed tamen
modici fuimus ἀποθεώσει, ut scripseram. erimus uberiores, si et **5**
ille libenter accipiet et hi subringentur qui villam me moleste
ferunt habere quae Catuli fuerat, a Vettio me emisse non
cogitant, qui domum negant oportuisse me aedificare, vendere
aiunt oportere. sed quid ad hoc si, quibus sententiis dixi quod

6, 8 sed *et* et *add. Sternkopf*   7 cetero *codd.*   **13** 1.2 a *om. codd.*   3 exempla
duo (*i.e.* ii) *Constans*: exemplari (*vel* -are *vel* -aria *vel* -ar) *codd.*   iam *add.*
Hand   9 eram *margo ed. Cratandrinae, ex cod. antiquo*: erat in *codd.*   2.1 te
ego: tenuisse *codd.*   facerem *Pius*: feceram *codd.*   2 nolui *codd.*   3 ne
qua mihi liceret *Victorius*: neque mihi (*vel* me) licet *codd.*   relabi *Pluygers*:
labi *codd.*   5 ΑΠΘΩCΙ *codd.*   scripseram. erimus *ego*: scripserimus *codd.*
2.9 oportere *ego*: oportuisse *codd.*

10 etiam ipsi probarent, laetati sunt tamen me contra Pompei
voluntatem dixisse? finis sit. quoniam qui nihil possunt ii me
nolunt amare, demus operam ut ab iis qui possunt diligamur.
3 dices 'vellem iam pridem'. scio te voluisse et me asinum
germanum fuisse. sed iam tempus est me ipsum a me amari,
quando ab illis nullo modo possum.

Domum meam quod crebro invisis est mihi valde gratum.
5 viaticam Crassipes praeripit. tu 'de via recta in hortos?'
videtur commodius. ad te postridie scilicet; quid enim tua?
sed viderimus.

Bibliothecam mihi tui pinxerunt cum structione et sittybis.
eos velim laudes.

LETTER 14 (*Att.* 4.12)

Scr. Antii ex. m. Iun., ut vid., an. 56

CICERO ATTICO SAL.

Egnatius Romae est, sed ego cum eo de re †Halimeti† vehementer Antii egi. graviter se acturum cum Aquilio confirmavit.
videbis ergo hominem si voles. Macroni vix videor praesto
esse. Idibus enim auctionem Larini video et biduum praeterea.
5 id tu, quoniam Macronem tanti facis, ignoscas mihi velim. sed
si me diligis, postridie Kal. cena apud me cum Pilia. prorsus
id facies. Kalendis cogito in hortis Crassipedis quasi in dever-
sorio cenare; facio fraudem senatus consulto. inde domum
cenatus, ut sim mane praesto Miloni. ibi te igitur videbo; et
10 praemonebo. domus te nostra tota salutat.

10 etiam *ego*: et *codd.*   11 sit *Graevius*: sed *codd.*   3.5 viaticam *ego*:
uiaticum *codd.*   8 cum structione *Birt*: constructione *codd.*   **14** 6 Pilia
Aldus: petilia *codd.*   10 promonebo *codd.*

LETTER 15 (*Fam.* 5.12)

Scr. Cumis (?) c. prid. Id. Apr. an. 55

M. CICERO S.D. L. LVCCEIO Q.F.

Coram me tecum eadem haec agere saepe conantem deterruit **1**
pudor quidam paene subrusticus quae nunc expromam
absens audacius; epistula enim non erubescit.

Ardeo cupiditate incredibili neque, ut ego arbitror, repre-
hendenda nomen ut nostrum scriptis illustretur et celebretur **5**
tuis. quod etsi mihi saepe ostendis te esse facturum, tamen
ignoscas velim huic festinationi meae. genus enim scriptorum
tuorum, etsi erat semper a me vehementer exspectatum,
tamen vicit opinionem meam meque ita vel cepit vel incendit
ut cuperem quam celerrime res nostras monumentis com- **10**
mendari tuis. neque enim me solum commemoratio posteritatis
ac spes quaedam immortalitatis rapit sed etiam illa cupiditas
ut vel auctoritate testimoni tui vel indicio benevolentiae vel
suavitate ingeni vivi perfruamur.

Neque tamen haec cum scribebam eram nescius quantis **2**
oneribus premerere susceptarum rerum et iam institutarum.
sed quia videbam Italici belli et civilis historiam iam a te
paene esse perfectam, dixeras autem mihi te reliquas res ordiri,
deesse mihi nolui quin te admonerem ut cogitares coniunctene **5**
malles cum reliquis rebus nostra contexere an, ut multi Graeci
fecerunt, Callisthenes Phocicum bellum, Timaeus Pyrrhi,
Polybius Numantinum, qui omnes a perpetuis suis historiis ea
quae dixi bella separaverunt, tu quoque item civilem coniu-
rationem ab hostilibus externisque bellis seiungeres. equidem **10**
ad nostram laudem non multum video interesse, sed ad
properationem meam quiddam interest non te exspectare
dum ad locum venias ac statim causam illam totam et tempus

15 1.12 ac spes quaedam *Hofmann*: ad spem quandam *codd.*   2.6 nostras
Lambinus   7 Phocicum *Westermann*: troicum *M*

arripere; et simul, si uno in argumento unaque in persona
15 mens tua tota versabitur, cerno iam animo quanto omnia
uberiora atque ornatiora futura sint.

Neque tamen ignoro quam impudenter faciam qui primum
tibi tantum oneris imponam (potest enim mihi denegare
occupatio tua), deinde etiam ut ornes me postulem. quid si
3 illa tibi non tanto opere videntur ornanda? sed tamen,
qui semel verecundiae fines transierit, eum bene et naviter
oportet esse impudentem. itaque te plane etiam atque etiam
rogo ut et ornes ea vehementius etiam quam fortasse sentis et
5 in eo leges historiae neglegas gratiamque illam de qua suavis-
sime quodam in prohoemio scripsisti, a qua te flecti non magis
potuisse demonstras quam Herculem Xenophontium illum
a Voluptate, eam, si me tibi vehementius commendabit, ne
aspernere amorique nostro plusculum etiam quam concedet
10 veritas largiare.

Quod si te adducemus ut hoc suscipias, erit, ut mihi
4 persuadeo, materies digna facultate et copia tua. a principio
enim coniurationis usque ad reditum nostrum videtur mihi
modicum quoddam corpus confici posse, in quo et illa poteris
uti civilium commutationum scientia vel in explicandis causis
5 rerum novarum vel in remediis incommodorum, cum et
reprehendes ea quae vituperanda duces et quae placebunt
exponendis rationibus comprobabis et, si liberius, ut consuesti,
agendum putabis, multorum in nos perfidiam, insidias, pro-
ditionem notabis. multam etiam casus nostri varietatem tibi
10 in scribendo suppeditabunt plenam cuiusdam voluptatis,
quae vehementer animos hominum in legendo te scriptore
tenere possit. nihil est enim aptius ad delectationem lectoris
quam temporum varietates fortunaeque vicissitudines. quae
etsi nobis optabiles in experiendo non fuerunt, in legendo
15 tamen erunt iucundae. habet enim praeteriti doloris secura
5 recordatio delectationem; ceteris vero nulla perfunctis propria

3.6 flecti *Victorius*: effecti *M*

molestia, casus autem alienos sine ullo dolore intuentibus,
etiam ipsa misericordia est iucunda. quem enim nostrum ille
moriens apud Mantineam Epaminondas non cum quadam
miseratione delectat? qui tum denique sibi evelli iubet 5
spiculum postea quam ei percontanti dictum est clipeum esse
salvum, ut etiam in vulneris dolore aequo animo cum laude
moreretur. cuius studium in legendo non erectum Themistocli
fuga †redituque† retinetur? etenim ordo ipse annalium
mediocriter nos retinet quasi enumeratione fastorum; at viri 10
saepe excellentis ancipites variique casus habent admirationem,
exspectationem, laetitiam, molestiam, spem, timorem; si vero
exitu notabili concluduntur, expletur animus iucundissima
lectionis voluptate.

Quo mihi acciderit optatius si in hac sententia fueris, ut 6
a continentibus tuis scriptis, in quibus perpetuam rerum
gestarum historiam complecteris, secernas hanc quasi fabulam
rerum eventorumque nostrorum. habet enim varios actus
multasque mutationes et consiliorum et temporum. ac non 5
vereor ne adsentatiuncula quadam aucupari tuam gratiam
videar cum hoc demonstrem, me a te potissimum ornari cele-
brarique velle. neque enim tu is es qui quid sis nescias et qui
non eos magis qui te non admirentur invidos quam eos qui
laudent adsentatores arbitrere; neque autem ego sum ita 10
demens ut me sempiternae gloriae per eum commendari velim
qui non ipse quoque in me commendando propriam ingeni
gloriam consequatur. neque enim Alexander ille gratiae causa 7
ab Apelle potissimum pingi et a Lysippo fingi volebat, sed quod
illorum artem cum ipsis tum etiam sibi gloriae fore putabat.
atque illi artifices corporis simulacra ignotis nota faciebant,
quae vel si nulla sint, nihilo sint tamen obscuriores clari viri. 5
nec minus est Spartiates Agesilaus ille perhibendus, qui neque
pictam neque fictam imaginem suam passus est esse, quam

5.5 evelli *Kayser*: auelli *M*   9 interituque *Ferrarius*   13 concluduntur
M corr.: excl- *M*   6.5 multasque mutationes *ego*: multasque actiones
M: mutationesque *Madvig*   8 qui quid *Cratander*: quid *M*

qui in eo genere laborarunt. unus enim Xenophontis libellus
in eo rege laudando facile omnes imagines omnium statuasque
10 superavit.

Atque hoc praestantius mihi fuerit et ad laetitiam animi et
ad memoriae dignitatem si in tua scripta pervenero quam si
in ceterorum quod non ingenium mihi solum suppeditatum
fuerit tuum, sicut Timoleonti a Timaeo aut ab Herodoto
15 Themistocli, sed etiam auctoritas clarissimi et spectatissimi
viri et in rei publicae maximis gravissimisque causis cogniti
atque in primis probati, ut mihi non solum praeconium, quod,
cum in Sigeum venisset, Alexander ab Homero Achilli tribu-
tum esse dixit, sed etiam grave testimonium impertitum clari
20 hominis magnique videatur. placet enim Hector ille mihi
Naevianus, qui non tantum 'laudari' se laetatur sed addit
etiam 'a laudato viro'.

8   Quod si a te non impetro, hoc est, si quae te res impedierit
(neque enim fas esse arbitror quicquam me rogantem abs te
non impetrare), cogar fortasse facere quod non nulli saepe
reprehendunt: scribam ipse de me, multorum tamen exemplo
5 et clarorum virorum. sed, quod te non fugit, haec sunt in hoc
genere vitia: et verecundius ipsi de sese scribant necesse est si
quid est laudandum et praetereant si quid reprehendendum
est. accedit etiam ut minor sit fides, minor auctoritas, multi
denique reprehendant et dicant verecundiores esse praecones
10 ludorum gymnicorum, qui, cum ceteris coronas imposuerint
victoribus eorumque nomina magna voce pronuntiarint, cum
ipsi ante ludorum missionem corona donentur, alium praeconem adhibeant, ne sua voce se ipsi victores esse praedicent.
9 haec nos vitare cupimus et, si recipis causam nostram, vita-
bimus idque ut facias rogamus.

Ac ne forte mirere cur, cum mihi saepe ostenderis te
accuratissime nostrorum temporum consilia atque eventus
5 litteris mandaturum, a te id nunc tanto opere et tam multis
verbis petamus, illa nos cupiditas incendit de qua initio scripsi,
festinationis, quod alacres animo sumus ut et ceteri viventibus

nobis ex libris tuis nos cognoscant et nosmet ipsi vivi gloriola
nostra perfruamur.

His de rebus quid acturus sis, si tibi non est molestum, **10**
rescribas mihi velim. si enim suscipis causam, conficiam commentarios reium omnium; sin autem differs me in tempus
aliud, coram tecum loquar. tu interea non cessabis et ea quae
habes instituta perpolies nosque diliges.   **5**

LETTER 16 (*Att.* 4.10)

Scr. in Cumano ix Kal. Mai. an. 55

CICERO ATTICO SAL.

Puteolis magnus est rumor Ptolomaeum esse in regno. si quid **1**
habes certius, velim scire. ego hic pascor bibliotheca Fausti.
fortasse tu putabas his rebus Puteolanis et Lucrinensibus. ne
ista quidem desunt, sed mehercule ut a ceteris oblectationibus
deseror et voluptatibus cum propter aetatem tum propter rem **5**
publicam, sic litteris sustentor et recreor maloque in illa tua
sedecula quam habes sub imagine Aristotelis sedere quam in
istorum sella curuli tecumque apud te ambulare quam cum
eo quocum video esse ambulandum. sed de illa ambulatione
fors viderit aut si quis est qui curet deus. nostram ambulationem **2**
et Laconicum eaque quae circa sunt velim quoad poteris invisas et urgeas Philotimum ut properet, ut possim tibi aliquid
in eo genere respondere.

Pompeius in Cumanum Parilibus venit. misit ad me statim **5**
qui salutem nuntiaret. ad eum postridie mane vadebam cum
haec scripsi.

---

16 1.4 ut *add. Bosius*   5 et voluptatibus...tum *ego*: et uoluptatum
codd.   **2.**2 circa *cod. Mediceus 49.18*   sunt *cod. Ambrosianus*: sint *ceteri*
codd.   quoad (quod) *Graevius*: quo *codd.* (cum *cod. Ambrosianus*)
poteris *cod. Ambrosianus*: poterit *ceteri codd.*

LETTER 17 (*Q.fr.* 2.9)

Scr., ut vid., an. 55

MARCVS QVINTO FRATRI SALVTEM

1 Tu metuis ne me interpelles? primum, si in isto essem, tu scis quid sit interpellare otiantem. sed mehercule mihi docere videris istius generis humanitatem, qua quidem ego nihil utor abs te. tu vero ut me et appelles et interpelles et obloquare et 5 colloquare velim; quid enim mihi suavius? non mehercule quisquam μουσοπάτακτος libentius sua recentia poemata legit quam ego te audio quacumque de re, publica privata, rustica urbana. sed mea factum est insulsa verecundia ut te proficiscens non tollerem. opposuisti semel ἀνавτίλεκτον causam, Ciceronis 2 nostri valetudinem; conticui. iterum Cicerones; quievi. nunc mihi iucunditatis plena epistula hoc adspersit molestiae, quod videris ne mihi molestus esses veritus esse atque etiam nunc vereri. litigarem tecum, si fas esset; sed mehercule, istuc si 5 umquam suspicatus ero, nihil dicam aliud nisi verebor ne quando ego tibi, cum sum una, molestus sim. video te ingemuisse. sic fit: 'εἰ 'δεῖν' ἔφησας – numquam enim dicam 'ἔδρασας'. Marium autem nostrum in lecticam mehercule coniecissem, non illam regis Ptolomaei Asicianam; memini enim, cum 10 hominem portarem ad Baias Neapoli octaphoro Asiciano machaerophoris centum sequentibus, miros risus nos edere cum ille ignarus sui comitatus repente aperuit lecticam et paene ille timore, ego risu corrui. hunc, ut dico, certe sustulissem ut aliquando subtilitatem veteris urbanitatis et humanissimi 15 sermonis attingerem; sed hominem infirmum in villam 3 apertam ac ne rudem quidem etiam nunc invitare nolui. hoc

---

17 1.2 otiantem. sed *ego*: antea te is *codd.*   8 insulsa] infusa *codd.*
9 ἀνавτίλεκτον *Victorius*: ΑΝΤΙΕΚΤΟΝ *codd.*   10 Cicerones *Manutius*:
ceteri omnes *codd.*   2.7 εἰ δεῖν' ἔφησας *Watt* (ἔλεξας *Rothstein*): ΕΙΔΕΝΑΙΑΕ
ΖΗCΑC *vel sim. codd.*   13 hunc *Manutius*: tunc *codd.*

vero mihi peculiare fuerit, hic etiam isto frui; nam illorum praediorum scito mihi vicinum Marium lumen esse. apud Anicium
videbimus ut paratum sit. nos enim ita philologi sumus ut vel
cum fabris habitare possimus; habemus hanc philosophiam 5
non ab Hymetto sed ab Arce nostra. Marius et valetudine est
et natura imbecillior. de interpellatione, tantum sumam a **4**
vobis temporis ad scribendum quantum dabitis; utinam nihil
detis, ut potius vestra iniuria quam ignavia mea cessem!

De re publica nimium te laborare doleo et meliorem civem
esse quam Philoctetam, qui accepta iniuria ea spectacula 5
quaerebat quae tibi acerba esse video. amabo te, advola (con-
solabor te et omnem abstergebo dolorem) et adduc, si me
amas, Marium; sed adproperate. hortus domi est.

LETTER 18 (*Fam.* 7.1)

Scr. Romae m. Sept. parte post an. 55

M. CICERO S.D. M. MARIO

Si te dolor aliqui corporis aut infirmitas valetudinis tuae tenuit **1**
quo minus ad ludos venires, fortunae magis tribuo quam
sapientiae tuae; sin haec quae ceteri mirantur contemnenda
duxisti et, cum per valetudinem posses, venire tamen noluisti,
utrumque laetor, et sine dolore corporis te fuisse et animo 5
valuisse, cum ea quae sine causa mirantur alii neglexeris,
modo ut tibi constiterit fructus oti tui; quo quidem tibi perfrui
mirifice licuit cum esses in ista amoenitate paene solus relictus.
neque tamen dubito quin tu in illo cubiculo tuo, ex quo tibi
Stabianum perforando patefecisti sinum, per eos dies matutina 10
tempora lectiunculis consumpseris, cum illi interea qui te istic
reliquerunt spectarent communes mimos semisomni. reliquas

3.4 videbimus *Aldus*: uidemus *codd*.   6 Arce nostra *ego*: araxira *vel sim. codd*.
4.1 tantum] tamen *codd*.   **18** 1.9 in *Schütz*: ex *M*   10 perforando
Reid: perforasti et *M*

vero partes diei tu consumebas iis delectationibus quas tibi
ipse ad arbitrium tuum compararas; nobis autem erant ea
15 perpetienda quae Sp. Maecius probavisset.

2   Omnino, si quaeris, ludi apparatissimi, sed non tui stomachi;
coniecturam enim facio de meo. nam primum honoris causa
in scaenam redierant ii quos ego honoris causa de scaena
decessisse arbitrabar. deliciae vero tuae, noster Aesopus, eius
5 modi fuit ut ei desinere per omnes homines liceret. is iurare
cum coepisset, vox eum defecit in illo loco, 'si sciens fallo'.
quid tibi ego alia narrem? nosti enim reliquos ludos; qui ne
id quidem leporis habuerunt quod solent mediocres ludi.
apparatus enim spectatio tollebat omnem hilaritatem; quo
10 quidem apparatu non dubito quin animo aequissimo carueris.
quid enim delectationis habent sescenti muli in 'Clytaemestra'
aut in 'Equo Troiano' creterrarum tria milia aut armatura
varia peditatus et equitatus in aliqua pugna? quae popularem
admirationem habuerunt, delectationem tibi nullam attulis-
3 sent. quod si tu per eos dies operam dedisti Protogeni tuo, dum
modo is tibi quidvis potius quam orationes meas legerit, ne
tu haud paulo plus quam quisquam nostrum delectationis
habuisti. non enim te puto Graecos aut Oscos ludos desiderasse,
5 praesertim cum Oscos vel in senatu vestro spectare possis,
Graecos ita non ames ut ne ad villam quidem tuam via Graeca
ire soleas. nam quid ego te athletas putem desiderare, qui
gladiatores contempseris? in quibus ipse Pompeius confitetur
se et operam et oleum perdidisse. reliquae sunt venationes
10 binae per dies quinque, magnificae, nemo negat; sed quae
. potest homini esse polito delectatio cum aut homo imbecillus
a valentissima bestia laniatur aut praeclara bestia venabulo
transverberatur? quae tamen, si videnda sunt, saepe vidisti,
neque nos qui haec spectavimus quicquam novi vidimus.
15 extremus elephantorum dies fuit. in quo admiratio magna
vulgi atque turbae, delectatio nulla exstitit; quin etiam miseri-

cordia quaedam consecuta est atque opinio eius modi, esse
quandam illi beluae cum genere humano societatem.

His ego tamen diebus, ludis scaenicis, ne forte videar tibi **4**
non modo beatus sed liber omnino fuisse, dirupi me paene in
iudicio Galli Canini, familiaris tui. quod si tam facilem populum haberem quam Aesopus habuit, libenter mehercule artem
desinerem tecumque et cum similibus nostri viverem. nam me **5**
cum antea taedebat, cum et aetas et ambitio me hortabatur et
licebat denique quem nolebam non defendere, tum vero hoc
tempore vita nulla est. neque enim fructum ullum laboris
exspecto et cogor non numquam homines non optime de me
meritos rogatu eorum qui bene meriti sunt defendere.   **10**

Itaque quaero causas omnes aliquando vivendi arbitratu **5**
meo teque et istam rationem oti tui et laudo vehementer et
probo, quodque nos minus intervisis, hoc fero animo aequiore
quod, si Romae esses, tamen neque nos lepore tuo neque te,
si qui est in me, meo frui liceret propter molestissimas occu- **5**
pationes meas. quibus si me relaxaro (nam ut plane exsolvam
non postulo), te ipsum, qui multos annos nihil aliud com-
mentaris, docebo profecto quid sit humaniter vivere. tu modo
istam imbecillitatem valetudinis tuae sustenta et tuere, ut facis,
ut nostras villas obire et mecum simul lecticula concursare **10**
possis.

Haec ad te pluribus verbis scripsi quam soleo non oti **6**
abundantia sed amoris erga te, quod me quadam epistula sub-
invitaras, si memoria tenes, ut ad te aliquid eius modi scriberem
quo minus te praetermisisse ludos paeniteret. quod si adsecutus
sum, gaudeo; sin minus, hoc me tamen consolor, quod posthac **5**
ad ludos venies nosque vises neque [in] epistulis relinques meis
spem aliquam delectationis tuae.

4.1 ludis scaenicis *removit Victorius*   6.4 praetermisse *M*   6 in *re-*
movit Mendelssohn, sententiam tamen non adsecutus

LETTER 19 (*Q.fr.* 2.10)

Scr. in. m. Febr. an. 54

MARCVS QVINTO FRATRI SALVTEM

1 Epistulam hanc convicio efflagitarunt codicilli tui. nam res quidem ipsa et is dies quo tu es profectus nihil mihi ad scribendum argumenti sane dabat. sed quem ad modum, coram cum sumus, sermo nobis deesse non solet, sic epistulae nostrae **2** debent interdum alucinari. Tenediorum igitur libertas securi Tenedia praecisa est, cum eos praeter me et Bibulum et Calidium et Favonium nemo defenderet. de te a Magnetibus ab Sipylo mentio est honorifica facta, cum te unum dicerent **5** postulationi L. Sesti Pansae restitisse. reliquis diebus si quid erit quod te scire opus sit, aut etiam si nihil erit, tamen scribam cottidie aliquid. prid. Id. neque tibi neque Pomponio deero. **3** Lucreti poemata, ut scribis, ita sunt, multis luminibus ingeni, multae tamen artis; sed cum veneris. virum te putabo si Sallusti Empedoclea legeris, hominem non putabo.

LETTER 20 (*Fam.* 7.5)

Scr. Romae m. Apr. an. 54

CICERO CAESARI IMP. S.D.

1 Vide quam mihi persuaserim te me esse alterum, non modo in iis rebus quae ad me ipsum sed etiam in iis quae ad meos pertinent. C. Trebatium cogitaram, quocumque exirem, mecum ducere, ut eum meis omnibus studiis beneficiis quam **5** ornatissimum domum reducerem. sed postea quam et Pompei commoratio diuturnior erat quam putaram et mea quaedam tibi non ignota dubitatio aut impedire profectionem meam

19 2.3 Magnetibus *Victorius*: magis *codd.*

videbatur aut certe tardare, vide quid mihi sumpserim: coepi
velle ea Trebatium exspectare a te quae sperasset a me, neque
mehercule minus ei prolixe de tua voluntate promisi quam 10
eram solitus de mea polliceri.

Casus vero mirificus quidam intervenit quasi vel testis 2
opinionis meae vel sponsor humanitatis tuae. nam cum de hoc
ipso Trebatio cum Balbo nostro loquerer accuratius domi
meae, litterae mihi dantur a te, quibus in extremis scriptum
erat: 'M. Curti filium, quem mihi commendas, vel regem 5
Galliae faciam; vel hunc Leptae delega, si vis, tu ad me alium
mitte quem ornem.' sustulimus manus et ego et Balbus. tanta
fuit opportunitas ut illud nescio quid non fortuitum sed
divinum videretur.

Mitto igitur ad te Trebatium atque ita mitto ut initio mea 10
sponte, post autem invitatu tuo mittendum duxerim. hunc, 3
mi Caesar, sic velim omni tua comitate complectare ut omnia
quae per me possis adduci ut in meos conferre velis in unum
hunc conferas. de quo tibi homine haec spondeo, non illo
vetere verbo meo quod, cum ad te de Milone scripsissem, 5
iure lusisti sed more Romano quo modo homines non inepti
loquuntur, probiorem hominem, meliorem virum, pudentiorem
esse neminem. accedit etiam quod familiam ducit in iure civili,
singulari memoria, summa scientia.

Huic ego neque tribunatum neque praefecturam neque 10
ullius benefici certum nomen peto; benevolentiam tuam et
liberalitatem peto, neque impedio quo minus, si tibi ita
placuerit, etiam hisce eum ornes gloriolae insignibus. totum
denique hominem tibi ita trado, de manu, ut aiunt, in
manum tuam istam et victoria et fide praestantem. simus 15
enim putidiusculi, quamquam per te vix licet; verum, ut
video, licebit.

Cura ut valeas, et me, ut amas, ama.

LETTER 21 *(Fam. 7.6)*

Scr. in Cumano aut Pompeiano m. Mai. an. 54

CICERO S.D. TREBATIO

1 In omnibus meis epistulis quas ad Caesarem aut ad Balbum
mitto legitima quaedam est accessio commendationis tuae,
nec ea vulgaris sed cum aliquo insigni indicio meae erga te
benevolentiae. tu modo ineptias istas et desideria urbis et
5 urbanitatis depone et, quo consilio profectus es, id adsiduitate
et virtute consequere. hoc tibi tam ignoscemus nos amici quam
ignoverunt Medeae

> 'quae Corinthum arcem altam habebant matronae opulen-
> tae, optimates',

10 quibus illa 'manibus gypsatissimis' persuasit ne sibi vitio illae
verterent quod abesset a patria. nam

> 'multi suam rem bene gessere et publicam patria procul;
> multi, qui domi aetatem agerent, propterea sunt improbati.'

quo in numero tu certe fuisses nisi te extrusissemus.

2 Sed plura scribemus alias. tu, qui ceteris cavere didicisti, in
Britannia ne ab essedariis decipiaris caveto et (quoniam
Medeam coepi agere) illud semper memento:

> 'qui ipse sibi sapiens prodesse non quit, nequiquam sapit.'
5 Cura ut valeas.

21 1.12 procul ⟨sua⟩ *Tyrrell, metri causa*

LETTER 22 (*Att.* 4.15)

Scr. Romae vi Kal. Sext. an. 54

CICERO ATTICO SAL.

De Eutychide gratum, qui vetere praenomine novo nomine T.   **1**
erit Caecilius, ut est ex me et ex te iunctus Dionysius M.
Pomponius. valde mehercule mihi gratum est Eutychidem tua
erga me benevolentia cognosse suam illam in meo dolore συμπάθειαν neque tum mihi obscuram neque post ingratam fuisse.   **5**

Iter Asiaticum tuum puto tibi suscipiendum fuisse. num-   **2**
quam enim tu sine iustissima causa tam longe a tot tuis et
hominibus et rebus carissimis et suavissimis abesse voluisses.
sed humanitatem tuam amoremque in tuos reditus celeritas
declarabit. sed vereor ne lepore suo detineat diutius praetor   **5**
Clodius et homo pereruditus, ut aiunt, et nunc quidem deditus
Graecis litteris Pituanius. sed si vis homo esse, recipe te ad nos
ad quod tempus confirmasti. cum illis tamen cum salvi venerint
Romae vivere licebit.

Avere te scribis accipere aliquid a me litterarum. dedi, ac   **3**
multis quidem de rebus ἡμερολεγδὸν perscripta omnia; sed, ut
conicio, quoniam mihi non videris in Epiro diu fuisse, redditas
tibi non arbitror. genus autem mearum ad te quidem litterarum eius modi fere est ut non libeat cuiquam dare nisi de quo   **5**
exploratum sit tibi eum redditurum.

Nunc Romanas res accipe. a. d. IIII Non. Quint. Sufenas et   **4**
Cato absoluti, Procilius condemnatus. ex quo intellectum est
τρισαρεοπαγίτας ambitum, comitia, interregnum, maiestatem,
totam denique rem publicam flocci non facere, patrem
familias domi suae occidi nolle, neque tamen id ipsum abunde;   **5**

---

22 1.3 gratum est (-mst) *Buecheler*: gratum si (*vel* se) *codd.*   3-4 tua...
benevolentia *Baiter*: tuam...benevolentiam *codd.*   4 cognosse suam
Baiter: cognosces suam *vel* cognossi iam *codd.*   3.1 habere *codd. meliores*
5 fere] forte *codd. plerique*   4.1 IIII *Manutius*: III *codd.*   3 τρισ *Bosius*: tres
codd.   5 occidi *Schütz*: occidere *codd.*

nam absolverunt xxii, condemnarunt xxviii. Publius sane
diserto epilogo lacrimans mentes iudicum moverat. Hortalus
in ea causa fuit cuius modi solet. nos verbum nullum; verita
est enim pusilla, quae nunc laborat, ne animum Publi offen-
10 deret.

5   His rebus actis Reatini me ad sua Τέμπη duxerunt ut agerem
causam contra Interamnates apud consules et decem legatos,
qua lacus Velinus a M'. Curio emissus interciso monte in
Narem defluit; ex quo est illa siccata et umida tamen modice
5 Rosea. vixi cum Axio; quin etiam me ad Septem Aquas duxit.

6   Redii Romam Fontei causa a. d. vii Id. Quint. veni spectatum, primum magno et aequabili plausu – sed hoc ne curaris,
ego ineptus qui scripserim. deinde Antiphonti operam. is erat
ante manu missus quam productus. ne diutius pendeas, pal-
5 mam tulit. sed nihil tam pusillum, nihil tam sine voce, nihil
tam...verum haec tu tecum habeto. in Andromacha tamen
maior fuit quam Astyanax, in ceteris parem habuit neminem.
quaeris nunc de Arbuscula. valde placuit. ludi magnifici et
grati; venatio in aliud tempus dilata.

7   Sequere nunc me in campum. ardet ambitus. ʿσῆμα δέ τοι
ἐρέωʾ: faenus ex triente Id. Quint. factum erat bessibus. dices
ʻistuc quidem non moleste fero.ʼ o virum! o civem! Memmium Caesaris omnes opes confirmant. cum eo Domitium
5 consules iunxerunt, qua pactione epistulae committere non
audeo. Pompeius fremit, queritur, Scauro studet; sed utrum
fronte an mente dubitatur. ἐξοχή in nullo est; pecunia omnium
dignitatem exaequat. Messalla languet, non quo aut animus
desit aut amici, sed coitio consulum et Pompeius obsunt. ea
10 comitia puto fore ut ducantur. tribunicii candidati iurarunt se

7 deserte *codd.*   lacrimans *ego*: criminans *vel* cruminar *codd. meliores*
9 publio *codd. plerique*   9–10 offenderem *Manutius*   5.1 Reatini] erat
in (i)me *codd.*   2 consules *ego*: consulem *codd.*   3 qua *ego*: quod *codd.*
4 Narem *Lambinus*: nar *codd.*   5 quin] qui *Manutius*   6.1–2 spectatum
Graevius: spectaculum *codd.*   3 is erat *Victorius*: miserat *codd.*   7.3 istum
codd.   5 cons. *vel* consulem *codd.*   9 consulum et] consulis *codd.*   ea *Manu-*
tius: ex *codd. plerique*

arbitrio Catonis petituros. apud eum HS quingena deposuerunt ut, qui a Catone damnatus esset, id perderet et competitoribus tribueretur.

Haec ego pridie scribebam quam comitia fore putabantur. **8** sed ad te v Kal. Sext., si facta erunt et tabellarius non erit profectus, tota comitia perscribam. quae si, ut putantur, gratuita fuerint, plus unus Cato potuerit quam omnes leges omnesque iudices.   5

Messius defendebatur a nobis de legatione revocatus; nam **9** eum Caesari legarat Appius. Servilius edixit ut adesset. tribus habet Pomptinam, Velinam, Maeciam. pugnatur acriter; agitur tamen satis. deinde me expedio ad Drusum, inde ad Scaurum. parantur orationibus indices gloriosi. fortasse accedent etiam consules designati. in quibus si Scaurus non fuerit, in hoc iudicio valde laborabit.

Ex Quinti fratris litteris suspicor iam eum esse in Britannia. **10** suspenso animo exspecto quid agat. illud quidem sumus adepti, quod multis et magnis indiciis possumus iudicare, nos Caesari et carissimos et iucundissimos esse. Dionysium velim salvere iubeas et eum roges ut te hortetur quam primum venias, ut 5 possit Ciceronem meum atque etiam me ipsum erudire.

LETTER 23 (*Att.* 5.1)

Scr. in Formiano iii aut prid. Non. Mai. an. 51

CICERO ATTICO SAL.

Ego vero et tuum in discessu vidi animum et meo sum ipse **1** testis; quo magis erit tibi videndum ne quid novi decernatur, ut hoc nostrum desiderium ne plus sit annuum.

*   *   *

12 esset] est *codd.*   et] ea *vel* et a *codd.*   8.4–5 omnes leges omnesque *Wesenberg*: omnes qui *codd.*   9.2 legerat *vel* legaret *codd.*   5–6 accident *vel* occident *codd.*

3 Nunc venio ad transversum illum extremae epistulae tuae versiculum in quo me admones de sorore. quae res se sic habet: ut veni in Arpinas, cum ad me frater venisset, in primis nobis sermo isque multus de te fuit; ex quo ego veni ad ea quae fueramus
5 ego et tu inter nos de sorore in Tusculano locuti. nihil tam vidi mite, nihil tam placatum quam tum meus frater erat in sororem tuam, ut, etiam si qua fuerat ex ratione sumpta offensio, non appareret. ille sic dies. postridie ex Arpinati profecti sumus. ut in Arcano Quintus maneret dies fecit; ego Aquini, sed pran-
10 dimus in Arcano (nosti hunc fundum). quo ut venimus, humanissime Quintus 'Pomponia' inquit, 'tu invita mulieres, ego vero adscivero pueros.' nihil potuit, mihi quidem ut visum est, dulcius, idque cum verbis tum etiam animo ac vultu. at illa audientibus nobis 'ego ipsa sum' inquit 'hic hospita'; id
15 autem ex eo, ut opinor, quod antecesserat Statius ut prandium nobis videret. tum Quintus 'en' inquit mihi, 'haec ego patior
4 cottidie.' dices 'quid, quaeso, istuc erat?' magnum; itaque me ipsum commoverat; sic absurde et aspere verbis vultuque responderat. dissimulavi dolens. discubuimus omnes praeter illam, cui tamen Quintus de mensa misit; illa reiecit. quid
5 multa? nihil meo fratre lenius, nihil asperius tua sorore mihi visum est; et multa praetereo quae tum mihi maiori stomacho quam ipsi Quinto fuerunt. ego inde Aquinum. Quintus in Arcano remansit et Aquinum ad me postridie mane venit mihique narravit nec secum illam dormire voluisse et cum dis-
10 cessura esset fuisse eius modi qualem ego vidissem. quid quaeris? vel ipsi hoc dicas licet, humanitatem ei meo iudicio illo die defuisse. haec ad te scripsi, fortasse pluribus quam necesse fuit, ut videres tuas quoque esse partes instituendi et monendi.
5 Reliquum est ut ante quam proficiscare mandata nostra exhaurias, scribas ad me omnia, Pomptinum extrudas, cum profectus eris cures ut sciam, sic habeas, nihil mehercule te mihi nec carius esse nec suavius.

23 3.7 sumptus *codd. aliquot*   4.1 quaeso *Manutius*: quasi *codd.*

A. Torquatum amantissime dimisi Minturnis, optimum 5
virum; cui me ad te scripsisse aliquid in sermone significes
velim.

LETTER 24 (*Fam.* 13.1)

Scr. Athenis ex. m. Iun. vel in. m. Quint. an. 51

M. CICERO S.D. C. MEMMIO

Etsi non satis mihi constiterat cum aliquane animi mei molestia 1
an potius libenter te Athenis visurus essem, quod iniuria quam
accepisti dolore me adficeret, sapientia tua qua fers iniuriam
laetitia, tamen vidisse te mallem; nam quod est molestiae non
sane multo levius est cum te non video, quod esse potuit 5
voluptatis certe, si vidissem te, plus fuisset. itaque non dubitabo
dare operam ut te videam, cum id satis commode facere potero.
interea quod per litteras et agi tecum et, ut arbitror, confici
potest, agam nunc, ac te illud primum rogabo, ne quid invitus 2
mea causa facias, sed id quod mea intelleges multum, tua
nullam in partem interesse ita mihi des si tibi ut id libenter
facias ante persuaseris.

Cum Patrone Epicurio mihi omnia sunt, nisi quod in 5
philosophia vehementer ab eo dissentio. sed et initio Romae,
cum te quoque et tuos omnes observabat, me coluit in primis
et nuper, cum ea quae voluit de suis commodis et praemiis
consecutus est, me habuit suorum defensorum et amicorum
fere principem et iam a Phaedro, qui nobis cum pueri essemus, 10
ante quam Philonem cognovimus, valde ut philosophus, postea
tamen ut vir bonus et suavis et officiosus probabatur, traditus
mihi commendatusque est.

Is igitur Patro cum ad me Romam litteras misisset, uti te 3
sibi placarem peteremque ut nescio quid illud Epicuri parietinarum sibi concederes, nihil scripsi ad te ob eam rem quod

---

24 2.2–3 multum *post* partem *codd., transposuit Aldus*

aedificationis tuae consilium commendatione mea nolebam
5 impediri. idem, ut veni Athenas, cum idem ut ad te scriberem
rogasset, ob eam causam impetravit quod te abiecisse illam
4 aedificationem constabat inter omnes amicos tuos. quod si ita
est et si iam tua plane nihil interest, velim, si qua offensiuncula
facta est animi tui perversitate aliquorum (novi enim gentem
illam), des te ad lenitatem vel propter summam tuam humani-
5 tatem vel etiam honoris mei causa. equidem, si quid ipse
sentiam quaeris, nec cur ille tanto opere contendat video nec
cur tu repugnes, nisi tamen multo minus tibi concedi potest
quam illi laborare sine causa. quamquam Patronis et orationem
et causam tibi cognitam esse certo scio; honorem, officium,
10 testamentorum ius, Epicuri auctoritatem, Phaedri obtestationem, sedem, domicilium, vestigia summorum hominum sibi
tuenda esse dicit. totam hominis vitam rationemque quam
sequitur in philosophia derideamus licet si hanc eius contentionem volumus reprehendere. sed mehercules, quoniam
15 illi ceterisque quos illa delectant non valde inimici sumus,
nescio an ignoscendum sit huic si tanto opere laborat; in quo
etiam si peccat, magis ineptiis quam improbitate peccat.
5 Sed ne plura (dicendum enim aliquando est), Pomponium
Atticum sic amo ut alterum fratrem. nihil est illo mihi nec
carius nec iucundius. is (non quo sit ex istis; est enim omni
liberali doctrina politissimus, sed valde diligit Patronem, valde
5 Phaedrum amavit) sic a me hoc contendit, homo minime
ambitiosus, minime in rogando molestus, ut nihil umquam
magis, nec dubitat quin ego a te nutu hoc consequi possem
etiam si aedificaturus esses. nunc vero, si audierit te aedificationem deposuisse neque tamen me a te impetrasse, non te in
10 me illiberalem sed me in se neglegentem putabit. quam ob
rem peto a te ut scribas ad tuos posse tua voluntate decretum
illud Areopagitarum, quem ὑπομνηματισμὸν illi vocant,
tolli.
Sed redeo ad prima. prius velim tibi persuadeas ut hoc mea

causa libenter facias quam ut facias. sic tamen habeto, si
feceris quod rogo, fore mihi gratissimum.
Vale.

LETTER 25 (*Att.* 5.14)

Scr. Trallibus, ut vid., vi Kal. Sext. an. 51

CICERO ATTICO SAL.

Ante quam aliquo loco consedero, neque longas a me neque **1**
semper mea manu litteras exspectabis; cum autem erit spatium,
utrumque praestabo. nunc iter conficiebamus aestuosa et
pulverulenta via. dederam Epheso pridie; has dedi Trallibus. in
provincia mea fore me putabam Kal. Sext. ex ea die, si me **5**
amas, παράπηγμα ἐνιαύσιον commoveto. interea tamen haec
mihi quae vellem adferebantur, primum otium Parthicum,
dein confectae pactiones publicanorum, postremo seditio
militum sedata ab Appio stipendiumque eis usque ad Id. Quint.
persolutum.   **10**

Nos Asia accepit admirabiliter. adventus noster fuit nemini **2**
ne minimo quidem sumptui. spero meos omnes servire laudi
meae; tamen magno timore sum, sed bene speramus. omnes
iam nostri praeter Tullium tuum venerunt. erat mihi in animo
recta proficisci ad exercitum, aestivos menses reliquos rei **5**
militari dare, hibernos iuris dictioni.

Tu velim, si me nihilo minus nosti curiosum in re publica **3**
quam te, scribas ad me omnia, quae sint, quae futura sint.
nihil mihi gratius facere potes; nisi tamen id erit mihi gratissimum, si quae tibi mandavi confeceris in primisque illud
ἐνδόμυχον, quo mihi scis nihil esse carius.   **5**

Habes epistulam plenam festinationis et pulveris; reliquae
subtiliores erunt.

25 1.3 praestabo] est (ē) dabo *vel* dabo *vel* stabo *codd. plerique*   5–6 me
amas *Victorius*: meas *codd.*   παράπηγμα *Tunstall*: ΠΑΓΓΕΓΜΑ *vel sim.*
codd.   2.3 paramus *codd.*   3.5 ἐνδόμυχον *Victorius*: ΕΝΟΜΥΛΟΝ *vel
sim. codd.*

LETTER 26 (*Fam.* 15.1)

Scr. in finibus Lycaoniae et Cappadociae xiii Kal. Oct. an. 51

M. TVLLIVS M.F. CICERO PRO COS. S.D. COS.
PR. TR. PL. SENATVI

1 S. v. v. b. e. e. q. v.

Etsi non dubie mihi nuntiabatur Parthos transisse Euphratem cum omnibus fere suis copiis, tamen, quod arbitrabar a
M. Bibulo pro consule certiora de his rebus ad vos scribi posse,
5 statuebam mihi non necesse esse publice scribere ea quae de
alterius provincia nuntiarentur. postea vero quam certissimis
auctoribus, legatis, nuntiis, litteris sum certior factus, vel quod
tanta res erat vel quod nondum audieramus Bibulum in
Syriam venisse vel quia administratio huius belli mihi cum
10 Bibulo paene est communis, quae ad me delata essent scribenda
ad vos putavi.

2 Regis Antiochi Commageni legati primi mihi nuntiarunt
Parthorum magnas copias Euphratem transire coepisse. quo
nuntio adlato, cum essent non nulli qui ei regi minorem fidem
habendam putarent, statui exspectandum esse si quid certius
5 adferretur. a. d. XIII Kal. Oct., cum exercitum in Ciliciam
ducerem, in finibus Lycaoniae et Cappadociae mihi litterae
redditae sunt a Tarcondimoto, qui fidelissimus socius trans
Taurum amicissimusque populo Romano existimatur, Paco-
rum, Orodi regis Parthorum filium, cum permagno equitatu
10 Parthico transisse Euphratem et castra posuisse Tybae, mag-
numque tumultum esse in provincia Syria excitatum. eodem
die ab Iamblicho, phylarcho Arabum, quem homines opinantur
bene sentire amicumque esse rei publicae nostrae, litterae de
isdem rebus mihi redditae sunt.

3 His rebus adlatis, etsi intellegebam socios infirme animatos
esse et novarum rerum exspectatione suspensos, sperabam
tamen eos ad quos iam accesseram quique nostram

mansuetudinem integritatemque perspexerant amiciores
populo Romano esse factos, Ciliciam autem firmiorem fore si 5
aequitatis nostrae particeps facta esset. et ob eam causam et ut
opprimerentur ii qui ex Cilicum gente in armis essent et ut
hostis is qui esset in Syria sciret exercitum populi Romani non
modo non cedere iis nuntiis adlatis sed etiam propius accedere,
exercitum ad Taurum institui ducere.   10

Sed si quid apud vos auctoritas mea ponderis habet, in iis **4**
praesertim rebus quas vos audistis, ego paene cerno, magno
opere vos et hortor et moneo ut his provinciis, serius vos
quidem quam decuit sed aliquando tamen, consulatis. nos
quem ad modum instructos et quibus praesidiis munitos ad tanti 5
belli opinionem miseritis, non estis ignari. quod ego negotium
non stultitia occaecatus sed verecundia deterritus non recusavi.
neque enim umquam ullum periculum tantum putavi quod
subterfugere mallem quam vestrae auctoritati obtemperare.

Hoc autem tempore res sese sic habet ut, nisi exercitum **5**
tantum quantum ad maximum bellum mittere soletis mature
in has provincias miseritis, summum periculum sit ne amit-
tendae sint omnes eae provinciae quibus vectigalia populi
Romani continentur. quam ob rem autem in hoc provinciali **5**
dilectu spem habeatis aliquam causa nulla est. neque multi
sunt et diffugiunt qui sunt metu oblato; et quod genus hoc
militum sit iudicavit vir fortissimus, M. Bibulus, in Asia, qui,
cum vos ei permisissetis, dilectum habere noluerit. nam
sociorum auxilia propter acerbitatem atque iniurias imperi 10
nostri aut ita imbecilla sunt ut non multum nos iuvare possint aut ita alienata a nobis ut neque exspectandum ab iis
neque committendum iis quicquam esse videatur. regis **6**
Deiotari et voluntatem et copias, quantaecumque sunt,
nostras esse duco. Cappadocia est inanis, reliqui reges tyrannique neque opibus satis firmi nec voluntate sunt. mihi in hac
paucitate militum animus certe non deerit, spero ne consilium
quidem. quid casurum sit incertum est. utinam saluti nostrae 5
consulere possimus! dignitati certe consulemus.

26 3.4 mansuetudinem *Ferrarius*: consuetudinem *codd.*

LETTER 27 (*Fam.* 2.12)

Scr., ut vid., in castris ad Pyramum c. v Kal. Quint. an. 50

M. CICERO IMP. S.D. M. CAELIO AEDILI CVRVLI

1 Sollicitus equidem eram de rebus urbanis. ita tumultuosae contiones, ita molestae Quinquatrus adferebantur; nam citeriora nondum audieramus. sed tamen nihil me magis sollicitabat quam in his molestiis non me, si quae ridenda
5 essent, ridere tecum; sunt enim multa, sed ea non audeo scribere. illud moleste fero, nihil me adhuc his de rebus habere tuarum litterarum. qua re, etsi, cum tu haec leges, ego iam annuum munus confecero, tamen obviae mihi velim sint tuae litterae quae me erudiant de omni re publica, ne hospes plane
10 veniam. hoc melius quam tu facere nemo potest.

2 Diogenes tuus, homo modestus, a me cum Philone Pessinuntem discessit. iter habebant ad Adiatorigem, quamquam omnia nec benigna nec copiosa cognorant.

Vrbem, urbem, mi Rufe, cole et in ista luce vive! omnis
5 peregrinatio, quod ego ab adulescentia iudicavi, obscura et sordida est iis quorum industria Romae potest illustris esse. quod cum probe scirem, utinam in sententia permansissem! cum una mehercule ambulatiuncula atque uno sermone nostro
3 omnes fructus provinciae non confero. spero me integritatis laudem consecutum: non erat minor ex contemnenda quam est ex conservata provincia. spem triumphi inicis: satis gloriose triumpharem, non essem quidem tam diu in desiderio rerum
5 mihi carissimarum. sed, ut spero, propediem te videbo. tu mihi obviam mitte epistulas te dignas.

---

27 1.3 audiebamus *codd.* 2.1–2 Pessinuntem *Baiter* (-ta *Martyni-Laguna*): pessi nuncte *M* (*in altero exemplo* pessinunte) ad Adiatorigem *Taurellus*: adiatoregem *M* 3.3 inicis: satis *ego*: inquisatis *M* (*in altero exemplo* inquis satis)

LETTER 28 (*Fam.* 9.25)

Scr. Laodiceae fort. med. m. Mart. an. 50

CICERO IMP. PAETO

Summum me ducem litterae tuae reddiderunt. plane nescie- **1**
bam te tam peritum esse rei militaris; Pyrrhi te libros et
Cineae video lectitasse. itaque obtemperare cogito praceptis
tuis; hoc amplius, navicularum habere aliquid in ora maritima.
contra equitem Parthum negant ullam armaturam meliorem 5
inveniri posse. sed quid ludimus? nescis quo cum imperatore
tibi negotium sit. Παιδείαν Κύρου, quam contrieram legendo,
totam in hoc imperio explicavi. sed iocabimur alias coram, ut **2**
spero, brevi tempore.

Nunc ades ad imperandum, vel ad parendum potius; sic
enim antiqui loquebantur. cum M. Fabio, quod scire te
arbitror, mihi summus usus est valdeque eum diligo cum prop- 5
ter summam probitatem eius ac singularem modestiam tum
quod in iis controversiis quas habeo cum tuis combibonibus
Epicuriis optima opera eius uti soleo. is, cum ad me Laodiceam **3**
venisset mecumque ego eum esse vellem, repente percussus
est atrocissimis litteris, in quibus scriptum erat fundum
Herculanensem a Q. Fabio fratre proscriptum esse, qui fundus
cum eo communis esset. id M. Fabius pergraviter tulit existi- 5
mavitque fratrem suum, hominem non sapientem, impulsu
inimicorum suorum eo progressum esse.

Nunc, si me amas, mi Paete, negotium totum suscipe,
molestia Fabium libera. auctoritate tua nobis opus est et
consilio et etiam gratia. noli pati litigare fratres et iudiciis **10**
turpibus conflictari. Matonem et Pollionem inimicos habet
Fabius. quid multa? non mehercule tam perscribere possum
quam mihi gratum feceris si otiosum Fabium reddideris. id
ille in te positum esse putat mihique persuadet.

28 3.12 tam *removit nescio quis*: *anne* tantum?

LETTER 29 (*Fam.* 15.6)

Scr. Tarsi post. parte m. Quint. an. 50

M. CICERO S.D. M. CATONI

1 'Laetus sum laudari me' inquit Hector, opinor, apud Naevium
'abs te, pater, a laudato viro.' ea est enim profecto iucunda
laus quae ab iis proficiscitur qui ipsi in laude vixerunt. ego
vero vel gratulatione litterarum tuarum vel testimoniis
5 sententiae dictae nihil est quod me non adsecutum putem,
idque mihi cum amplissimum tum gratissimum est, te libenter
amicitiae dedisse quod liquido veritati dares. et si non modo
omnes verum etiam multi Catones essent in civitate nostra, in
qua unum exstitisse mirabile est, quem ego currum aut quam
10 lauream cum tua laudatione conferrem? nam ad meum sensum
et ad illud sincerum ac subtile iudicium nihil potest esse
laudabilius quam ea tua oratio quae est ad me perscripta a
meis necessariis.

2   Sed causam meae voluntatis (non enim dicam cupiditatis)
exposui tibi superioribus litteris. quae etiam si parum iusta
tibi visa est, hanc tamen habet rationem, non ut nimis con-
cupiscendus honos sed tamen, si deferatur a senatu, minime
5 aspernandus esse videatur. spero autem illum ordinem pro
meis ob rem publicam susceptis laboribus me non indignum
honore, usitato praesertim, existimaturum. quod si ita erit,
tantum ex te peto, quod amicissime scribis, ut, cum tuo iudicio
quod amplissimum esse arbitraris mihi tribueris, si id quod
10 maluero acciderit, gaudeas. sic enim fecisse te et sensisse et
scripsisse video, resque ipsa declarat tibi illum honorem
nostrum supplicationis iucundum fuisse, quod scribendo adfuisti. haec enim senatus consulta non ignoro ab amicissimis
eius cuius de honore agitur scribi solere.

15   Ego, ut spero, te prope diem videbo, atque utinam re publica
meliore quam timeo!

29 2.3 nimis] minus *codd.*

LETTER 30 (*Att.* 6.6)

Scr. Sidae c. iii Non. Sext. an. 50

CICERO ATTICO SAL.

Ego dum in provincia omnibus rebus Appium orno, subito **1**
sum factus accusatoris eius socer. 'id quidem' inquis 'di
adprobent!' ita velim, teque ita cupere certo scio. sed crede
mihi, nihil minus putaram ego, qui de Ti. Nerone, qui mecum
egerat, certos homines ad mulieres miseram; qui Romam **5**
venerunt factis sponsalibus. sed hoc spero melius. mulieres
quidem valde intellego delectari obsequio et comitate adule-
scentis. cetera noli ἐξακανθίζειν.

Sed heus tu, πυροὺς εἰς δῆμον Athenis? placet hoc tibi? etsi **2**
non impediebant mei certe libri; non enim ista largitio fuit in
cives sed in hospites liberalitas. me tamen de Academiae
προπύλῳ iubes cogitare, cum iam Appius de Eleusine non
cogitet?   **5**

De Hortensio te certo scio dolere. equidem excrucior;
decreram enim valde cum eo familiariter vivere.

Nos provinciae praefecimus Coelium. 'puerum' inquies 'et **3**
fortasse fatuum et non gravem et non continentem.' adsentior;
fieri non potuit aliter. nam quas multo ante tuas acceperam
litteras in quibus ἐπέχειν te scripseras quid esset mihi faciendum
de relinquendo, eae me pungebant. videbam enim quae tibi **5**
essent ἐποχῆς causae, et erant eaedem mihi. puero traderem?
id rei publicae non utile. fratri autem? illud non utile nobis.
nam praeter fratrem nemo erat quem sine contumelia quaestori,
nobili praesertim, anteferrem. tamen, dum impendere Parthi
videbantur, statueram fratrem relinquere, aut etiam rei pub- **10**
licae causa contra senatus consultum ipse remanere; qui postea

30 1.4 quin de *Madvig*   2.4 cum iam *Manutius*: quoniam *codd.*   3.6
traderem *cod. Tornesianus deperditus, teste Bosio*: tradere *codd.*   7 id...
utile *addidi*: illud non rei publicae, hoc non utile nobis *Madvig*

quam incredibili felicitate discesserunt, sublata dubitatio est.
videbam sermones: 'hui, fratrem reliquit! num est hoc non
plus annum obtinere provinciam? quid quod senatus eos
voluit praeesse provinciis qui non praefuissent? at hic trien-   15
nium.'

Ergo haec ad populum: quid quae tecum? numquam 4
essem sine cura, si quid iracundius aut contumeliosius aut
neglegentius, quae fert vita hominum. quid si quid filius puer
et puer bene sibi fidens? qui esset dolor? quem pater non
dimittebat teque id censere moleste ferebat. at nunc Coelius 5
non dico equidem 'quod egerit', sed tamen multo minus
laboro. adde illud: Pompeius, eo robore vir, iis radicibus,
Q. Cassium sine sorte delegit, Caesar Antonium: ego sorte
datum offenderem, ut etiam inquireret in eum quem reliquis-
sem? hoc melius, et huius rei plura exempla, senectuti quidem 10
nostrae profecto aptius. at te apud eum, di boni, quanta in
gratia posui! eique legi litteras non tuas sed librari tui.

Amicorum litterae me ad triumphum vocant, rem a nobis,
ut ego arbitror, propter hanc παλιγγενεσίαν nostram non
neglegendam. qua re tu quoque, mi Attice, incipe id cupere, 15
quo nos minus inepti videamur.

LETTER 31 (*Fam.* 16.5)

Scr. Leucade vii Id. Nov. an. 50

TVLLIVS ET CICERO ET QQ. TIRONI
HVMANISSIMO ET OPTIMO S.P.D.

Vide quanta sit in te suavitas. duas horas Thyrrei fuimus: 1
Xenomenes hospes tam te diligit quasi vixerit tecum. is omnia
pollicitus est quae tibi essent opus; facturum puto. mihi place-
bat, si firmior esses, ut te Leucadem deportaret, ut ibi te plane
confirmares. videbis quid Curio, quid Lysoni, quid medico 5
placeat. volebam ad te Marionem remittere quem, cum

meliuscule tibi esset, ad me mitteres; sed cogitavi unas litteras
Marionem adferre posse, me autem crebras exspectare. quod **2**
poteris igitur; et facies, si me diligis, ut cottidie sit Acastus in
portu. multi erunt quibus recte litteras dare possis qui ad me
libenter perferant. equidem Patras euntem neminem praeter-
mittam.   5

Ego omnem spem tui diligenter curandi in Curio habeo.
nihil potest illo fieri humanius, nihil nostri amantius. ei te
totum trade. malo te paulo post valentem quam statim im-
becillum videre. cura igitur nihil aliud nisi ut valeas; cetera
ego curabo.   10

Etiam atque etiam vale.

Leucade proficiscens VII Id. Nov.

LETTER 32 (*Att.* 7.4)

Scr. in Cumano, ut vid., c. Id. Dec. an. 50

CICERO ATTICO SAL.

Dionysium flagrantem desiderio tui misi ad te, nec mehercule **1**
aequo animo, sed fuit concedendum. quem quidem cognovi
cum doctum, quod mihi iam ante erat notum, tum sanctum,
plenum offici, studiosum etiam meae laudis, frugi hominem,
ac, ne libertinum laudare videar, plane virum bonum.   5

Pompeium vidi IIII Id. Dec.; fuimus una horas duas fortasse. **2**
magna laetitia mihi visus est adfici meo adventu; de triumpho
hortari, suscipere partes suas, monere ne ante in senatum
accederem quam rem confecissem, ne dicendis sententiis aliquem tribunum alienarem. quid quaeris? in hoc officio sermone **5**
eius nihil potuit esse prolixius. de re publica autem ita mecum
locutus est quasi non dubium bellum haberemus: nihil ad spem
concordiae; plane illum a se alienatum cum ante intellegeret,

tum vero proxime iudicasse; venisse Hirtium a Caesare, qui
10 esset illi familiarissimus, ad se non accessisse et, cum ille a. d.
VIII Id. Dec. vesperi venisset, Balbus de tota re constituisset
a. d. VII ad Scipionem ante lucem venire, multa de nocte eum
profectum esse ad Caesarem. hoc illi τεκμηριῶδες videbatur
3 esse alienationis. quid multa? nihil me aliud consolatur nisi
quod illum, cui etiam inimici alterum consulatum, fortuna
summam potentiam dederit, non arbitror fore tam amentem
ut haec in discrimen adducat. quod si ruere coeperit, ne ego
5 multa timeo quae non audeo scribere. sed ut nunc est, a. d.
III Non. Ian. ad urbem cogito.

LETTER 33 (*Att.* 7.10)

Scr. ad urbem xiii Kal. Febr. an. 49

CICERO ATTICO SAL.

Subito consilium cepi ut ante quam luceret exirem, ne qui
conspectus fieret aut sermo, lictoribus praesertim laureatis. de
reliquo neque hercule quid agam neque quid acturus sim
scio; ita sum perturbatus temeritate nostri amentissimi consili.
5 tibi vero quid suadeam, cuius ipse consilium exspecto? Gnaeus
noster quid consili ceperit capiatve nescio adhuc, in oppidis
coartatus et stupens. omnes, si in Italia consistet, erimus una;
sin cedet, consili res est. adhuc certe, nisi ego insanio, stulte
omnia et incaute. tu, quaeso, crebro ad me scribe vel quod
10 in buccam venerit.

11 venisset ⟨et⟩ *Madvig*   3.3 dederit *Pius*: dederet *M*   **33** 7 et] sed
codd.   omnes] omnino *Watt*   consistet *Pius*: consistat *codd.*   8 certe
Victorius: certa *vel* incerta *vel* incerti *codd.*

LETTER 34 (*Fam.* 14.18)

Scr. Formiis ix Kal. Febr. an. 49

TVLLIVS TERENTIAE SVAE ET PATER SVAVISSIMAE
FILIAE, CICERO MATRI ET SORORI S.D.P.

Considerandum vobis etiam atque etiam, animae meae, **1**
diligenter puto quid faciatis, Romaene sitis an mecum an
aliquo tuto loco. id non solum meum consilium est sed etiam
vestrum.

Mihi veniunt in mentem haec: Romae vos esse tuto posse **5**
per Dolabellam eamque rem posse nobis adiumento esse si
quae vis aut si quae rapinae fieri coeperint; sed rursus illud
me movet, quod video omnes bonos abesse Roma et eos
mulieres suas secum habere. haec autem regio in qua ego sum
nostrorum est cum oppidorum tum etiam praediorum, ut et **10**
multum esse mecum et, cum aberitis, commode et in nostris
esse possitis. mihi plane non satis constat adhuc utrum sit **2**
melius. vos videte quid aliae faciant isto loco feminae et ne,
cum velitis, exire non liceat. id velim diligenter etiam atque
etiam vobiscum et cum amicis consideretis. domus ut pro-
pugnacula et praesidium habeat Philotimo dicetis. et velim **5**
tabellarios instituatis certos ut cottidie aliquas a vobis litteras
accipiam. maxime autem date operam ut valeatis, si nos vultis
valere.

VIIII Kal. Formiis.

34 1.2 mecum an *Wesenberg*: mecum in *codd.*   11 aberitis *ego*: abi-
eritis *M*

LETTER 35 (*Fam.* 7.27)

Scr. in Italia an. 49 ante m. Apr.

M. CICERO S.D. T. FADIO

1 Miror cur me accuses cum tibi id facere non liceat. quod si
liceret, tamen non debebas. 'ego enim te in consulatu obser-
varam,' ais, et fore ut te Caesar restituat: multa tu quidem
dicis, sed tibi nemo credit. tribunatum plebi dicis te mea causa
5 petiisse: utinam semper esses tribunus! intercessorem non
quaereres. negas me audere quod sentiam dicere: quasi tibi,
cum impudenter me rogares, parum fortiter responderim.

2 Haec tibi scripsi ut isto ipso in genere in quo aliquid posse
vis te nihil esse cognosceres. quod si humaniter mecum questus
esses, libenter tibi me et facile purgassem; non enim ingrata
mihi sunt quae fecisti, sed quae scripsisti molesta. me autem,
5 propter quem ceteri liberi sunt, tibi liberum non visum
demiror. nam si falsa fuerunt quae tu ad me, ut ais, detulisti,
quid tibi ego debeo? si vera, tu es optimus testis quid mihi
populus Romanus debeat.

LETTER 36 (*Att.* 8.1)

Scr. in Formiano xv vel xiv Kal. Mart. an. 49

CICERO ATTICO SAL.

1 Cum ad te litteras dedissem, redditae mihi litterae sunt a
Pompeio: cetera de rebus in Piceno gestis quas ad se Vibullius
scripsisset, de dilectu Domiti, quae sunt vobis nota, nec tam
laeta erant in iis litteris quam ad me Philotimus scripserat.

35 T. FADIO *ego*: GALLO *M*   1.2 te ⟨inquis⟩ *Lambinus*   3 ais, et
ego: et ais *M*   2.7 quid *om. M*   36 1.2 quas *ego*: qu(a)e *codd.*   3 tam]
tamen *codd.*: tamen tam *Bosius*   4 quam ⟨quae⟩ *Orelli*

ipsam tibi epistulam misissem sed iam subito fratris puer 5
proficiscebatur; cras igitur mittam. sed in ea Pompei epistula
erat in extremo ipsius manu 'tu censeo Luceriam venias;
nusquam eris tutius.' id ego in eam partem accepi, haec oppida
.atque oram maritimam illum pro relicto habere, nec sum
miratus eum qui caput ipsum reliquisset reliquis membris non 10
parcere. ei statim rescripsi, hominemque certum misi de 2
comitibus meis, me non quaerere ubi tutissimo essem; si me
vellet sua aut rei publicae causa Luceriam venire, statim esse
venturum; hortatusque sum ut oram maritimam retineret, si
rem frumentariam sibi ex provinciis suppeditari vellet. hoc me 5
frustra scribere videbam; sed uti in urbe retinenda tunc, sic
nunc in Italia non relinquenda testificabar sententiam meam.
sic enim parari video, ut Luceriam omnes copiae contrahantur
et ne is quidem locus sit stabilis sed ex eo ipso, si urgeamur,
paretur fuga; quo minus mirere si invitus in eam causam 3
descendo in qua neque pacis neque victoriae ratio quaesita sit
umquam sed semper flagitiosae et calamitosae fugae. eundum,
ut quemcumque fors tulerit casum subeam potius cum iis qui
dicuntur esse boni quam videar a bonis dissentire. etsi prope 5
diem video bonorum, id est lautorum et locupletum, urbem
refertam fore, municipiis vero his relictis refertissimam; quo
ego in numero essem, si hos lictores molestissimos non haberem,
nec me M'. Lepidi, L. Vulcati, Ser. Sulpici comitum paeniteret, quorum nemo nec stultior est quam L. Domitius nec in- 10
constantior quam Ap. Claudius. unus Pompeius me movet, 4
beneficio non auctoritate; quam enim ille habeat auctoritatem
in hac causa? qui, cum omnes Caesarem metuebamus, ipse
eum diligebat, postquam ipse metuere coepit, putat omnes
hostes illi esse oportere. ibimus tamen Luceriam, nec eum 5
fortasse delectabit noster adventus; dissimulare enim non
potero mihi quae adhuc acta sint displicere.

5 sed] miser *codd.*   2.9 sit *add. Müller (post* stabilis *Ernesti)*   3.3 *fort.*
⟨sed⟩ eundum *vel* eundum ⟨tamen⟩   4.1 habet *Kayser*

Ego si somnum capere possem, tam longis te epistulis non obtunderem. tu, si tibi eadem causa est, me remunerere sane velim.

LETTER 37 (*Att.* 8.13)

Scr. in Formiano Kal. Mart. an. 49

CICERO ATTICO SAL.

1 Lippitudinis meae signum tibi sit librari manus et eadem causa brevitatis; etsi nunc quidem quod scriberem nihil erat. omnis exspectatio nostra erat in nuntiis Brundisinis; si nactus hic esset Gnaeum nostrum, spes dubia pacis, sin ille ante
5 tramisisset, exitiosi belli metus.

Sed videsne in quem hominem inciderit res publica, quam acutum, quam vigilantem, quam paratum? si mehercule neminem occiderit neque cuiquam quicquam ademerit, ab iis qui
2 eum maxime timuerant maxime diligetur. multum mecum municipales homines loquuntur, multum rusticani; nihil prorsus aliud curant nisi agros, nisi villulas, nisi nummulos suos. et vide quam conversa res sit: illum quo antea confidebant metuunt,
5 hunc amant quem timebant. id quantis nostris peccatis vitiisque evenerit non possum sine molestia cogitare. quae autem impendere putarem scripseram ad te, et iam tuas litteras exspectabam.

37 1.3 si] nisi *codd.*   2.4 sit *Lambinus*: est *codd.*

LETTER 38 (*Att.* 9.18)

Scr. in Formiano v Kal. Apr. an. 49

CICERO ATTICO SAL.

Vtrumque ex tuo consilio; nam et oratio fuit ea nostra ut bene **1**
potius ille de nobis existimaret quam gratias ageret, et in eo
mansimus, ne ad urbem. illa fefellerunt, facilem quod puta-
ramus; nihil vidi minus. damnari se nostro iudicio, tardiores
fore reliquos, si nos non veniremus, dicere. ego dissimilem **5**
illorum esse causam. cum multa, 'veni igitur et age de pace.'
'meone' inquam 'arbitratu?' 'an tibi' inquit 'ego praescri-
bam?' 'sic' inquam 'agam, senatui non placere in Hispanias
iri nec exercitus in Graeciam transportari, multaque' inquam
'de Gnaeo deplorabo.' tum ille, 'ego vero ista dici nolo.' 'ita **10**
putabam' inquam, 'sed ego eo nolo adesse quod aut sic mihi
dicendum est aut non veniendum, multaque quae nullo modo
possem silere si adessem.' summa fuit ut ille, quasi exitum
quaerens, ut deliberarem. non fuit negandum. ita discessimus.
credo igitur hunc me non amare. at ego me amavi, quod mihi **15**
iam pridem usu non venit.

Reliqua, o di! qui comitatus, quae, ut tu soles dicere, νέκυια! **2**
in qua erat ἥρως Celer. o rem perditam! o copias desperatas!
quid quod Servi filius, quod Titini in iis castris fuerunt quibus
Pompeius circumsederetur? sex legiones; multum vigilat,
audet. nullum video finem mali. nunc certe promenda tibi **5**
sunt consilia. hoc fuerat extremum.

Illa tamen κατακλεὶς illius est odiosa, quam paene praeterii, **3**
si sibi consiliis nostris uti non liceret, usurum quorum posset

---

38 1.5 reliquos *Victorius*: belli quos *codd.* veniremus *Faërnus*: ueneri-
mus *codd.* 10 de Gnaeo *Victorius*: digne eo *codd.* 12–13 aut non veniendum *post* adessem *codd. deteriores* 13 possim *codd.* 15 me amavi
Victorius: mea(m) aut *codd.* 2.2 ἥρως Celer *Lehmann*: ero sceler(um) *vel*
(a)ero sceleri *codd.* 4 sex legiones] sed legionis *codd.*

ad omniaque esse descensurum. vidisti igitur virum, ut
scripseras? ingemuisti certe. 'cedo reliqua.' quid? continuo
5 ipse in †Pelanum†, ego Arpinum; inde exspecto equidem
λαλαγεῦσαν illam tuam. 'tu malim' inquies 'actum ne agas;
etiam illum ipsum quem sequimur multa fefellerunt.'

4　Sed ego tuas litteras exspecto. nihil est enim ut antea 'videamus hoc quorsum evadat'. extremum fuit de congressu nostro;
quo quidem non dubito quin istum offenderim. eo maturius
agendum est. amabo te, epistulam, et πολιτικήν. valde tuas
5 litteras nunc exspecto.

LETTER 39 (*Fam.* 14.7)

Scr. in portu Caietano nave conscensa vii Id. Iun.

TVLLIVS TERENTIAE SVAE S.P.

1 Omnes molestias et sollicitudines quibus et te miserrimam
habui, id quod mihi molestissimum est, et Tulliolam, quae
nobis nostra vita dulcior est, deposui et eieci. quid causae
autem fuerit postridie intellexi quam a vobis discessi. χολὴν
5 ἄκρατον noctu eieci. statim ita sum levatus ut mihi deus aliquis
medicinam fecisse videatur. cui quidem tu deo, quem ad
modum soles, pie et caste satis facies [id est Apollini et
Aesculapio].

2 Navem spero nos valde bonam habere. in eam simul atque
conscendi, haec scripsi. deinde conscribam ad nostros familiares
multas epistulas, quibus te et Tulliolam nostram diligentissime
commendabo. cohortarer vos quo animo fortiores essetis nisi
5 vos fortiores cognossem quam quemquam virum. et tamen eius
modi spero negotia esse ut et vos istic commodissime sperem

3.3-4 *ita distinxi; at vulgo* 'vidisti...scripseras? ingemuisti?' certe.　　ut]
aut *vel* aut ut *codd.*　　5 Pedanum *nescio quis*: Pedi Norbanum *O. E. Schmidt*
equidem *Lambinus*: quidem *codd.*　　6 λαλαγεῦσαν *Bosius*: *varia, velut*
ΛΛΛΤΕΛCAN *codd.* malim *Boot*: mal(l)em *vel* malum *codd.* 39 1.7-8 id
...Aesculapio *glossema esse suspicatus est Manutius*

esse et me aliquando cum similibus nostri rem publicam
defensuros. tu primum valetudinem tuam velim cures; deinde, 3
si tibi videbitur, villis iis utere quae longissime aberunt a
militibus. fundo Arpinati bene poteris uti cum familia urbana
si annona carior fuerit.

Cicero bellissimus tibi salutem plurimam dicit. etiam atque 5
etiam vale.

D. vii Id. Iun.

LETTER 40 (*Att.* 11.4)

Scr. in castris Pompei Id. Quint. an. 48

CICERO ATTICO SAL.

Accepi ab Isidoro litteras et postea datas binas. ex proximis
cognovi praedia non venisse. videbis ergo ut sustentetur per te.
de Frusinati, si modo fruituri sumus, erit mihi res opportuna.
meas litteras quod requiris, impedior inopia rerum, quas nullas
habeo litteris dignas, quippe cui nec quae accidunt nec quae 5
aguntur ullo modo probentur. utinam coram tecum olim
potius quam per epistulas! hic tua, ut possum, tueor apud hos.
cetera Celer. ipse fugi adhuc omne munus, eo magis quod ita
nihil poterat agi ut mihi et meis rebus aptum esset.

LETTER 41 (*Att.* 11.5)

Scr. Brundisii prid. Non. Nov. an. 48

CICERO ATTICO SAL.

Quae me causae moverint, quam acerbae, quam graves, 1
quam novae, coegerintque impetu magis quodam animi uti

3.1 tu] ut *codd.*   40 2 per te *Manutius*: partim *codd.*   3 Frusinati *Her-
vagius*: frusinatis *codd.*   fruituri *Lehmann*: futur(a)e *codd.*   41 1.2 quo-
dam] coram *codd.*

quam cogitatione, non possum ad te sine maximo dolore
scribere. fuerunt quidem tantae ut id quod vides effecerint.
5 itaque nec quid ad te scribam de meis rebus nec quid a te
petam reperio; rem et summam negoti vides.

Equidem ex tuis litteris intellexi et iis quas communiter cum
aliis scripsisti et iis quas tuo nomine, quod etiam mea sponte
videbam, te subita re quasi debilitatum novas rationes tuendi
10 mei quaerere.

2   Quod scribis placere ut propius accedam iterque per oppida
noctu faciam, non sane video quem ad modum id fieri possit.
neque enim ita apta habeo deversoria ut tota tempora diurna
in iis possim consumere neque ad id quod quaeris multum
5 interest utrum me homines in oppido videant an in via. sed
tamen hoc ipsum sicut alia considerabo quem ad modum
commodissime fieri posse videatur.

3   Ego propter incredibilem et animi et corporis molestiam
conficere plures litteras non potui; iis tantum rescripsi a quibus
acceperam. tu velim et Basilo et quibus praeterea videbitur,
etiam Servilio, conscribas, ut tibi videbitur, meo nomine. quod
5 tanto intervallo nihil omnino ad vos scripsi, his litteris profecto
intellegis rem mihi deesse de qua scribam, non voluntatem.

4   Quod de Vatinio quaeris, neque illius neque cuiusquam mihi
praeterea officium deest, si reperire possent qua in re me
iuvarent. Quintus aversissimo a me animo Patris fuit. eodem
. Corcyra filius venit. inde profectos eos una cum ceteris
5 arbitror.

4 tantae ut *Victorius*: tanta fuit *codd.*   3.5 scripsi, his *Wesenberg*: scriptis
codd.   4.2 deesset *Corradus*   4 Corcyra *Victorius*: corcyram *codd.*

LETTER 42 (*Fam.* 14.12)

Scr. Brundisii prid. Non. Nov. an. 48

TVLLIVS TERENTIAE SVAE S.D.

Quod nos in Italiam salvos venisse gaudes, perpetuo gaudeas velim. sed perturbati dolore animi magnisque meorum iniuriis metuo ne id consili ceperimus quod non facile explicare possimus. qua re, quantum potes, adiuva; quid autem possis mihi in mentem non venit. in viam quod te des hoc tempore nihil 5 est. et longum est iter et non tutum; et non video quid prodesse possis si veneris.

Vale.

D. prid. Non. Nov. Brundisio.

LETTER 43 (*Fam.* 14.20)

Scr. in Venusino Kal. Oct. an. 47

TVLLIVS S.D. TERENTIAE SVAE

In Tusculanum nos venturos putamus aut Nonis aut postridie. ibi ut sint omnia parata. plures enim fortasse nobiscum erunt et, ut arbitror, diutius ibi commorabimur. labrum si in balineo non est, ut sit; item cetera quae sunt ad victum et ad valetudinem necessaria. 5

Vale.

Kal. Oct. de Venusino.

42 2 meorum *addidi*

LETTER 44 *(Fam.* 9.1)

Scr. Romae ex. an. 47 aut in. an. 46

CICERO M. VARRONI S.

1 Ex iis litteris quas Atticus a te missas mihi legit quid ageres
et ubi esses cognovi; quando autem te visuri essemus, nihil
sane ex isdem litteris potui suspicari. in spem tamen venio
appropinquare tuum adventum. qui mihi utinam solacio sit!
5 etsi tot tantisque rebus urgemur ut nullam adlevationem
quisquam non stultissimus sperare debeat. sed tamen aut tu
2 potes me aut ego te fortasse aliqua re iuvare. scito enim me,
postea quam in urbem venerim, redisse cum veteribus amicis,
id est cum libris nostris, in gratiam. etsi non idcirco eorum
usum dimiseram quod iis suscenserem sed quod eorum me
5 subpudebat; videbar enim mihi, cum me in res turbulentis-
simas infidelissimis sociis demisissem, praeceptis illorum non
satis paruisse. ignoscunt mihi, revocant in consuetudinem
pristinam teque, quod in ea permanseris, sapientiorem quam
me dicunt fuisse. quam ob rem, quoniam placatis iis utor,
10 videor sperare debere, si te viderim, et ea quae premant et ea
quae impendeant me facile laturum.

Quam ob rem, sive in Tusculano sive in Cumano, sive ad
me sive ad te placebit, sive, quod minime velim, Romae, dum
modo simul simus, perficiam profecto ut id utrique nostrum
15 commodissimum esse videatur.

---

44 2.6 demissum *codd.*   10–11 acque...aeque *M*   11 laturum *duo*
codd.; turum *M* (transi *superscr. manus vetus*)   12–13 sive ad me sive *addidi*
15 diuidetur *M*: diiudicetur *duo codd. et vulg.*

LETTER 45 (*Fam.* 9.18)

Scr. in Tusculano paulo ante vii Kal. Sext. an. 46

CICERO S.D. PAETO

Cum essem otiosus in Tusculano propterea quod discipulos **1**
obviam miseram, ut eadem me quam maxime conciliarent
familiari suo, accepi tuas litteras plenissimas suavitatis; ex
quibus intellexi probari tibi meum consilium, quod, ut
Dionysius tyrannus, cum Syracusis pulsus esset, Corinthi **5**
dicitur ludum aperuisse, sic ego sublatis iudiciis, amisso regno
forensi ludum quasi habere coeperim. quid quaeris? me **2**
quoque delectat consilium. multa enim consequor: primum,
id quod maxime nunc opus est, munio me ad haec tempora.
id cuius modi sit nescio; tantum video, nullius adhuc consilium
me huic anteponere, nisi forte mori melius fuit. in lectulo, **5**
fateor, sed non accidit; in acie non fui. ceteri quidem, Pompeius,
Lentulus tuus, Scipio, Afranius foede perierunt. at Cato praeclare. iam istuc quidem cum volemus licebit; demus modo
operam ne tam necesse nobis sit quam illi fuit, id quod agimus.
ergo hoc primum. **10**

Sequitur illud: ipse melior fio, primum valetudine, quam **3**
intermissis exercitationibus amiseram; deinde ipsa illa, si qua
fuit in me, facultas orationis, nisi me ad has exercitationes
rettulissem, exaruisset. extremum illud est, quod tu nescio an
primum putes: plures iam pavones confeci quam tu pullos **5**
columbinos. tu istic te Hateriano iure delectas, ego me hic
Hirtiano. veni igitur, si vir es, et disce a me προλεγομένας quas
quaeris; etsi sus Minervam. sed, quo modo video, si aestima- **4**
tiones tuas vendere non potes neque ollam denariorum implere,
Romam tibi remigrandum est; satius est hic cruditate quam

---

45 1.1 pr(a)eterea *codd.*   2.4 consilium *Ernesti:* consilio *codd.*   3.7 disce
a me *Bengel:* disceam *M*   4.1 sed...si *locum varie vexatum distinguendo
sanavi, quod postmodo suo Marte fecit M. Demmel*

istic fame. video te bona perdidisse; spero idem istuc familiares
5 tuos. actum igitur de te est nisi provides. potes mulo isto, quem
tibi reliquum dicis esse, quoniam cantherium comedisti,
Romam pervehi. sella tibi erit in ludo, tamquam hypodidas-
calo, proxima; eam pulvinus sequetur.

LETTER 46 (*Fam.* 7.28)

Scr. Romae m. Sext., ut vid., an. 46

M. CICERO S.D. CVRIO

1 Memini cum mihi desipere videbare quod cum istis potius
viveres quam nobiscum. erat enim multo domicilium huius
urbis, cum quidem haec urbs, aptius humanitati et suavitati
tuae quam tota Peloponnesus, nedum Patrae. nunc contra et
5 vidisse mihi multum tum videris cum prope desperatis his
rebus te in Graeciam contulisti et hoc tempore non solum
sapiens qui hinc absis sed etiam beatus. quamquam quis qui
aliquid sapiat nunc esse beatus potest?

2 Sed quod tu, cui licebat, pedibus es consecutus, ut ibi esses
'ubi nec Pelopidarum' (nosti cetera), nos idem prope modum
consequimur alia ratione. cum enim salutationi nos dedimus
amicorum, quae fit hoc etiam frequentius quam solebat quod
5 quasi avem albam videntur bene sentientem civem videre,
abdo me in bibliothecam. itaque opera efficio tanta quanta
fortasse tu senties; intellexi enim ex tuo sermone quodam,
cum meam maestitiam et desperationem accusares domi tuae,
dicere te ex meis libris animum meum desiderare.

3 Sed mehercule et tum rem publicam lugebam, quae non
solum a suis erga me sed etiam a meis erga se beneficiis erat

---

4 idem istic *Gronovius*: item istic *Orelli*   **46** 1.3 urbs ⟨fuit⟩ *Wesenberg*
5 tum *addidi*   2.9 dicere *removit Graevius*: discere *Madvig, parum feliciter*
3.2 a suis erga mc *ego*: suis erga me *vulgo*: a me *cod. Harleianus 2773*: a suis
cod. Parisinus 17812: om. *M*   a meis] meis *vulgo*

mihi vita mea carior, et hoc tempore, quamquam me non
ratio solum consolatur, quae plurimum debet valere, sed
etiam dies, quae stultis quoque mederi solet, tamen doleo ita 5
rem communem esse dilapsam ut ne spes quidem melius
aliquando fore relinquatur. nec vero nunc quidem culpa in eo
est in cuius potestate omnia sunt, nisi forte id ipsum esse non
debuit; sed alia casu, alia etiam nostra culpa sic acciderunt ut
de praeteritis non sit querendum. reliquam spem nullam video. 10
qua re ad prima redeo: sapienter haec reliquisti si consilio,
feliciter si casu.

LETTER 47 (*Fam.* 6.14)

Scr. Romae ex. m. Nov. an. 46

CICERO LIGARIO

Me scito omnem meum laborem, omnem operam, curam, **1**
studium in tua salute consumere. nam cum te semper maxime
dilexi tum fratrum tuorum, quos aeque atque te summa
benevolentia sum complexus, singularis pietas amorque
fraternus nullum me patitur offici erga te studique munus aut 5
tempus praetermittere. sed quae faciam fecerimque pro te ex
illorum te litteris quam ex meis malo cognoscere. quid autem
sperem, aut confidam et exploratum habeam, de salute tua,
id tibi a me declarari volo.

Nam si quisquam est timidus in magnis periculosisque rebus 10
semperque magis adversos rerum exitus metuens quam
sperans secundos, is ego sum et, si hoc vitium est, eo me non
carere confiteor. ego idem tamen, cum a. d. v Kal. inter- **2**
calares priores rogatu fratrum tuorum venissem mane ad
Caesarem atque omnem adeundi et conveniendi illius in-
dignitatem et molestiam pertulissem, cum fratres et propinqui
tui iacerent ad pedes et ego essem locutus quae causa, quae 5

3.3 vita (*Kleyn*) mea add. *Wesenberg*

tuum tempus postulabat, non solum ex oratione Caesaris,
quae sane mollis et liberalis fuit, sed etiam ex oculis et vultu,
ex multis praeterea signis, quae facilius perspicere potui quam
scribere, hac opinione discessi ut mihi tua salus dubia non esset.
3   Quam ob rem fac animo magno fortique sis et, si turbidis-
sima sapienter ferebas, tranquilliora laete feras. ego tamen
tuis rebus sic adero ut difficillimis neque Caesari solum sed
etiam amicis eius omnibus, quos mihi amicissimos esse
5 cognovi, pro te, sicut adhuc feci, libentissime supplicabo.
Vale.

LETTER 48 (*Fam.* 9.26)

Scr. Romae med. m. interc. post., ut vid., an. 46

CICERO PAETO S.D.

1 Accubueram hora nona cum ad te harum exemplum in
codicillis exaravi. dices 'ubi?' apud Volumnium Eutrapelum,
et quidem supra me Atticus, infra Verrius, familiares tui.
miraris tam exhilaratam esse servitutem nostram? quid ergo
5 faciam? te consulo, qui philosophum audis. angar, excruciem
me? quid adsequar? deinde, quem ad finem? 'vivas' inquis
'in litteris.' an quicquam me aliud agere censes aut posse vivere
nisi in litteris viverem? sed est earum etiam non satietas sed
quidam modus; a quibus cum discessi, etsi minimum mihi est
10 in cena, quod tu unum ζήτημα Dioni philosopho posuisti, tamen
quid potius faciam prius quam me dormitum conferam non
reperio.
2   Audi reliqua. infra Eutrapelum Cytheris accubuit. 'in eo
igitur' inquis 'convivio Cicero ille

"quem aspectabant, cuius ob os Grai ora obvertebant sua"?'

non mehercule suspicatus sum illam adfore. sed tamen ne

Aristippus quidem ille Socraticus erubuit cum esset obiectum 5
habere eum Laida. 'habeo' inquit, 'non habeor a Laide'
(Graece hoc melius; tu, si voles, interpretabere). me vero
nihil istorum ne iuvenem quidem movit umquam, ne nunc
senem. convivio delector; ibi loquor quod in solum, ut
dicitur, et gemitum in risus maximos transfero. an tu id melius 3
qui etiam [in] philosophum irriseris, cum ille si quis quid
quaereret dixisset, cenam te quaerere a mane dixeris? ille
baro te putabat quaesiturum unum caelum esset an innumera-
bilia. quid ad te? at hercule cena numquid ad te, ibi prae- 5
sertim?

Sic igitur vivitur. cottidie aliquid legitur aut scribitur. 4
dein, ne amicis nihil tribuamus, epulamur una non modo non
contra legem, si ulla nunc lex est, sed etiam intra legem, et
quidem aliquanto. qua re nihil est quod adventum nostrum
extimescas. non multi cibi hospitem accipies, multi ioci.   5

LETTER 49 (*Fam.* 9.23)

Scr. in Cumano xiii Kal. Dec., ut vid., an. 46

CICERO PAETO

Heri veni in Cumanum, cras ad te fortasse; sed cum certum
sciam, faciam te paulo ante certiorem. etsi M. Caeparius, cum
mihi in silva Gallinaria obviam venisset quaesissemque quid
ageres, dixit te in lecto esse quod ex pedibus laborares. tuli
scilicet moleste, ut debui, sed tamen constitui ad te venire, 5
ut et viderem te et viserem et cenarem etiam; non enim
arbitror cocum etiam te arthriticum habere. exspecta igitur
hospitem cum minime edacem tum inimicum cenis sump-
tuosis.

2.6 Laida *post* inquit *add. nescio quis ('cur non...ante* habeo?' *Purser*)   a
Laide *removit Muretus*   3.2 in *removit Cratander*   cum] et cum *vel sim.*
viri docti

LETTER 50 (*Fam.* 7.4)

Scr. in Cumano xiii Kal. Dec., ut vid., an. 46

M. CICERO S.D. M. MARIO

A. d. xiiii Kal. in Cumanum veni cum Libone tuo, vel nostro potius. in Pompeianum statim cogito, sed faciam ante te certiorem. te cum semper valere cupio tum certe dum hic sumus; vides enim quanto post una futuri simus. qua re, si
5 quod constitutum cum podagra habes, fac ut in alium diem differas. cura igitur ut valeas, et me hoc biduo aut triduo exspecta.

LETTER 51 (*Fam.* 7.26)

Scr. in Tusculano inter m. Oct. an. 46 et Febr. an. 45

CICERO S.D. GALLO

1 Cum decimum iam diem graviter ex intestinis laborarem neque iis qui mea opera uti volebant me probarem non valere quia febrim non haberem, fugi in Tusculanum, cum quidem biduum ita ieiunus fuissem ut ne aquam quidem gustarem.
5 itaque confectus languore et fame magis tuum officium desideravi quam a te requiri putavi meum. ego autem cum omnes morbos reformido tum eum in quo Epicurum tuum Stoici male accipiunt quia dicat στραγγουρικὰ καὶ δυσεντερικὰ πάθη sibi molesta esse; quorum alterum morbum edacitatis
10 esse putant, alterum etiam turpioris intemperantiae. sane δυσεντερίαν pertimueram; sed visa est mihi vel loci mutatio vel animi etiam relaxatio vel ipsa fortasse iam senescentis morbi remissio profuisse.

50 1 xiiii *Schiche*: viii *codd.*   4 simus *Victorius*: sumus *codd.*   **51** 1.7 eum in quo *ego*: quod *M*: quo *Manutius*: in quo *nescio quis*   8 στραγγουρικὰ *Orelli*: γγουρικα *M*

Ac tamen, ne mirere unde hoc acciderit quo modove 2
commiserim, lex sumptuaria, quae videtur λιτότητα attulisse,
ea mihi fraudi fuit. nam dum volunt isti lauti terra nata, quae
lege excepta sunt, in honorem adducere, fungos, helvellas,
herbas omnes ita condiunt ut nihil possit esse suavius. in eas 5
cum incidissem in cena augurali apud Lentulum, tanta me
διάρροια arripuit ut hodie primum videatur coepisse consistere.
ita ego, qui me ostreis et murenis facile abstinebam, a beta
et a malva deceptus sum. posthac igitur erimus cautiores.   10

Tu tamen, cum audisses ab Anicio (vidit enim me nause-
antem), non modo mittendi causam iustam habuisti sed
etiam visendi. ego hic cogito commorari quoad me reficiam.
nam et vires et corpus amisi; sed si morbum depulero, facile,
ut spero, illa revocabo.   15

LETTER 52 (*Fam.* 5.16)

Scr. aestate vel autumno, ut vid., an. 46

M. CICERO S.D. TITIO

Etsi unus ex omnibus minime sum ad te consolandum accom- 1
modatus, quod tantum ex tuis molestiis cepi doloris ut con-
solatione ipse egerem, tamen, cum longius a summi luctus
acerbitate meus abesset dolor quam tuus, statui nostrae
necessitudinis esse meaeque in te benevolentiae non tacere 5
tanto in tuo maerore tam diu sed adhibere aliquam modicam
consolationem, quae levare dolerem tuum posset si minus
sanare potuisset.

Est autem consolatio pervulgata quidem illa maxime, quam 2
semper in ore atque in animo habere debemus, homines nos
ut esse meminerimus, ea lege natos ut omnibus telis fortunae
proposita sit vita nostra, neque esse recusandum quo minus
ea qua nati sumus condicione vivamus, neve tam graviter eos 5
casus feramus quos nullo consilio vitare possimus eventisque

aliorum memoria repetendis nihil accidisse novi nobis cogite-
3 mus. sed neque hae neque ceterae consolationes quae sunt a
sapientissimis viris usurpatae memoriaeque litteris proditae
tantum videntur proficere debere quantum status ipse nostrae
civitatis et haec perturbatio temporum perditorum, cum
5 beatissimi sint qui liberos non susceperunt, minus autem miseri
qui his temporibus amiserunt quam si eosdem bona aut denique aliqua re publica perdidissent.

4 Quod si tuum te desiderium movet aut si tuarum rerum
cogitatione maeres, non facile exhauriri tibi istum dolorem
posse universum puto; sin illa te res cruciat quae magis amoris
est, ut eorum qui occiderunt miserias lugeas, ut ea non dicam
5 quae saepissime et legi et audivi, nihil mali esse in morte, ex
qua si resideat sensus immortalitas illa potius quam mors
ducenda sit, sin sit amissus nulla videri miseria debeat quae
non sentiatur, hoc tamen non dubitans confirmare possum,
ea misceri, parari, impendere rei publicae quae qui reliquerit
10 nullo modo mihi quidem deceptus esse videatur. quid est enim
iam non modo pudori, probitati, virtuti, rectis studiis, bonis
artibus sed omnino libertati ac saluti loci? non mehercule
quemquam audivi hoc gravissimo et pestilentissimo anno
adulescentulum aut puerum mortuum qui mihi non a dis
15 immortalibus ereptus ex his miseriis atque ex iniquissima
condicione vitae videretur.

5 Qua re, si tibi unum hoc detrahi potest, ne quid iis quos
amasti mali putes contigisse, permultum erit ex maerore tuo
deminutum. relinquetur enim simplex illa iam cura doloris
tui, quae non cum illis communicabitur sed ad te ipsum
5 proprie referetur; in qua non est iam gravitatis et sapientiae
tuae, quam tu a puero praestitisti, ferre immoderatius casum
incommodorum tuorum, qui sit ab eorum quos dilexeris
miseria maloque seiunctus. etenim eum semper te et privatis in
rebus et publicis praestitisti tuenda tibi ut sit gravitas et
10 constantiae serviendum. nam quod adlatura est ipsa diutur-

nitas, quae maximos luctus vetustate tollit, id nos praecipere
consilio prudentiaque debemus. etenim si nulla fuit umquam **6**
liberis amissis tam imbecillo mulier animo quae non aliquando
lugendi modum fecerit, certe nos, quod est dies adlatura, id
consilio ante ferre debemus neque exspectare temporis
medicinam, quam repraesentare ratione possimus. **5**

His ego litteris si quid profecissem, existimabam optandum
quiddam me esse adsecutum; sin minus forte valuissent, officio
tamen esse functum viri benevolentissimi atque amicissimi.
quem me tibi et fuisse semper existimes velim et futurum esse
confidas. **10**

LETTER 53 *(Fam. 15.18)*

Scr. Romae m. Dec. an. 46

M. CICERO S.D. C. CASSIO

Longior epistula fuisset nisi eo ipso tempore petita esset a me **1**
cum iam iretur ad te, longior autem si φλύαρον aliquem
habuissem; nam σπουδάζειν sine periculo vix possumus.
'ridere igitur' inquies 'possumus?' non mehercule facillime;
verum tamen aliam aberrationem a molestiis nullam habemus. **5**
'ubi igitur' inquies 'philosophia?' tua quidem in culina, mea
molesta est; pudet enim servire. itaque facio me alias res agere
ne convicium Platonis audiam.

De Hispania nihil adhuc certi, nihil omnino novi. te abesse **2**
mea causa moleste fero, tua gaudeo. sed flagitat tabellarius.
valebis igitur meque, ut a puero fecisti, amabis.

---

53 1.2 autem si] autem *Mendelssohn, alii alia*   3 habuissem *Lambinus*:
habuisset *codd.*

LETTER 54 (*Fam.* 16.18)

Scr. Romae, ut vid., post m. Oct. an. 47

TVLLIVS TIRONI S.

1 Quid igitur? non sic oportet? equidem censeo sic, addendum etiam 'suo'. sed, si placet, invidia vitetur; quam quidem ego saepe contempsi.

Tibi διαφόρησιν gaudeo profuisse; si vero etiamTusculanum,
5 di boni, quanto mihi illud erit amabilius! sed si me amas, quod quidem aut facis aut perbelle simulas, quod tamen in modum procedit – sed, utut est, indulge valetudini tuae; cui quidem tu adhuc, dum mihi deservis, servisti non satis. ea quid postulet non ignoras: πέψιν, ἀκοπίαν, περίπατον σύμμετρον,
10 τρῖψιν, εὐλυσίαν κοιλίας. fac bellus revertare, ut non modo te sed etiam Tusculanum nostrum plus amem.

2 Parhedrum excita ut hortum ipse conducat; sic holitorem ipsum commovebis. Helico nequissimus HS ∞ dabat, nullo aprico horto, nullo emissario, nulla maceria, nulla casa. iste nos tanta impensa derideat? calface hominem, ut ego Motho-
3 nem; itaque abutor coronis. de Crabra quid agatur, etsi nunc quidem etiam nimium est aquae, tamen velim scire. horologium mittam et libros, si erit sudum. sed tu nullosne tecum libellos? an pangis aliquid Sophocleum? fac opus appareat.

5 A. Ligurius, Caesaris familiaris, mortuus est, bonus homo et nobis amicus. te quando exspectemus fac ut sciam. cura te diligenter.
Vale.

---

54 1.3 saepe] semper *cod. Palatinus*   7 utut *Manutius*: ut *codd.*   10
ut *add. Orelli*

LETTER 55 (*Fam. 9.10*)

Scr. Romae in. an. 45

M. CICERO S.D. P. DOLABELLAE

Non sum ausus Salvio nostro nihil ad te litterarum dare; nec **1**
mehercule habebam quid scriberem nisi te a me mirabiliter
amari, de quo etiam nihil scribente me te non dubitare certo
scio. omnino mihi magis litterae sunt exspectandae a te quam
a me tibi; nihil enim Romae geritur quod te putem scire **5**
curare, nisi forte scire vis me inter Niciam nostrum et Vidium
iudicem esse. profert alter, opinor, duobus versiculis expensum
Niciae, alter Aristarchus hos ὀβελίζει; ego tamquam criticus
antiquus iudicaturus sum utrum sint τοῦ ποιητοῦ an παρεμβε-
βλημένοι.   **10**

Puto te nunc dicere 'oblitusne es igitur fungorum illorum **2**
quos apud Niciam et ingentium †cularum cum sophia
septimae†?' quid ergo? tu adeo mihi excussam severitatem
veterem putas ut ne in foro quidem reliquiae pristinae frontis
appareant? sed tamen suavissimum συμβιωτὴν nostrum **5**
praestabo integellum, nec committam ut, si ego eum con-
demnaro, tu restituas, ne non habeat Bursa Plancus apud quem
litteras discat.

Sed quid ago? cum mihi sit incertum tranquillone sis animo **3**
an ut in bello in aliqua maiuscula cura negotiove versere,
labor longius. cum igitur mihi erit exploratum te libenter esse
risurum, scribam ad te pluribus. te tamen hoc scire volo,
vehementer populum sollicitum fuisse de P. Sullae morte ante **5**
quam certum scierit. nunc quaerere desierunt quo modo
perierit; satis putant se scire quod sciunt. ego ceteroqui animo
aequo fero. unum vereor, ne hasta Caesaris refrixerit.

55 2.1 te *add. Aldus*   7 ne non *Sedgwick*: ne *codd.*: ut *Wesenberg*

LETTER 56 (*Att.* 12.15)

Scr. Asturae vii Id. Mart. an. 45

CICERO ATTICO SAL.

Apud Appuleium, quoniam in perpetuum non placet, in dies
ut excuser videbis. in hac solitudine careo omnium colloquio,
cumque mane me in silvam abstrusi densam et asperam, non
exeo inde ante vesperum. secundum te nihil est mihi amicius
5 solitudine. in ea mihi omnis sermo est cum litteris. eum tamen
interpellat fletus; cui repugno quoad possum, sed adhuc pares
non sumus. Bruto, ut suades, rescribam. eas litteras cras
habebis. cum erit cui des, dabis.

LETTER 57 (*Att.* 12.16)

Scr. Asturae vi Id. Mart. an. 45

CICERO ATTICO SAL.

Te tuis negotiis relictis nolo ad me venire; ego potius accedam,
si diutius impediere. etsi ne discessissem quidem e conspectu
tuo, nisi me plane nihil ulla res adiuvaret. quod si esset
aliquod levamen, id esset in te uno, et cum primum ab aliquo
5 poterit esse, a te erit. nunc tamen ipsum sine te esse non
possum. sed nec tuae domi probabatur nec meae poteram nec,
si propius essem uspiam, tecum tamen essem. idem enim te
impediret quo minus mecum esses quod nunc etiam impedit.
mihi nihil adhuc aptius fuit hac solitudine; quam vereor ne
10 Philippus tollat. heri enim vesperi venerat. me scriptio et
litterae non leniunt sed obturbant.

57 2 decessissem *codd.*

LETTER 58 (*Att.* 12.32)

Scr. Asturae v Kal. Apr. an. 45

CICERO ATTICO SAL.

Haec ad te mea manu. vide, quaeso, quid agendum sit. **1**
Publilia ad me scripsit matrem suam cum Publilio locutam et
ut mecum loqueretur ad me cum illo venturam et se una, si
ego paterer. orat multis et supplicibus verbis ut liceat et ut
sibi rescribam. res quam molesta sit vides. rescripsi me etiam **5**
gravius esse adfectum quam tum cum illi dixissem me solum
esse velle; qua re nolle me hoc tempore eam ad me venire.
putabam si nihil rescripsissem illam cum matre venturam;
nunc non puto. apparebat enim illas litteras non esse ipsius.
illud autem quod fore video ipsum volo vitare, ne illi ad me **10**
veniant, et una est vitatio ut ego evolem. nollem, sed necesse est.
te hoc nunc rogo ut explores ad quam diem hic ita possim
esse ut ne opprimar. ages, ut scribis, temperate.

Ciceroni velim hoc proponas, ita tamen si tibi non iniquum **2**
videbitur, ut sumptus huius peregrinationis, quibus, si Romae
esset domumque conduceret, quod facere cogitabat, facile
contentus futurus erat, accommodet ad mercedes Argileti et
Aventini, et cum ei proposueris ipse velim reliqua moderere, **5**
quem ad modum ex iis mercedibus suppeditemus ei quod opus
sit praestabo nec Bibulum nec Acidinum nec Messallam, quos
Athenis futuros audio, maiores sumptus facturos quam quod
ex eis mercedibus recipietur. itaque velim videas primum
conductores qui sint et quanti, deinde ut sint qui ad **10**
diem solvant, et quid viatici, quid instrumenti satis sit.

---

58 1.2-3 locutam...mecum *addidi*   loqueretur] ut loquerer *ed. Romana*:
locutam *Iunius*   7 nolle me *Victorius*: nole me *vel* nollem me *codd.*   10
illi *duo codd. Parisini*: ill(a)e *cod. Mediceus 49.18 et dett.*   11 evolem *addidi*
(avolem *Madvig*)   2.2-4 quibus...futurus erat *post* Aventini (*v. 5*)
transp. Madvig   10-11 ut sint...solvant *Lambinus*: ut sit...soluat *codd.*

iumento certe Athenis nihil opus sit. quibus autem in via utatur domi sunt plura quam opus erit, quod etiam tu animadvertis.

LETTER 59 (*Fam.* 9.11)

Scr., ut vid., in Attici Nomentano paulo post xii Kal. Mai. an. 45

CICERO DOLABELLAE S.

1 Vel meo ipsius interitu mallem litteras meas desiderares quam eo casu quo sum gravissime adflictus; quem ferrem certe moderatius si te haberem. nam et oratio tua prudens et amor erga me singularis multum levaret. sed quoniam brevi tempore,
5 ut opinio nostra est, te sum visurus, ita me adfectum offendes ut multum a te possim iuvari; non quo ita sim fractus ut aut hominem me esse oblitus sim aut fortunae succumbendum putem, sed tamen hilaritas illa nostra et suavitas, quae te praeter ceteros delectabat, erepta mihi omnis est; firmitatem
10 tamen et constantiam, si modo fuit aliquando in nobis, eandem cognosces quam reliquisti.

2 Quod scribis proelia te mea causa sustinere, non tam id laboro ut si qui mihi obtrectent a te refutentur quam intellegi cupio, quod certe intellegitur, me a te amari. quod ut facias te etiam atque etiam rogo, ignoscasque brevitati litterarum
5 mearum; nam et celeriter una futuros nos arbitror et nondum satis sum confirmatus ad scribendum.

12 sit] est *nescio quis*: erit *Wesenberg*   via *Pius*: (u)illa *codd.*   13 erit *Wesenberg*: erat *codd.*

LETTER 60 (*Att.* 13.10)

Scr. in Tusculano xiv Kal. Quint., ut vid., an. 45

CICERO ATTICO SAL.

Minime miror te et graviter ferre de Marcello et plura vereri **1**
periculi genera. quis enim hoc timeret quod neque acciderat
antea nec videbatur natura ferre ut accidere posset? omnia
igitur metuenda. sed illud παρὰ τὴν ἱστορίαν, tu praesertim,
me reliquum consularem. quid? tibi Servius quid videtur? **5**
quamquam hoc nullam ad partem valet scilicet, mihi praesertim qui non minus bene actum cum illis putem. quid enim
sumus aut quid esse possumus? domin an foris? quod nisi mihi
hoc venisset in mentem, scribere ista nescio quae, quo verterem
me non haberem.   **10**

Ad Dolabellam, ut scribis, ita puto faciendum, κοινότερα **2**
quaedam et πολιτικώτερα. faciendum certe aliquid est; valde
enim desiderat.

Brutus si quid egerit, curabis ut sciam; cui quidem quam **3**
primum agendum puto, praesertim si statuit. sermunculum
enim omnem aut restinxerit aut sedarit. sunt enim qui
loquantur etiam mecum. sed haec ipse optime, praesertim si
etiam tecum loquetur.   **5**

Mihi est in animo proficisci xi Kal. hic enim nihil habeo
quod agam, ne hercule illic quidem nec usquam, sed tamen
aliquid illic. hodie Spintherem exspecto. misit enim Brutus
ad me. per litteras purgat Caesarem de interitu Marcelli; in
quem, ne si insidiis quidem ille interfectus esset, caderet ulla **10**
suspicio. nunc vero, cum de Magio constet, nonne furor eius
causam omnem sustinet? plane quid sit non intellego. explana-
bis igitur. quamquam nihil habeo quod dubitem nisi ipsi
Magio quae fuerit causa amentiae; pro quo quidem etiam

60 3.7 quod] quid *codd.*   8-9 ad me. Brutus *Boot*

15 sponsor sum factus. et nimirum id fuit. solvendo enim non
erat. credo eum petisse a Marcello aliquid et illum, ut erat,
constantius respondisse.

LETTER 61 (*Att.* 13.16)

Scr. in Arpinati vi Kal. Quint. an. 45

CICERO ATTICO SAL.

1 Nos cum flumina et solitudines sequeremur quo facilius
sustentare nos possemus, pedem e villa adhuc egressi non
sumus; ita magnos et adsiduos imbres habebamus. illam
'Ακαδημικὴν σύνταξιν totam ad Varronem traduximus. primo
5 fuit Catuli, Luculli, Hortensi; deinde, quia παρὰ τὸ πρέπον
videbatur, quod erat hominibus nota non illa quidem ἀπαι-
δευσία sed in his rebus ἀτριψία, simul ac veni ad villam eosdem
illos sermones ad Catonem Brutumque transtuli. ecce tuae
2 litterae de Varrone. nemini visa est aptior Antiochia ratio. sed
tamen velim scribas ad me, primum placeatne tibi aliquid ad
illum, deinde, si placebit, hocne potissimum.

Quid Servilia? iamne venit? Brutus ecquid agit et quando?
5 de Caesare quid auditur? ego ad Nonas, quem ad modum
dixi. tu cum Pisone, si quid poteris.

LETTER 62 (*Att.* 13.33a)

Scr. in Tusculano fort. vii Id. Quint. an. 45

CICERO ATTICO SAL.

1 De Varrone loquebamur: lupus in fabula. venit enim ad me
et quidem id temporis ut retinendus esset. sed ego ita egi ut

---

16 ut erat ⟨mos⟩ *Sedgwick*   **61** 1.1, 4 solitudines *et* primo *cod. Tornesianus
et alter deperditus, ut vid.*: solitudinem *et* modo *codd. superstites*

non scinderem paenulam. memini enim tuum 'et multi erant
nosque imparati'. quid refert? paulo post C. Capito cum
T. Carrinate. horum ego vix attigi paenulam. tamen reman- 5
serunt ceciditque belle. sed casu sermo a Capitone de urbe
augenda, a ponte Mulvio Tiberim perduci secundum montis
Vaticanos, campum Martium coaedificari, illum autem campum Vaticanum fieri quasi Martium campum. 'quid ais?'
inquam; 'at ego ad tabulam ut, si recte possem, Scapulanos 10
hortos.' 'cave facias' inquit; 'nam ista lex perferetur; vult
enim Caesar.' audire me facile passus sum, fieri autem moleste
fero. sed tu quid ais? quamquam quid quaero? nosti dili-
gentiam Capitonis in rebus novis perquirendis. non concedit
Camillo. facies me igitur certiorem de Idibus. ista enim me res 15
adducebat. eo adiunxeram ceteras, quas consequi tamen biduo
aut triduo post facile potero. te tamen in via confici minime
volo; quin etiam Dionysio ignosco. de Bruto quod scribis, feci 2
ut ei liberum esset, quod ad me attineret. scripsi enim ad eum
heri, Idibus iam eius opera mihi nihil opus esse.

LETTER 63 (*Att.* 13.52)

Scr. in Puteolano, ut vid., xiv Kal. Ian. an. 45

CICERO ATTICO SAL.

O hospitem mihi tam gravem ἀμεταμέλητον! fuit enim per- 1
iucunde. sed cum secundis Saturnalibus ad Philippum vesperi
venisset, villa ita completa a militibus est ut vix triclinium ubi
cenaturus ipse Caesar esset vacaret; quippe hominum cɔ cɔ.
sane sum commotus quid futurum esset postridie; at mihi 5
Barba Cassius subvenit, custodes dedit. castra in agro, villa

---

62 1.7 perduci *Bosius*: pauci *codd.*: duci *margo ed. Cratandri*   8 coaedificari *Lambinus*: cum (tum) (a)ed- *codd.*: totum aed- *Manutius*   2.3 iam
ego: maii(s) *vel* maias *codd.*: *del. Manutius*   63 1.1 tam gravem] gravem
tamen *Boot* (*mallem* tam gravem ἀμ- ⟨tamen⟩)   5 at *Ernesti*: ac *codd.*

defensa est. ille tertiis Saturnalibus apud Philippum ad H.
vii, nec quemquam admisit; rationes, opinor, cum Balbo. inde
ambulavit in litore. post H. viii in balneum. tum audivit de
10 Mamurra, vultum non mutavit. unctus est, accubuit. ἐμετικὴν
agebat; itaque et edit et bibit ἀδεῶς et iucunde, opipare sane
et apparate nec id solum sed

'bene cocto et
condito, sermone bono et, si quaeris, libenter.'

2 praeterea tribus tricliniis accepti οἱ περὶ αὐτὸν valde copiose.
libertis minus lautis servisque nihil defuit. nam lautiores
eleganter accepi. quid multa? homines visi sumus. hospes
tamen non is cui diceres 'amabo te, eodem ad me cum
5 revertere.' semel satis est. σπουδαῖον οὐδὲν in sermone, φιλόλογα multa. quid quaeris? delectatus est et libenter fuit. Puteolis
se aiebat unum diem fore, alterum ad Baias.

Habes hospitium sive ἐπισταθμείαν odiosam mihi, dixi, non
molestam. ego paulisper hic, deinde in Tusculanum.
10   Dolabellae villam cum praeteriret, omnis armatorum copia
dextra sinistra ad equum nec usquam alibi. hoc ex Nicia.

LETTER 64 (*Att.* 13.42)

Scr. in Tusculano ex. m. Dec. an. 45

CICERO ATTICO SAL.

1 Venit ille ad me 'καὶ μάλα κατηφής'. et ego '"σὺ δὲ δὴ τί
σύννους;"' 'rogas?' inquit, 'cui iter instet et iter ad bellum,
idque cum periculosum tum etiam turpe!' 'quae vis igitur?'
inquam. 'aes' inquit 'alienum, et tamen ne viaticum quidem
5 habeo.' hoc loco ego sumpsi quiddam de tua eloquentia; nam
tacui. at ille: 'sed me maxime angit avunculus.' 'quidnam?'

2.4 cui *Victorius*: qui *codd.*   **64** 1.2 cui] quo *codd.*   5 habeo *om. codd.*
superstites

inquam. 'quod mihi' inquit 'iratus est.' 'cur pateris?' inquam.
'malo enim ita dicere quam cur committis?' 'non patiar'
inquit; 'causam enim tollam.' et ego: 'rectissime quidem; sed
si grave non est, velim scire quid sit causae.' 'quia, dum 10
dubitabam quam ducerem, non satis faciebam matri; ita ne
illi quidem. nunc nihil mihi tanti est. faciam quod volunt.'
'feliciter velim' inquam, 'teque laudo. sed quando?' 'nihil ad
me' inquit 'de tempore, quoniam rem probo.' 'at ego' inquam
'censeo prius quam proficiscaris. ita patri quoque morem 15
gesseris.' 'faciam' inquit 'ut censes.' hic dialogus sic conclusus
est.

Sed heus tu, diem meum scis esse III Non. Ian.; aderis igitur. 2

Scripseram iam: ecce tibi orat Lepidus ut veniam. opinor, 3
augures vult habere ad templum effandum. eatur; μὴ σκόρδου.
videbimus te igitur.

LETTER 65 (*Fam.* 13.27)

Scr. an. 46 vel 45

CICERO SERVIO S.

Licet eodem exemplo saepius tibi huius generis litteras mittam, 1
cum gratias agam quod meas commendationes tam diligenter
observes, quod feci in aliis et faciam, ut video, saepius; sed
tamen non parcam operae et, ut vos soletis in formulis, sic ego
in epistulis 'de eadem re alio modo'. 5

C. Avianius igitur Hammonius incredibiles mihi gratias per 2
litteras egit et suo et Aemili Avianiani, patroni sui, nomine:
nec liberalius nec honorificentius potuisse tractari nec se
praesentem nec rem familiarem absentis patroni sui. id mihi

14 probo. at *Victorius*: probat *codd.*   3.2 vult *Boot*: nil *vel* ni(c)hil *codd.*
effandum *Beroaldus*: afflandum (adf-) *codd.*: efflandum '*vetus codex*' *Lambini*
μὴ σκόρδου *Tyrrell*: MIACK- *codd.*   65 1.4 vos soletis *Victorius*: uoletis
codd.

5 cum iucundum est eorum causa quos tibi ego summa necessitudine et summa coniunctione adductus commendaveram,
quod M. Aemilius unus est ex meis familiarissimis atque intimis
maxime necessarius, homo et magnis meis beneficiis devinctus
et prope omnium qui mihi debere aliquid videntur gratissimus,
10 tum multo iucundius te esse in me tali voluntate ut plus prosis
amicis meis quam ego praesens fortasse prodessem, credo,
quod magis ego dubitarem quid illorum causa facerem quam
tu quid mea.

3 Sed hoc non dubito, quin existimes mihi esse gratum. illud
te rogo, ut illos quoque gratos esse homines putes; quod ita
esse tibi promitto atque confirmo. qua re velim quicquid
habent negoti des operam, quod commodo tuo fiat, ut te
5 obtinente Achaiam conficiant.

Ego cum tuo Servio iucundissime et coniunctissime vivo
magnamque cum ex ingenio eius singularique studio tum ex
virtute et probitate voluptatem capio.

LETTER 66 (*Att.* 14.1)

Scr. in suburbano Mati vii Id. Apr. an. 44

CICERO ATTICO SAL.

1 Deverti ad illum de quo tecum mane. nihil perditius; ex-
plicari rem non posse: 'etenim si ille tali ingenio exitum non
reperiebat, quis nunc reperiet?' quid quaeris? perisse omnia
aiebat (quod haud scio an ita sit; verum ille gaudens) adfir-
5 mabatque minus diebus xx tumultum Gallicum; in sermonem
se post Id. Mart. praeterquam Lepido venisse nemini; ad
summam, non posse istaec sic abire. o prudentem Oppium!
qui nihilo minus illum desiderat, sed loquitur nihil quod
quemquam bonum offendat. sed haec hactenus.

2 Tu quaeso quicquid novi (multa autem exspecto) scribere

4.2 *fort.* singularique ⟨in me⟩   66 1.6 lepidi *codd.*

ne pigrere, in his de Sexto satisne certum, maxime autem de
Bruto nostro. de quo quidem ille ad quem deverti Caesarem
solitum dicere, 'magni refert hic quid velit, sed quicquid vult
valde vult'; idque eum animadvertisse cum pro Deiotaro 5
Nicaeae dixerit; valde vehementer eum visum et libere dicere;
atque etiam (ut enim quidque succurrit libet scribere) proxime, cum Sesti rogatu apud eum fuissem exspectaremque
sedens quoad vocarer, dixisse eum, 'ego dubitem quin summo
in odio sim, cum M. Cicero sedeat nec suo commodo me 10
convenire possit? atqui si quisquam est facilis, hic est. tamen
non dubito quin me male oderit.' haec et eius modi multa. sed
ad propositum: quicquid erit, non modo magnum sed etiam
parvum, scribes. equidem nihil intermittam.

LETTER 67 (*Att.* 14.13B)

Scr. in Puteolano vi Kal. Mai. an. 44

CICERO ANTONIO COS. S.D.

Quod mecum per litteras agis unam ob causam mallem coram **1**
egisses; non enim solum ex oratione, sed etiam ex vultu et
oculis et fronte, ut aiunt, meum erga te amorem perspicere
potuisses. nam cum te semper amavi, primum tuo studio, post
etiam beneficio provocatus, tum his temporibus res publica te 5
mihi ita commendavit ut cariorem habeam neminem. litterae **2**
vero tuae cum amantissime tum honorificentissime scriptae sic
me adfecerunt ut non dare tibi beneficium viderer sed accipere
a te ita petente ut inimicum meum, necessarium tuum, me
invito servare nolles, cum id nullo negotio facere posses. 5
    Ego vero tibi istuc, mi Antoni, remitto atque ita ut me a te, **3**
cum his verbis scripseris, liberalissime atque honorificentissime
tractatum existimem, idque cum totum, quoquo modo se res
haberet, tibi dandum putarem, tum do etiam humanitati et

2.4–5 uolet...uolet *codd.*

5 naturae meae. nihil enim umquam non modo acerbum in me
fuit sed ne paulo quidem tristius aut severius quam necessitas
rei publicae postulavit. accedit ut ne in ipsum quidem Cloe-
lium meum insigne odium fuerit umquam, semperque ita
statui, non esse insectandos inimicorum amicos, praesertim
10 humiliores, nec his praesidiis nosmet ipsos esse spoliandos.

4 Nam de puero Clodio tuas partes esse arbitror ut eius
animum tenerum, quem ad modum scribis, iis opinionibus
imbuas ut ne quas inimicitias residere in familiis nostris
arbitretur. contendi cum P. Clodio cum ego publicam causam,
5 ille suam defenderet. nostras concertationes res publica
diiudicavit. si viveret, mihi cum illo nulla contentio iam
5 maneret. qua re, quoniam hoc a me sic petis ut, quae tua
potestas est, ea neges te me invito usurum, puero quoque hoc
a me dabis, si tibi videbitur, non quo aut aetas nostra ab illius
aetate quicquam debeat periculi suspicari aut dignitas mea
5 ullam contentionem extimescat, sed ut nosmet ipsi inter nos
coniunctiores simus quam adhuc fuimus. interpellantibus
enim his inimicitiis animus tuus mihi magis patuit quam
domus. sed haec hactenus.

Illud extremum: ego quae te velle quaeque ad te pertinere
10 arbitrabor semper sine ulla dubitatione summo studio faciam.
hoc velim tibi penitus persuadeas.

LETTER 68 (*Att.* 14.21)

Scr. Puteolis v Id. Mai. an. 44

CICERO ATTICO SAL.

1 Cum paulo ante dedissem ad te Cassi tabellario litteras, v Id.
venit noster tabellarius et quidem, portenti simile, sine tuis
litteris. sed cito conieci Lanuvii te fuisse. Eros autem festinavit
ut ad me litterae Dolabellae perferrentur, non de re mea

(nondum enim meas acceperat) sed rescripsit ad eas quarum 5
exemplum tibi miseram sane luculente.

Ad me autem, cum Cassi tabellarium dimisissem, statim 2
Balbus. o dei boni, quam facile perspiceres timere otium! et
nosti virum, quam tectus. sed tamen Antoni consilia narrabat;
illum circumire veteranos ut acta Caesaris sancirent idque
se facturos esse iurarent, ut arma omnes haberent eaque duum- 5
viri omnibus mensibus inspicerent. questus est etiam de sua
invidia eaque omnis eius oratio fuit ut amare videretur
Antonium. quid quaeris? nihil sinceri.

Mihi autem non est dubium quin res spectet ad castra. acta 3
enim illa res est animo virili, consilio puerili. quis enim hoc
non vidit, regni heredem relictum? quid autem absurdius?
'hoc metuere, alterum in metu non ponere'! quin etiam hoc
ipso tempore multa ὑποσόλοικα. Ponti Neapolitanum a matre 5
tyrannoctoni possideri! legendus mihi saepius est 'Cato maior'
ad te missus. amariorem enim me senectus facit. stomachor
omnia. sed mihi quidem βεβίωται; viderint iuvenes. tu mea
curabis, ut curas.

Haec scripsi seu dictavi apposita secunda mensa apud 4
Vestorium. postridie apud Hirtium cogitabam et quidem
Πεντέλοιπον. sic hominem traducere ad optimates paro. λῆρος
πολύς! nemo est istorum qui otium non timeat. qua re talaria
videamus; quidvis enim potius quam castra.   5

Atticae salutem plurimam velim dicas. exspecto Octavi
contionem et si quid aliud, maxime autem ecquid Dolabella
tinniat an in meo nomine tabulas novas fecerit.

68 2.5 ut arma] ut eam *codd.*   4.8 tinniat an] tinnitam *codd.*

LETTER 69 (*Att.* 15.1*a*)

Scr. in Sinuessano xv Kal. Iun. an. 44

CICERO ATTICO SAL.

1 Heri dederam ad te litteras exiens e Puteolano deverteramque
in Cumanum. ibi bene valentem videram Piliam. quin etiam
paulo post Cumis eam vidi; venerat enim in funus, cui funeri
ego quoque operam dedi. Cn. Lucceius, familiaris noster,
5 matrem efferebat. mansi igitur eo die in Sinuessano atque inde
mane postridie Arpinum proficiscens hanc epistulam exaravi.

2 Erat autem nihil novi quod aut scriberem aut ex te quaere-
rem, nisi forte hoc ad rem putas pertinere: Brutus noster misit
ad me orationem suam habitam in contione Capitolina
petivitque a me ut eam ne ambitiose corrigerem ante quam
5 ederet. est autem oratio scripta elegantissime sententiis, verbis,
ut nihil possit ultra. ego tamen si illam causam habuissem,
scripsissem ardentius. ὑπόθεσις vides quae sit et persona dicen-
tis. itaque eam corrigere non potui. quo enim in genere Brutus
noster esse vult et quod iudicium habet de optimo genere
10 dicendi, id ita consecutus est in ea oratione ut elegantius esse
nihil possit; sed ego secutus aliud sum, sive hoc recte sive non
recte. tu tamen velim orationem legas, nisi forte iam legisti,
certioremque me facias quid iudices ipse. quamquam vereor
ne cognomine tuo lapsus ὑπεραττικὸς sis in iudicando. sed si
15 recordabere Δημοσθένους fulmina, tum intelleges posse et
Ἀττικώτατα et gravissime dici. sed haec coram. nunc nec sine
epistula nec cum inani epistula volui ad te Metrodorum
venire.

69 1.1 heri *Lambinus*: here *vel* hercle *codd.*   2 bene] pene (*i.e.* paene)
codd.   3 post *add. Lambinus*   Cumis *cod. Tornesianus deperditus, teste Bosio*:
clam iis *vel* damus *codd.*   4 Lucceius *ego*: lucul(l)us *codd.*   2.2 noster]
non *codd.*   7 et *add. Orelli*   8 eam] iam *codd.*   11 secutus *Pius*: solus
codd.   sive hoc] spe hoc *codd.*   16 et *add. Lambinus*

LETTER 70 (*Att.* 15.11)

Scr. fort. Antii c. vii Id. Iun. an. 44

CICERO ATTICO SAL.

Antium veni ante H. vi. Bruto iucundus noster adventus. **1**
deinde multis audientibus, Servilia, Tertulla, Porcia, quaerere
quid placeret. aderat etiam Favonius. ego, quod eram medi-
tatus in via, suadere ut uteretur Asiatica curatione frumenti;
nihil esse iam reliqui quod ageremus nisi ut salvus esset; in eo 5
etiam ipsi rei publicae esse praesidium. quam orationem cum
ingressus essem, Cassius intervenit. ego eadem illa repetivi.
hoc loco fortibus sane oculis Cassius (Martem spirare diceres)
se in Siciliam non iturum. 'egone ut beneficium accepissem
contumeliam?' 'quid ergo agis?' inquam. at ille in Achaiam 10
se iturum. 'quid tu' inquam, 'Brute?' 'Romam' inquit, 'si
tibi videtur.' 'mihi vero minime; tuto enim non eris.' 'quid?
si possem esse, placeretne?' 'atque ut omnino neque nunc
neque ex praetura in provinciam ires; sed auctor non sum ut
te urbi committas.' dicebam ea quae tibi profecto in mentem 15
veniunt cur non esset tuto futurus.

Multo inde sermone querebantur, atque id quidem Cassius **2**
maxime, amissas occasiones Decimumque graviter accusabant.
ad ea negabam oportere praeterita, adsentiebar tamen. cumque ingressus essem dicere quid oportuisset, nec vero quicquam
novi sed ea quae cottidie omnes, nec tamen illum locum 5
attingerem, quemquam praeterea oportuisse tangi, sed senatum
vocare, populum ardentem studio vehementius incitare, totam
suscipere rem publicam, exclamat tua familiaris 'hoc vero

70 1.1 ante H. vi *ego*: ante K. vi *vel* ante vi kal. (*vel sim.*) *codd.*: a. d. vi
Idus *olim vulgo*   5 saluos esse *codd.*   8 spirare *Victorius*: sperare *codd.*
2.2 accusabant *cod. Torn. deperditus*: accusabat *codd.*   3 ad ea *ego*: ea
codd.: ego *Victorius*   3–4 cumque *Manutius*: quamquam *codd.*   7 vocare
cod. Torn., *teste Bosio*: uocari *codd.*   incitare *cod. Torn.*: incitari *codd.*   8
suscipi *Orelli*

neminem umquam audivi!' ego me repressi. sed et Cassius
10 mihi videbatur iturus (etenim Servilia pollicebatur se cura-
turam ut illa frumenti curatio de senatus consulto tolleretur)
et noster Brutus cito deiectus est de illo inani sermone quo se
Romae velle esse dixerat. constituit igitur ut ludi absente se
fierent suo nomine. proficisci autem mihi in Asiam videbatur
15 ab Antio velle.
3   Ne multa, nihil me in illo itinere praeter conscientiam meam
delectavit. non enim fuit committendum ut ille ex Italia prius
quam a me conventus esset discederet. hoc dempto munere
amoris atque offici sequebatur ut mecum ipse ' ἡ δεῦρ' ὁδός σοι
5 τί δύναται νῦν, θεοπρόπε; ' prorsus dissolutum offendi navigium
vel potius dissipatum. nihil consilio, nihil ratione, nihil ordine.
itaque etsi ne antea quidem dubitavi, tamen nunc eo minus,
evolare hinc idque quam primum, 'ubi nec Pelopidarum
facta neque famam audiam.'

LETTER 71 (*Att.* 15.16*a*)

Scr. Asturae (?) *prid. Id. Iun. an. 44* (?)

CICERO ATTICO SAL.

Narro tibi, haec loca venusta sunt, abdita certe et, si quid
scribere velis, ab arbitris libera. sed nescio quo modo οἶκος
φίλος. itaque me referunt pedes in Tusculanum. et tamen haec
ῥωπογραφία ripulae videtur habitura celerem satietatem. equi-
5 dem etiam pluvias metuo, si Prognostica nostra vera sunt;
ranae enim ῥητορεύουσιν. tu, quaeso, fac sciam ubi Brutum
nostrum et quo die videre possim.

9 me *add. Malaespina*   12-13 quo se Romae *addidi* (se Romae *Boot,*
quo Romae *Tyrrell*)   3.7 dubitavi tamen] dubitabit habitam *codd.*
71 4 uidentur *codd.*   habituram *codd.*

LETTER 72 (*Att.* 15.27)

Scr. in Arpinati v Non. Quint. an. 44

CICERO ATTICO SAL.

Gaudeo id te mihi suadere quod ego mea sponte pridie feceram. **1**
nam cum ad te VI Non. darem, eidem tabellario dedi etiam ad
Sestium scriptas πάνυ φιλοστόργως. ille autem, quod Puteolos
persequitur, humane, quod queritur, iniuste. non enim ego
tam illum exspectare dum de Cosano rediret debui quam ille **5**
aut non ire ante quam me vidisset aut citius reverti. sciebat
enim me celeriter velle proficisci seseque ad me in Tusculanum
scripserat esse venturum.

Te, ut a me discesseris, lacrimasse moleste ferebam. quod si **2**
me praesente fecisses, consilium totius itineris fortasse mutas-
sem. sed illud praeclare, quod te consolata est spes brevi
tempore congrediendi; quae quidem exspectatio me maxime
sustentat. meae tibi litterae non deerunt. de Bruto scribam ad **5**
te omnia. librum tibi celeriter mittam de gloria. excudam
aliquid 'Ηρακλείδειον quod lateat in thesauris tuis.

De Planco memini. Attica iure queritur. quod me de **3**
Bacchide et de statuarum coronis certiorem fecisti, valde
gratum; nec quicquam posthac non modo tantum sed ne
tantulum quidem praeterieris. sed de Herode et †Metio†
meminero et de omnibus quae te velle suspicabor modo. o **5**
turpem sororis tuae filium! cum haec scriberem adventabat
αὐτῆ βουλύσει cenantibus nobis.

72 1.5 dum *Wesenberg*: cum *codd.*   3.2 et de *addidi* (de *Graevius*, et
Moricca)   certiorem me *codd.*   4 metio, mecio, macio, maetis *codd.*
7 αὐτῆ *Boot*: autem *vel* auti (?) *vel* aut *codd.*

LETTER 73 (*Att.* 16.6)

Scr. Vibone viii Kal. Sext. an. 44

CICERO ATTICO SAL.

1 Ego adhuc (perveni enim Vibonem ad Siccam) magis commode quam strenue navigavi; remis enim magnam partem, prodromi nulli. illud satis opportune, duo sinus fuerunt quos tramitti oporteret, Paestanus et Vibonensis, utrumque pedibus aequis tramisimus. veni igitur ad Siccam octavo die e Pompeiano, cum unum diem Veliae constitissem; ubi quidem fui sane libenter apud Talnam nostrum nec potui accipi, illo absente praesertim, liberalius. viiii Kal. igitur ad Siccam. ibi tamquam domi meae scilicet. itaque obduxi posterum diem. sed putabam, cum Regium venissem, fore ut illic ' δολιχὸν πλόον ὁρμαίνοντες ' cogitaremus corbitane Patras an actuariolis ad Leucopetram Tarentinorum atque inde Corcyram; et, si oneraria, statimne freto an Syracusis. hac super re scribam ad te Regio.

2 Sed mehercule, mi Attice, saepe mecum, ' ἡ δεῦρ' ὁδός σοι τί δύναται; ' cur ego tecum non sum? cur ocellos Italiae, villulas meas, non video? sed id satis superque, tecum me non esse. quid fugientem? periculumne? at id nunc quidem, nisi fallor, nullum est; ad ipsum enim revocat me auctoritas tua. scribis enim in caelum ferri profectionem meam, sed ita si ante Kal. Ian. redeam; quod quidem certe enitar. malo enim vel cum timore domi esse quam sine timore Athenis tuis. sed tamen perspice quo ista vergant mihique aut scribe aut, quod multo malim, adfer ipse. haec hactenus.

3 Illud velim in bonam partem accipias me agere tecum quod tibi maiori curae sciam esse quam ipsi mihi. nomina mea, per deos, expedi, exsolve. bella reliqua reliqui; sed opus est diligentia coheredibus pro Cluviano Kal. Sext. persolutum ut sit. cum

---

73 1.1 ad] et *codd.*   6 Veliae] uellem (*vel* uelleni ?) *codd.*   7 Talnam] tal(l)anam *vel sim. codd.*   11 leucopetras *codd.*   12 atque *Lambinus*: ast *codd.* 2.1 sed *addidi*   4 quid *cod. Torn.*: om. *codd.*   3.2 ipsi] ipse *codd.*

Publilio quo modo agendum sit videbis. non debet urgere, 5
quoniam iure non utimur. sed tamen ei quoque satis fieri plane
volo. Terentiae vero quid ego dicam? etiam ante diem, si potes.
quin si, ut spero, celeriter in Epirum, hoc quod satis dato debeo
peto a te ut ante provideas planeque expedias et solutum
relinquas. sed de his satis, metuoque ne tu nimium putes. 10

Nunc neglegentiam meam cognosce. de gloria librum ad te 4
misi, et in eo prohoemium id quod est in Academico tertio. id
evenit ob eam rem quod habeo volumen prohoemiorum. ex
eo eligere soleo cum aliquod σύγγραμμα institui. itaque iam in
Tusculano, qui non meminissem me abusum isto prohoemio, 5
conieci id in eum librum quem tibi misi. cum autem in navi
legerem Academicos, agnovi erratum meum. itaque statim
novum prohoemium exaravi et tibi misi. tu illud desecabis, hoc
adglutinabis. Piliae salutem dices et Atticae, deliciis atque
amoribus meis. 10

LETTER 74 (*Fam.* 12.3)

Scr. Romae paulo post vi Non. Oct. an. 44

CICERO CASSIO S.

Auget tuus amicus furorem in dies. primum in statua quam 1
posuit in rostris inscripsit 'parenti optime merito', ut non
modo sicarii sed iam etiam parricidae iudicemini. quid dico
'iudicemini'? iudicemur potius. vestri enim pulcherrimi facti
ille furiosus me principem dicit fuisse. utinam quidem fuissem! 5
molestus nobis non esset. sed hoc vestrum est; quod quoniam
praeteriit, utinam haberem quid vobis darem consili! sed ne
mihi quidem ipsi reperio quid faciendum sit. quid enim est
quod contra vim sine vi fieri possit?

Consilium omne autem hoc est illorum ut mortem Caesaris 2
persequantur. itaque a. d. vi Non. Oct. productus in contio-

4.2 id quod est *ego*: id est quod *vel* .i. (= id est) quod est *vel* idem quod
codd.: idem est quod *Wesenberg*

nem a Cannutio turpissime ille quidem discessit, sed tamen ea
dixit de conservatoribus patriae quae dici deberent de prodito-
5 ribus; de me quidem non dubitanter quin omnia de meo
consilio et vos fecissetis et Cannutius faceret. cetera cuius modi
sint ex hoc iudica quod legato tuo viaticum eripuerunt. quid
eos interpretari putas cum hoc faciunt? ad hostem scilicet
portari.
10   O rem miseram! dominum ferre non potuimus, conservo
servimus. et tamen me quidem favente magis quam sperante
etiam nunc residet spes in virtue tua. sed ubi sunt copiae?
de reliquo malo te ipsum tecum loqui quam nostra dicta
cognoscere.
15   Vale.

LETTER 75 (*Att.* 16.9)

Scr. in Puteolano prid. Non. Nov. an. 44

CICERO ATTICO SAL.

Binae uno die mihi litterae ab Octaviano, nunc quidem ut
Romam statim veniam; velle se rem agere per senatum. cui
ego non posse senatum ante Kal. Ian., quod quidem ita credo.
ille autem addit 'consilio tuo'. quid multa? ille urget, ego
5 autem σκήπτομαι. non confido aetati, ignoro quo animo. nil sine
Pansa tuo·volo. vereor ne valeat Antonius, nec a mari discedere
libet. at metuo ne quae ἀριστεία me absente. Varroni quidem
displicet consilium pueri, mihi non. firmas copias habet,
Brutum habere potest; et rem gerit palam, centuriat Capuae,
10 dinumerat. iam iamque video bellum. ad haec rescribe. tabellarium meum Kalendis Roma profectum sine tuis litteris miror.

75 4 addit *Manutius*: adiit *codd.*   7 at *ego*: et *codd.*   9 *anne* D. Brutum?

LETTER 76 (*Fam.* 12.22)

Scr. Romae post xiii Kal. Oct. et fort. post vi Non.
Oct. an. 44

CICERO CORNIFICIO S.

Nos hic cum homine gladiatore omnium nequissimo, collega **1**
nostro, Antonio, bellum gerimus, sed non pari condicione,
contra arma verbis. at etiam de te contionatur, nec impune;
nam sentiet quos lacessierit. ego autem acta ad te omnia
arbitror perscribi ab aliis; a me futura debes cognoscere, **5**
quorum quidem nunc est difficilis coniectura.

Oppressa omnia sunt, nec habent ducem boni nostrique **2**
tyrannoctoni longe gentium absunt. Pansa et sentit bene et
loquitur fortiter; Hirtius noster tardius convalescit. quid
futurum sit plane nescio; spes tamen una est aliquando
populum Romanum maiorum similem fore. ego certe rei **5**
publicae non deero et quicquid acciderit a quo mea culpa
absit animo forti feram. illud profecto quoad potero: tuam
famam et dignitatem tuebor.

LETTER 77 (*Fam.* 10.3)

Scr. Romae paulo post v Id. Dec. an. 44

CICERO PLANCO S.

Cum ipsum Furnium per se vidi libentissime tum hoc libentius **1**
quod illum audiens te videbar videre. nam et in re militari
virtutem et in administranda provincia iustitiam et in omni
genere prudentiam mihi tuam exposuit et praeterea mihi non
ignotam in consuetudine et familiaritate suavitatem tuam; **5**

76 1.2 nostro] uostro *fragm. Heilbronnense, ut vid.*: uestro *codd.*   6 nunc
ego: non *codd.*   **77** 1.2 videre *ego*: audire *codd.*   5 ignotam *cod. Parisinus*
14761: ignatam *vel* ignaram *ceteri*

adiunxit praeterea summam erga se liberalitatem. quae omnia
mihi iucunda, hoc extremum etiam gratum fuit.

2   Ego, Plance, necessitudinem constitutam habui cum domo
vestra ante aliquanto quam tu natus es, amorem autem erga
te ab ineunte pueritia tua, confirmata iam aetate familiari-
tatem cum studio meo tum iudicio tuo constitutam. his de
5 causis mirabiliter faveo dignitati tuae, quam me tecum
statuo habere communem. omnia summa consecutus es
virtute duce, comite fortuna, eaque es adeptus adulescens
multis invidentibus, quos ingenio industriaque fregisti. nunc,
me amantissimum tui, nemini concedentem qui tibi vetustate
10 necessitudinis potior possit esse, si audies, omnem tibi reliquae
vitae dignitatem ex optimo rei publicae statu adquires.

3   Scis profecto (nihil enim te fugere potuit) fuisse quoddam
tempus cum homines existimarent te nimis servire temporibus;
quod ego quoque existimarem, te si ea quae patiebare probare
etiam arbitrarer. sed cum intellegerem quid sentires, prudenter
5 te arbitrabar videre quid posses. nunc alia ratio est. omnium
rerum tuum iudicium est idque liberum. consul es designatus,
optima aetate, summa eloquentia, maxima orbitate rei publicae virorum talium. incumbe, per deos immortales, in eam
curam et cogitationem quae tibi summam dignitatem et
10 gloriam adferat; unus autem est, hoc praesertim tempore, per
tot annos re publica divexata, rei publicae bene gerendae
cursus ad gloriam.

4   Haec amore magis impulsus scribenda ad te putavi quam
quo te arbitrarer monitis et praeceptis egere. sciebam enim
ex iisdem te haec haurire fontibus ex quibus ipse hauseram.
qua re modum faciam. nunc tantum significandum putavi ut
5 potius amorem tibi ostenderem meum quam ostentarem
prudentiam. interea quae ad dignitatem tuam pertinere
arbitrabor studiose diligenterque curabo.

2.5 me *ego*: mihi *codd.*   6 habere *cod. Parisinus 14761*: habere (et) esse
ceteri: debere esse *Victorius*   3.7 ⟨in⟩ maxima *Ernesti*

LETTER 78 (*Fam.* 9.24)

Scr. Romae m. Ian., ut vid., an. 43

CICERO PAETO S.D.

Rufum istum, amicum tuum, de quo iterum iam ad me scribis, **1**
adiuvarem quantum possem etiam si ab eo laesus essem cum
te tanto opere viderem eius causa laborare; cum vero et ex tuis
litteris et ex illius ad me missis intellegam et iudicem magnae
curae ei salutem meam fuisse, non possum ei non amicus esse, **5**
neque solum tua commendatione, quae apud me, ut debet,
valet plurimum, sed etiam voluntate ac iudicio meo. volo enim
te scire, mi Paete, initium mihi suspicionis et cautionis et
diligentiae fuisse litteras tuas, quibus litteris congruentes
fuerunt aliae postea multorum. nam et Aquini et Fabrateriae **10**
consilia sunt inita de me, quae te video inaudisse, et quasi divinarent quam iis molestus essem futurus, nihil aliud egerunt nisi
me ut opprimerent. quod ego non suspicans incautior fuissem nisi
a te admonitus essem. quam ob rem iste tuus amicus apud me
commendatione non eget. utinam ea fortuna rei publicae sit ut **15**
ille me[um] gratissimum possit cognoscere! sed haec hactenus.

Te ad cenas itare desisse moleste fero; magna enim te **2**
delectatione et voluptate privasti. deinde etiam vereor (licet
enim verum dicere) ne nescio quid illud quod sciebas dediscas
et obliviscare cenulas facere. nam si tum cum habebas quos
imitarere non multum proficiebas, quid nunc te facturum **5**
putem? Spurinna quidem, cum ei rem demonstrassem et
vitam tuam superiorem exposuissem, magnum periculum
summae rei publicae demonstrabat nisi ad superiorem consuetudinem tum cum Favonius flaret revertisses; hoc tempore
ferri posse, si forte tu frigus ferre non posses. **10**

Et mehercule, mi Paete, extra iocum moneo te, quod **3**
pertinere ad beate vivendum arbitror, ut cum viris bonis,

---

78 1.16 me *Wesenberg*: meum *vel* me meum *codd.*   2.3 sciebas *ego*: solebas
codd.

iucundis, amantibus tui vivas. nihil est aptius vitae, nihil ad
beate vivendum accommodatius. nec id ad voluptatem refero
5 sed ad communitatem vitae atque victus remissionemque
animorum, quae maxime sermone efficitur familiari, qui est
in conviviis dulcissimus, ut sapientius nostri quam Graeci;
illi 'συμπόσια' aut 'σύνδειπνα', id est compotationes aut con-
cenationes, nos 'convivia', quod tum maxime simul vivitur.
10 vides ut te philosophando revocare coner ad cenas.

    Cura ut valeas; id foris cenitando facillime consequere.

4   Sed cave, si me amas, existimes me quod iocosius scribam
abiecisse curam rei publicae. sic tibi, mi Paete, persuade, me
dies et noctes nihil aliud agere, nihil curare, nisi ut mei cives
salvi liberique sint. nullum locum praetermitto monendi,
5 agendi, providendi. hoc denique animo sum, ut, si in hac
cura atque administratione vita mihi ponenda sit, praeclare
actum mecum putem.

    Etiam atque etiam vale.

LETTER 79 (*Fam.* 7.22)

Scr. Romae, fort. an. 44

CICERO TREBATIO S.

Illuseras heri inter scyphos, quod dixeram controversiam esse,
possetne heres, quod furtum antea factum esset, furti recte
agere. itaque, etsi domum bene potus seroque redieram, tamen
id caput ubi haec controversia est notavi et descriptum tibi
5 misi, ut scires id quod tu neminem sensisse dicebas Sex. Aelium,
M'. Manilium, M. Brutum sensisse. ego tamen Scaevolae et
Testae adsentior.

COMMENTARY

LETTER 1 (*Att.* 1.5)

This is the earliest of Cicero's extant letters. Atticus had returned to Greece from one of his periodical visits to Italy and was now on his recently bought estate near Buthrotum in Epirus, opposite the island of Corcyra (Corfù). On the letter-headings in the Atticus correspondence see Introd. p. 11.

1 Luci Cicero's cousin L. Cicero had been with him at Athens in 79 and assisted him in the Verres case. The children of brothers (*fratres patrueles*) can be termed simply *fratres* (*sorores*).

humanitate A key word in Cicero's vocabulary. It connotes thoughtfulness for other people (kindness, tact, courtesy) and also culture – hence the 'humanities'. For to the Roman way of thinking, or at any rate to Cicero's, the first was a natural product of the second. *mores* ('ways') may be good or bad according to the context.

adfinem Loosely = 'connexion by marriage'. L. Cicero's cousin Quintus had married Atticus' sister. In a legal sense neither Lucius nor Marcus Cicero was Atticus' *adfinis*.

2 quod...scribis Lit. 'as to the fact that you write...' (cf. Letter 10.1 n.). Translate simply: 'you write...'.

sorore Exactly when the marriage between Q. Cicero and Pomponia took place is uncertain. Quintus was away from Rome when Cicero wrote, but expected back any day (sec. 8).

quantae...curae In English a nominative would be used: 'how great an anxiety it has been to me', i.e. 'how anxious I have been'.

3 de litterarum missione 'on the subject of letter-dispatches'. Atticus had complained that Cicero was not writing often enough.

nequedum...audiebamus 'nor do we hear so far...' Past ('epistolary') tenses are often used in letters of matters present from the writer's standpoint but prospectively past to the reader.

4 negotio Apparently a business dispute between Atticus and a certain Acutilius.

ut et...et ut An unusual sequence. *et ut...et* would be normal.

[113]

satis consili 'enough (of) judgement', a common type of ('partitive') genitive. So *oti...plus* below.

Peducaeum Probably not the governor of Sicily under whom Cicero had served as Quaestor in 75 but his son, a close friend of Atticus.

duxi 'I should not have thought...' In such cases Latin quite logically prefers the indicative. *grave* = 'onerous', *leve putassem* = 'made light of'.

subodiosum 'a trifle tiresome'. The softening prefix *sub* is often attached to adjectives, adverbs, and verbs in familiar style. Here it politely makes little of what Cicero had gone through for Atticus' sake.

5 cuius The person meant is L. Lucceius, a wealthy politician and close friend of Pompey. He also wrote on contemporary Roman history, though it is doubtful whether his work was published (see Letter 15). Several letters of this period refer to his rift with Atticus, though leaving the circumstances obscure (see next letter). Cicero is apt to avoid using personal names in his letters when anything at all delicate is involved.

6 Tadiana re A certain Tadius seems to have acquired some property from Atticus which was then claimed on behalf of a girl *in legitima tutela*, i.e. under the guardianship of relatives (as distinct from guardians appointed by will). Atticus had told him not to worry, since the title (presumably Atticus' title) had been established by length of possession (*usucapio*), but Cicero corrects his friend's surprising ignorance of the law: in the case of a ward *in tutela legitima* title of ownership could not be so established. The matter was eventually settled to Tadius' satisfaction.

nihil...laboraretur *nihil est quod* = 'there is no reason why...'. Cicero could have written *laboraremus*, but Latin often prefers the less direct impersonal passive corresponding to expressions like 'on s'en occupe' in French and other modern languages.

mirabamur 'We are surprised', another epistolary tense. Or perhaps 'I am surprised'. It is often impossible to be sure whether the first person plural is used for the singular or not.

7 emptionem The estate at Buthrotum.

Tusculano Cicero's villa near the old Latin town of Tusculum (close to modern Frascati in the hills east of Rome), also probably a recent acquisition. Atticus had been asked to buy works of art in Greece to decorate it. A neuter form like *Tusculanum* may mean either (as here) a particular property in the district (= *praedium Tusculanum*) or the district itself (= *ager Tusculanus*).

velim...cures A polite substitute for an imperative (*cura*); cf. *velim recordere* and *velim iudices* in Letter 5.4. The simple subjunctive (without *ut*) is common in such expressions.

quod Or *quoad*? The manuscripts vary between the two in such expressions.

8 Tulliola Cicero often uses this affectionate diminutive (similarly 'Atticula' for Attica, 'Tertulla' for Tertia).

LETTER 2 (*Att.* 1.11)

1 faciebam 'I was doing it (i.e. what you ask)' – trying to mollify Lucceius.

hortator Equivalent to a participle, *hortans* (*adsidue*).

Sallustius Cn. Sallustius, a faithful friend of Cicero's.

arbitrium Atticus may have acted as umpire (*arbiter*) in a private dispute between Lucceius and someone else, and found against him. In that case *tuum* (an old conjecture) might have been expected rather than *suum*. But the latter may mean 'that arbitration he is always harping on'.

legatio *adlegatio* has usually been read, since *legatio* is generally a public mission. But *legare* and *legatus* are sometimes used of private missions. Possibly the use of the official term ('embassy') here is faintly humorous.

humanitati tuae 'your kind heart'. Atticus is often credited with the quality of *humanitas* (see on Letter 1.1), one aspect of which was readiness to overlook offence.

ei...erit Perhaps Cicero suspected that Lucceius had a genuine grievance.

2 te Added to the text because the evidence for a passive use of *arbitrari* in Cicero is meagre and doubtful.

designatum Cicero was standing for the praetorship, which he held in 66. The elections were normally held in July immediately after those for the consulship, but this year they had been held up, probably through the activities of an anti-senatorial Tribune, C. Cornelius.

nihil...iniquitatibus 'that candidates are the most harassed beings in Rome at the present time, with all manner of injustices'.

Philadelpho No doubt a slave or freedman who carried the letter.

3 Academiae Cicero constructed two *gymnasia* (something like lecture-halls) in his Tusculan villa, and called them 'Academy' and 'Lyceum' after the halls in which Plato and Aristotle had taught in Athens.

mire quam i.e. *mirum* (*est*) *quam*, apparently a colloquial usage.

libros From other references we gather that Atticus had bought a library in Greece which he was willing to sell to Cicero.

LETTER 3 (*Att.* 1.2)

1 consulibus i.e. elected Consuls (for 64). So the recently elected Murena in 63 is called *modo consulem* (*Mur.* 88). One is tempted to guess that the child was born on the actual day of the election. The expression is a kind of parody on the normal way of dating a happening to a particular year ('X and Y being Consuls') and also incidentally lets Atticus know who had been elected. Some editors, however, consider the words a spurious addition to the text.

filiolo me auctum This use of *auctus* is found in Plautus (*Truc.* 384 *quom tu es aucta liberis*) and elsewhere.

salva Terentia Virtually an abl. abs., 'Terentia being (doing) well', Latin having no present participle from *esse*.

nihil litterarum 'nothing in the way of writing', i.e. 'not a line'. 'Partitival' genitives like *nihil pecuniae = nulla pecunia* are common. The plural *litterae* ('writing') is used for one letter (= *epistula*) or more, but usually the former.

Catilinam The future conspirator, who was on trial for extortion in his province of Africa. In an earlier letter Cicero wrote that his guilt was plain as daylight, but appears to have undertaken his defence (see below) with a view to getting some cooperation in the consular elections, in which both were candidates. According to the Augustan antiquary Fenestella he actually did defend Catiline, but this is convincingly refuted by Cicero's commentator Asconius. He must have withdrawn at the last moment. *cogitamus* has a positive implication, 'plan' or 'propose'.

iudices...voluntate This shows that the challenging of the jury (*reiectio*) had already taken place, and that Cicero was Catiline's counsel, or one of them. The prosecutor, Cicero's future bugbear P. Clodius Pulcher, was in collusion with the defence (*praevaricatio*, itself an indictable offence). In a speech made some years later (*Pis*. 23) Cicero calls him *Catilinae praevaricator*.

humaniter 'philosophically'. More literally, 'like a human being (*homo*)', who knows that mortals must bear the misfortunes incidental to their lot. ἀνθρωπίνως has a similar sense in Greek.

2 familiares Atticus had close friends among the aristocracy, including the orator Hortensius, M. Cato, and L. Manlius Torquatus, Consul this year.

nobiles This term applied to persons descended in direct male line from one or more Consuls. At the other end of the spectrum were *novi homines* like Cicero, who had no Senators among their ancestors. The consulate at this period was generally held by *nobiles*, and it was thirty years since a *novus homo* had been elected.

honori *honos* often means 'public office'.

LETTER 4 (*Fam.* 5.1)

The writer's younger brother, Q. Caecilius Metellus Nepos, had served under their brother-in-law Pompey in the East until Pompey sent him home to be elected as Tribune for 63–62. The Tribunes had taken office as usual on 10 December 63, five days after the Catilinarian conspirators arrested in Rome had been put to death. Nepos immediately launched a campaign against Cicero's handling of the crisis and threatened him with a prosecution, at the same time proposing that Pompey should be recalled to deal with Catiline, who was still in arms in Etruria. A lively struggle ensued between the majority of the Senate and Nepos, aided by Julius Caesar, who was Praetor in 62. Both were deprived of their offices, or at any rate suspended, and in mid January Nepos threw in his hand, leaving Italy to rejoin Pompey (Caesar was reinstated). His brother Q. Caecilius Metellus Celer, who had been Praetor in 63 and a loyal supporter of Cicero, was now governor of Cisalpine Gaul at the head

of an army which blocked Catiline's escape route to the north. He
seems to have written this letter about 12 January, after news
received of a speech of Cicero's attacking Nepos (*Contra contionem Q.
Metelli*; see below). Its stiff and arrogant tone recalls Syme's remarks
in *The Roman revolution* (p. 20): 'Their heraldic badge was an elephant
... The Metelli prevailed by their mass and by their numbers. Their
sons became consuls by prerogative or inevitable destiny; and their
daughters were planted out in dynastic marriages.' But though one
of the haughtiest, the Metelli were not one of the oldest Roman
families. They were plebeians, and rose to the consulship early in the
third century.

PRO COS. i.e. *pro consule.* The noun *proconsul* does not seem to have
been in use at this period. After Sulla ex-Praetors governing provinces
were regularly given proconsular rank until 52, when a law of
Pompey's restored the status of *pro praetore.* The pre-Sullan practice
gave proconsular rank only to ex-Consuls and to ex-Praetors holding
military commands.

1   si vales, bene est This preliminary formula, with some variations,
occurs in Cicero's letters to his wife and is sometimes used by his correspondents (but very seldom by Cicero himself when writing to
friends). It is often abbreviated *s. v. b.* (*b.* = *benest*, as usually written
at this period; see critical n. I write *bene est* only for consistency).

pro reconciliata gratia In his reply (Letter 5) Cicero claims to be
unaware that he and Metellus Celer had ever fallen out, but we do
not have to believe him. The circumstances are unknown.

ludibrio See sec. 1 of Cicero's reply.

dictum Probably 'a phrase', with reference to a remark in an
anti-Ciceronian speech by Nepos on 3 January; see sec. 8 of Cicero's
reply. But the meaning could be 'something said', i.e. words as
opposed to acts, with reference to the same speech.

capite ac fortunis Nepos was removed from his office as Tribune
by the Senate and may have been threatened with worse in the
rejoinder which Cicero delivered on 7 or 8 January. This was the speech
later published under the title *Contra contionem Q. Metelli.* It is lost,
except for a few fragments.

pudor ipsius A rather difficult expression, best explained as 'his
own decency'. *pudor* is sensitivity to the opinion of others, keeping a

person from conduct liable to make him an object of disapproval; this should in turn make for respect and forbearance on their part. The words could be read as an admission that Nepos *had* shown some lack of *pudor*, but whether Celer meant them so is hard to say.

vos Cicero and the Senate.

circumventum 'beset'.

a quibus i.e. *ab iis quibus*, cf. Letter 13.2 *quibus sententiis*.

2 luctu et squalore Relations and friends of people threatened with punishment or disgrace customarily put on signs of mourning.

bellum gero Against Catiline.

nostrum An old form, = *nostrorum*.

clementia Claimed (with whatever degree of historical justification) as a traditional Roman virtue.

paenitebit Not to be taken as a threat of military action against the government. Metellus will have been thinking of Pompey.

sperabam cf. *Fam.* 7.32.1 *sperabam...me reliquisse.* In English a pluperfect would be normal ('I had not expected...'). See critical note.

LETTER 5 (*Fam.* 5.2)

Cicero's reply to the foregoing is a wholly admirable mixture of spirit, dignity, and tact – except that it might have been shorter. It seems to have served its purpose, for he and Celer were afterwards good friends, though the quarrel with Nepos lasted several years.

M. TVLLIVS M. F. If the manuscripts are to be trusted, Celer had omitted Cicero's filiation in *his* letter-heading. Cicero may have seen this as a discourtesy.

1 si...bene est Abbreviated this would be *s. t. e. q. v. b.*

propinquos A polite way of referring to the individual, Nepos. So *tuis propinquis* below and *a tuis* in sec. 10.

reticeres While still Praetor, about the end of October 63, Celer had been sent by the Senate to oppose Catiline. He must have revisited Rome in December before taking over his province of Cisalpine Gaul (cf. sec. 4).

illud adiunxi *illud* (like *hoc*, as in sec. 2 fin.) is very often used in anticipation, a signal to the reader to stay awake as it were. In translation it is better omitted or represented by a colon, and the following long period in indirect speech broken up. Thus: 'I added that you and I had made a division of duty in the preservation of the common-wealth: my part was to guard Rome..., yours to protect Italy from ...conspiracy. This partnership', etc.

societatem In his speech in defence of Sestius six years later Cicero refers to Celer, who died in 59, as *socio laborum, periculorum, consiliorum meorum* (131).

2 hoc in sermone 'in this line of talk'. *sermo*, which is hardly ever used of public speaking, probably suggests informality, as though this part of Cicero's speech had not been meant to be taken very seriously.

    iam 'and furthermore'. But perhaps *nam* should be read.

    testimonium tuae vocis 'a testimonial from *your* lips'.

3 provinciam Cisalpine Gaul. Early in his consulship Cicero had accepted this as his future province in exchange for the financially more profitable Macedonia in order to win over his undependable colleague, C. Antonius. Later, in May or June, he publicly gave it up.

    ipse *ipsi* would be easier.

    meae...tulerunt 'this was the way my own interests pointed'.

    eius mei consili Not to take a province. Cicero hated to be away from Rome for long, but this decision may have been one of the worst mistakes of his career.

    vestra i.e. *praetorum*. The eight Praetors drew lots for their future provinces, and apparently C. Antonius, who as Consul will have super-vised the proceedings, managed to get Cisalpine Gaul for Celer.

4 senatus consultum This probably assigned funds for adminis-trative and military purposes (*ornatio provinciae*).

    praescriptione Cicero as presiding Consul would be named in the preamble, which evidently contained an appreciative mention of Metellus Celer's services as Praetor. The ablative with *est* is of 'accompanying circumstance', so that the phrase is equivalent to *eam praescriptionem habet*.

    tuus adventus See on sec. 1 (*reticeres*).

6 existimes Note the sequence *existimes...ut ignoscas...satis habeas*, all depending on *velim*.

    restiterim This refers to a meeting of the Senate on 1 January at which Cicero and Metellus Nepos had clashed (cf. sec. 8 *praesenti restiti*). Sense is in favour of taking *restiterim* and *defenderim* as perfect subjunctives rather than as future perfects. Indicatives would be logical, but the mood is assimilated to that of the other verbs.

tam...qui maxime sc. *est amicus*. 'in public spirit I call no man my superior'. Perhaps an ironical reminiscence of the end of Celer's letter. For the idiom, cf. *Sull.* 87 *tam mitis quam qui lenissimus*.

defenderim In the speech *Contra contionem Q. Metelli*.

etiam tecum 'you should be satisfied that *I* do not protest to *you*'.

Claudia P. Clodius Pulcher's half-sister, whom Cicero elsewhere calls 'Clodia' (a vulgarized form which he naturally avoids in writing to her husband). In all probability she was the 'Lesbia' of Catullus' poems.

sorore Pompey's wife Mucia was half-sister to the Metelli.

7 certo scio Distinguish in Cicero's usage between *certo scio* = 'I feel certain', *certum scio* = 'I know for certain', and *certe scio* = 'I certainly know' ('it is certain that I know').

ullo So I read for *animo* in line with Cicero's normal usage.

privavit Nepos and another Tribune used their constitutional power of 'blocking' (*intercessio*) to stop Cicero addressing a public meeting after laying down his office as Consul. They would only allow him to take the customary oath – that as a magistrate he had done nothing against the law. Cicero turned the tables by changing the usual form of the oath and swearing that he and he alone had saved the state and the City. He was fond of recalling this incident in after years.

honori Predicative dative; see on Letter 1.2.

idem Perhaps read *item* (in a fifteenth-century edition). If *idem* is right, there seems to be a conflation of two ideas: *populus idem iuravit* and *populus me vere iurasse iuravit*. Plutarch in his life of Cicero (23) says that the people took the oath after him *en masse*.

8 ei...oportere This is probably the *dictum* to which Celer's letter refers.

hominem gravem In exclamations the simple accusative is sometimes found without any introductory word such as *o* or *en*.

qui...liberasset Almost the words used by the Senate on 3 December 63 in decreeing a Thanksgiving for Cicero's services; see *Cat.* 3.15.

agere sc. *cum populo.* This was the *contio Q. Metelli* to which Cicero's speech replied.

tertio quoque verbo 'with every other word'.

casu Cicero makes the same point elsewhere, as in *Cat.* 3.29 *curemque ut ea virtute non casu gesta esse videantur.*

9 lenis...expostulem The point has been already made in sec. 6.

sententia Regularly used of a speech in the Senate by a senator called upon in his turn. He might put forward a motion, so *sententia* can have that sense too. Or it may register agreement or disagreement with a previous motion and conveniently be translated 'vote'.

sedens i.e. without rising to make a speech. He would simply say 'I agree (*adsentior*) with so-and-so.'

adsensi Cicero uses the active form very seldom, and only in letters.

senati This second-declensional form of the genitive is common in earlier Latin.

sublevaretur Generally taken to mean that Metellus was reinstated in his office, but if so he would hardly have left Rome to rejoin Pompey. Perhaps he was given permission to go abroad.

10 ab officiis The preposition with *deseri* is usual even when the noun is impersonal.

per litteras 'in writing' or 'in a letter'.

ego...admonet Here Cicero amplifies what he has already said in the first sentence of sec. 6.

exercitus Metellus had referred to his army (*qui exercitui praesum*). Nothing specific should be read into Cicero's mention of it – he was not envisaging military intervention on Celer's part.

LETTER 6 (*Att.* 1.13)

Atticus had left Rome *en route* for Greece in late December 62. About the same time Pompey had returned from the East, having disbanded his army on arrival in Italy. After the activities of Metellus Nepos and some unsatisfactory correspondence, Cicero's attitude towards

Pompey was highly critical at first, but they were soon on cordial
terms. The other main item of Roman gossip was a scandal. The
festival of the 'Good Goddess' (Bona Dea), from whose rites all males
were rigorously excluded, was held in December at the house of the
City Praetor, Julius Caesar, who was also head of the state religion
(Pontifex Maximus). A young nobleman, P. Clodius Pulcher (Catiline's prosecutor in 65), was discovered among those present disguised
as a woman, and had to make his escape with the help of a slave girl.
It was rumoured that he was keeping a rendezvous with Caesar's
wife, Pompeia. At his subsequent trial for sacrilege he was acquitted,
thanks to extensive bribery, but his alibi was exploded by Cicero's
evidence. A lifelong feud was the result.

1   **M. Cornelio** Unknown.
   Tribus...Tabernis A place about 30 miles down the Appian
Way. Canusium was an important town in Apulia on the way to
Brundisium, where Atticus will have embarked.
   phaselo Atticus seems to have dispatched his third letter just as
the boat which was to take him to his ship was putting off.
   rhetorum pueri From a Greek expression, παῖδες ῥητόρων ('sons
of rhetors'), used by Lucian. Plato (*Laws*, 769b) has οἱ ζωγράφων παῖδες
('the sons of painters'), as we might say 'the painting fraternity'.
The following phrase is rhetorically balanced (note the metrically
equivalent clausulae, *spārsāe sǎle | (a)-mōrīs nŏtis*) and rather precious.
   graviorem 'rather weighty', in the literal sense.
   ita...videtur Something has dropped out. What is printed here is
a guess at what may have been in the original.
   caesis..profectum The town of Sicyon owed Atticus money (three
years later, as we learn from Pliny the Elder, all publicly owned
paintings in this famous art centre were made over to its creditors
and taken to Rome). After a halt at Buthrotum he intended to visit
the governor of Macedonia, C. Antonius, in order to bring official
pressure to bear. Cicero facetiously writes as though Atticus was a
general about to start on a campaign. The archaic spelling *victumeis*
for *victimis* seems to be part of the joke (possibly cited from an old play).
   Amaltheam Atticus had a temple and garden on his estate
consecrated to the nymph Amalthea, on whom Zeus had bestowed
the cornucopia (horn of plenty).

Sicyonem Elsewhere in Latin the gender, when determinable, is feminine, as sometimes also in Greek; but masculine in Xenophon and Polybius.

quid...temporis *quid* here is equivalent to *quantum*, with partitive genitive, probably a colloquialism.

neque Achaicis...neque Epiroticis i.e. as such. Confidential letters could only be entrusted to bearers who were on their way to Atticus personally, as presumably in the present case. For certain parts of this letter are 'fairly frank', though Cicero still cannot write with full freedom because the bearer was a mere 'who knows what' (see on sec. 4).

2   committendae As though the subject was *litterae*, not *res*; so in *Att.* 7.17.2 *tantas res atque eas quae in omnium manus venturae essent.*

primum...primum The jingle is probably intentional. *igitur* implies that what follows is as much as Cicero thinks it prudent to put in this letter.

rogatum The presiding Consul called upon senators to speak (*sententiam rogare*) in a regular order: first the Consuls-Elect, if there were any, then the ex-Consuls. Under a rule of Sulla's these spoke in an order determined by the Consul who presided at the first sitting of the year. After these came Praetors-Elect and Praetorii, and so on down the official scale. Senators holding magisterial or promagisterial office, like Pompey at this time, were not included. Cicero's choice as first speaker in 62 was no doubt a tribute to his achievements as Consul, though it may have owed something to the gratitude of his former client, the Consul L. Murena. But even in 61 he only went down one place.

pacificatorem Allobrogum C. Calpurnius Piso, Consul in 67, who had been governor of Gallia Narbonensis, where the Allobroges were the principal tribe. They were currently in revolt, and Cicero's phrase is best explained as a sarcasm, not referring to any military activity on Piso's part but to acts of oppression which led to the outbreak. Sallust (*Cat.* 49.2) mentions one such. The Consul who chose him belonged to the same noble *gens* (see next note).

homine perverso The Consul, M. Pupius Piso Frugi (originally a Calpurnius Piso, adopted by a M. Pupius). A man of unusual gifts, expert in rhetoric and philosophy, he had been Cicero's guide, philosopher, and friend when they were young, and is favourably mentioned in his later works. Cicero's animosity in 61 may have been largely due to his relegation to second place on the senatorial rota, but the sketch in the *Brutus* (236), though much kindlier, does not differ essentially from what follows here.

Catulus Q. Lutatius Catulus, by seniority and reputation Rome's leading conservative statesman. He had been Consul in 78 and Censor in 65.

Hortensius Q. Hortensius Hortalus, Consul in 69. Cicero, who was eight years younger, had superseded him as Rome's leading orator and advocate.

moroso 'peevish'.

facie...facetiis Note the assonance (also *parvo...pravo* above). There are other examples, e.g. *Fam.* 7.20.1 *Velia non est vilior quam Lupercal.*

speres...metuas In Latin this use of the second person sing. ('you' = 'one') belongs to good literary style as well as to colloquial language.

collega M. Valerius Messalla Niger.

3 hoc quod infectum est 'a certain infected spot', i.e. the disagreement between the Consuls over the Bona Dea affair.

cum...fieret 'at the offering of sacrifice'.

virgines The Vestals.

mentionem...factam The regular expression for raising a matter in public.

Q. Cornificio An ex-Praetor, an unsuccessful competitor of Cicero for the consulship of 63.

nostrum i.e. *consularium.*

rogationem promulgasse 'gave notice of a bill'. A law had to be published at least 24 days (*trinum nundinum*) before being put to vote in a popular assembly. The bill was to set up a special tribunal to try Clodius.

nuntium remisisse 'sent notice of divorce'. Asked why he had done this if he did not believe Clodius guilty, Caesar made his famous reply, that *his* wife must be above suspicion (Plut. *Vit. Caes.* 10 *et al.*).

boni viri Usually simply *boni*. Cicero divided Roman society in its political aspect into *boni*, respectable folk who supported law and order, and *improbi*, radicals and trouble-makers. I normally translate 'the honest men', an expression once common in English political terminology (cf. 'les honnêtes hommes', 'les gens de bien').

Lycurgei Probably with reference to the fourth-century Athenian orator, who was famous for his savage prosecutions, rather than the Spartan law-giver. The subjunctive *fuissemus* has a concessive force ('though I had been').

†iniecta This word makes no sense here. *neglecta* has sometimes been read instead. *incepta* is another possibility.

4 amicus Pompey does not in fact seem to have been a particular friend of Atticus, though they were acquainted, so that the expression is to be taken as semi-ironical.

ἐν τοῖς πολιτικοῖς 'in political affairs', 'politically'.

terrae filio i.e. an obscure person of unknown origin; cf. Minucius Felix, 22.11 *ignobiles et ignotos terrae filios nominamus.* The description of Pompey is frank enough, but does not go into factual detail.

5 praetores Of 62, including Cicero's brother Quintus, who finally drew the governorship of Asia. Atticus was invited to join his staff, but declined.

τοποθεσίαν A topographical description; literally, 'plan, survey'. There is such a description of Syracuse in *Verr.* 2.4.117. The speech in question may have been the one against Metellus referred to below.

mendose fuisse Adverbs instead of adjectives are often used predicatively with the verb 'to be'.

orationibus There is nothing to show which speeches Atticus had been reading other than the one against Metellus.

Ἀττικώτερα 'more Attic', with a play on the cognomen 'Atticus'.

Metellinam The speech *Contra contionem Q. Metelli.* See on Letter 4.

φιλορήτορα 'an amateur of oratory'.

6 novi...quidnam 'What news?' *novi* is substantival. For the genitive see on sec. 1 *quid...temporis.*

etiam 'Why, yes.' So often in the Letters, as *Att.* 4.18.4 *quid aliud novi? etiam.*

Autronianam domum Formerly belonging to P. Autronius Paetus, now in exile for his share in Catiline's plot. *domus* is used of town houses, as opposed to *horti* or *suburbanum* (close to town) and *villa* (in the country). They were often called by the name of their owner, past or present. The price of 13,400,000 sesterces is very high but not incredible. Still, Constans may have been right to read ⌈XXXIII⌉ (3,300,000). In our manuscripts the numeral is written without the horizontal and lateral strokes (= hundreds of thousands); these may have originally been mistaken for figures.

bene emisse Cicero had recently bought Crassus' house on the Palatine, overlooking the Forum, for HS 3,500,000, all or part of which he borrowed. This purchase was considered ostentatious by some.

Teucris Cicero had been promised a loan by his former colleague C. Antonius, and Teucris (feminine form of Teucer) seems to have been an otherwise unknown go-between. The widely held belief that this was a nickname (variously explained) for Antonius himself is unlikely.

lentum negotium 'a slow-coach'. The use of *negotium* of persons is no doubt rather colloquial, though Cicero has it once in a speech to the Senate.

est in spe 'I have hopes of her.' So *Att.* 3.18.1 *an est aliquid in spe?* and elsewhere.

LETTER 7 (*Att.* 2.14)

Cicero had been spending the holiday month of April (59) on his properties by the sea-side. He writes this from his villa near Formiae.

1   sermone Bibuli No more is known of this. M. Calpurnius Bibulus was now Consul, Caesar's colleague and diehard political opponent.

Βοώπιδος 'Ox-Eyes', Homeric epithet of Hera. This nickname for P. Clodius Pulcher's half-sister Clodia (see on Letter 5.6) had a double relevance. Clodia had remarkable eyes (Cicero twice elsewhere refers to them as 'burning') and her relations with her brother were supposed to be similar to those of Hera with Zeus.

Sampsiceramus One of Cicero's nicknames for Pompey, actually the name of the ruler of Emesa in Syria.

vapulare 'that his name is mud'; literally 'that he is taking a beating'.

actiones Caesar's legislation on land and the ratification of Pompey's measures in the East. *actio* is often used of political action, the conduct of a political programme.

εὐανατρέπτους 'easily overturned'.

ruere 'plunge'. Often in Cicero of politicians resorting to violence.

ἐντυραννεῖσθαι 'be tyrannized over'.

2   pangendo Cicero had been collecting materials for a work on geography, but it did not get far.

ad quam...Aemiliam The text seems beyond restoration. It somehow has to do with the fact that the inhabitants of Formiae belonged to the Aemilian tribe (i.e. voting fraction) and probably also with the Basilica Aemilia in Rome. A basilica, a public building for judicial and business purposes, was a natural haunt of loungers and gossips.

horam quartam About 10 a.m. at this time of year. According to Martial (4.8.1), callers (*salutantes*) came during the first *two* hours of the day.

C. Arrius Arrii figure in inscriptions at Formiae.

contubernalis 'tent-mate'. Arrius was spending all his time in Cicero's house.

Sebosus Possibly a geographer, Statius Sebosus, mentioned by the elder Pliny. Q. Lutatius Catulus, Rome's leading conservative states-man in the seventies and sixties, had died about two years previously.

fundum *fundus* and *villa* are often used interchangeably.

probe sc. *scribis*. The first person plural *adgrediamur* merely implies a friendly interest in the other person's doings, in this case Cicero's literary undertakings.

LETTER 8 (*Att.* 3.3)

Cicero fled from Rome probably in the third week of March 58. This letter places him *en route* for Vibo Valentia (Bivone) in the toe of Italy. He probably wrote it near a parting of roads, perhaps at Teanum Sidicinum or Capua.

vivere Cicero writes more than once that he would have preferred suicide to flight but for the dissuasion of Atticus and others.

converti iter Originally Cicero had meant to make directly for

Brundisium but he changed his plan in order to stay on his friend Sicca's property near Vibo and also with a thought of settling in Sicily or Malta. This did not work out.

si veneris Atticus remained in Rome.

LETTER 9 (*Fam.* 14.2)

Cicero sailed from Brundisium on 29 April and reached Thessalonica (Salonika) on 23 May. He stayed there until November at the official residence of the Quaestor, Cn. Plancius.

SVIS In the letter itself only Terentia is addressed, except at the end (*valete*).

1 **longiores** 'of any length' rather than 'longer (than those I write to you)'.

nisi si = *nisi*. So in comedy, but also in literary prose.

quid scribam *habeo* implies *scio* and so can be followed by an indirect question, a common idiom if the manuscripts are to be trusted (*quod* and *quid* are constantly confused by copyists).

praestare debui 'I ought to have given it to you.' *praestare* often = 'render what is due'. In expressing past obligation or ability (*posse*) Latin puts the infinitive in the present tense and the governing verb in the past, as indeed does English except where a present would be ambiguous, as with 'ought' (originally a past tense) and 'could'.

timidi In letters to Atticus Cicero sometimes admits that he lost his nerve in the March crisis.

fuissemus, praestitissem Such combinations of first person plural (for singular) and singular are not particularly unusual.

2 **Pisonem** Cicero's son-in-law, C. Calpurnius Piso Frugi. He was Quaestor this year and died before Cicero returned to Rome.

tribunis pl. These would come into office on 10 December. Among them Milo and P. Sestius were particularly zealous on Cicero's behalf.

Crassum Evidently regarded as an unfriendly influence. Cicero never liked him and they were sometimes on openly bad terms.

eius modi...subleventur These words have to function like an adjective qualifying *casum*.

P. Valerius Probably a friend of Cicero's and Atticus' who crops up again fourteen years later.

a Vestae sc. *aede*, as regularly. Terentia's half-sister Fabia was a Vestal Virgin.

Tabulam Valeriam Not a bank or auction room, as often supposed, but the meeting place of the Tribunes, so called from a painting placed near by commemorating a victory of M. Valerius Maximus Messalla in the First Punic War. Terentia seems to have been summoned to appear by a hostile Tribune, perhaps Clodius himself, probably in connexion with her husband's confiscated property.

hem 'Alas!' This interjection is common in comedy, later very rare.

opem People who needed Cicero's services in court would approach him through his wife.

3   domo On the Palatine, now confiscated and demolished.

illud Anticipatory, as often; see on Letter 5.1.

quae...partem i.e. *in partem eius impensae quae facienda est.*

conficitur...premet As in English, the present is often used in conditions with reference to the future. The change to the future here may indicate the alternative more remotely, as being less desirable, or may signify continuity ('continue to afflict').

miseras Editors used to read *misera*, but cf. *Sull.* 1 *pristinae fortunae reliquiis miseris et adflictis.*

4   vos Other members of the family (Quintus senior, Atticus, Piso) will be included.

D. Probably for *dedi* or *dabam*, though the manuscripts usually have *data* where they do not abbreviate.

LETTER 10 (*Att.* 3.13)

1   quod 'as to the fact that'. Translate 'although'.

comitia The consular elections were normally held in July.

meque...feram 'and I shall not take it hard that for no very long time I have been beguiled by hope'. More often understood: 'nor shall I regret that the hope which buoyed me up has not lasted long' (Winstedt). Literally *temporis non longinqui spe* = 'by a hope of (i.e. directed towards) a not remote point of time'.

2 ut...audieris *ut = quo modo*. The subjunctives are probably assimilated to *videas* rather than potential ('you could never see or hear').

tam sc. *integra*.

cum...sum Cicero often complains that he was misled by treacherous friends, the orator Hortensius in particular, who deliberately gave him bad advice (to leave Rome). He seems to have continued to believe this, though after his restoration he publicly claimed that his withdrawal had been an act of exalted patriotism, to avoid a civil war.

nunc 'as matters stand'. *nunc* comes back from the past to the present. *iam* = 'presently'.

incolumem The word is often used of the preservation of a man's status as a member of the community. Roman governors on their return to Rome not infrequently had to face prosecution for misconduct in their provinces. Condemnation meant exile. Quintus had been threatened with prosecution, but it did not happen.

LETTER 11 (*Att.* 4.3)

This was written between three and four months after Cicero's triumphant return to Rome.

1 quid...ea For the shift from singular to plural cf. Plaut. *Trin.* 1168 *si quid stulte fecit, ut ea missa facias omnia*.

non quo 'Not that...'. Regularly followed by a subjunctive.

sensus 'sentiments', 'way of thinking'.

2 armatis hominibus They are regarded as instruments, so *ab* is not required.

area Cicero's house was being rebuilt at the public expense.

porticus Catuli This had been erected by the elder Catulus (Cos. 102) where the house of C. Gracchus' associate M. Fulvius Flaccus had once stood, Clodius had demolished it and put up a colonnade of his own.

Quinti His house adjoined his brother's.

nescio an nulli In Ciceronian Latin *nescio* (*haud scio*) *an* implies an affirmative: 'I am inclined to think they don't exist.'

ruere The historic infinitives, often found in lively narrative, lend a certain excitement.

vero Emphasizing the time contrast, as in *Fam.* 13.24.1 *cum antea . . . tum vero, postea quam* sqq.

nolebat Clodius had evaded Milo's efforts to bring him to trial earlier in the year. Milo was about to try again.

†Decimum† dissignatorem This henchman of Clodius is also mentioned in *Dom.* 50 (*Decumis*), but his real name is uncertain. Cicero would not have referred to him publicly by simple praenomen. Decimius, Decius (a supporter of Antony's by that name is mentioned in the *Philippics*), or Docimus are sufficiently similar to have been corrupted in both places to the familiar 'Decimus'. *dissignatores* acted as ushers in the theatre and/or as undertakers arranging funeral processions, perhaps *inter alia*.

Gellium Another of Clodius' satellites, known chiefly from Cicero's assault in *Sest.* 110f. He seems to have been brother to L. Gellius Poplicola, Cos. 72, and the elder of the two Gellii lampooned by Catullus in several epigrams.

. **3   descenderem** On the way from the Palatine to the Forum.

Tetti Damionis Clodius had a freedman called Damio, mentioned by Asconius, but this is someone else.

diaeta The healing art was anciently divided into three branches: dietetic (including general regimen), pharmaceutic, and surgical.

omnes...reddidit Clodius' atrocities made all previous villains look like pillars of virtue. L. Manlius Acidinus Fulvianus, Cos. 179, was a typical 'good man and good citizen'. No doubt Cicero liked the jingle *Catilinas Acidinos. postea* can be given its usual sense 'thereafter' (not = *in posterum*).

Milonis Originally a Papius, he was adopted by his maternal grandfather and became T. Annius Milo. As Tribune in 57 he organized gangs to fight Clodius (whom he finally killed) with his own weapons, and played an important part in bringing about Cicero's recall from exile. It appears that he had two houses, one in the Cermalus, a part of the Palatine near the Tiber, the other (inherited from his grandfather) on the Clivus Capitolinus, the road running up the Capitol on the other side of the valley.

hora quinta Just after 11 a.m.

P. Sullae A relative of the Dictator, who was found guilty of electoral malpractice in 66 along with Autronius Paetus and retired to Naples. In 62 Cicero successfully defended him against a charge of complicity in Catiline's plot and borrowed money from him to pay for his house.

Q. Flaccus Otherwise unknown, but perhaps a scion of an ancient noble family, now in decay, the Fulvii Flacci.

cupivit sc. *occidere*. The words following *ille* seem hopelessly corrupt, but probably mean that Clodius took refuge in the recesses of Sulla's house.

Marcellinus Cn. Cornelius Lentulus Marcellinus, Consul-Designate.

calumnia...exemit 'talked out the time with a filibuster (*calumnia dicendi*)'; cf. *Q. fr.* 2.1.3 *Clodius...diem dicendo eximere coepit.*

Appio Clodius' eldest brother, Ap. Claudius Pulcher, Praetor this year. The praenomen 'Appius', being almost confined to the patrician Claudii, does duty for nomen or cognomen without the usual implication of familiarity. 'Servius' and 'Faustus' are similarly used.

familiari tuo Probably Hortensius. Though Atticus was his close friend, he may have written to the effect that Hortensius' conduct was sometimes lacking in consistency. The expression *constantia vitae* is common with Cicero.

ille Clodius, who was standing for the curule aedileship. The elections had been held up, and Clodius was actually elected in the following January.

Milo sqq. 'Milo on his side posted up Marcellinus' proposal, which the latter had read out from a written draft, calling for a trial to cover the whole case – the site, the fires, and my own narrow escape, all to take place before the elections'.

dies comitiales Days on which assemblies could meet for legislation or election. Milo's announcement meant that Clodius could not be legally elected until the Tribunes went out of office on 9 December. For Milo as Tribune had the right of *spectio*, i.e. he could 'keep watch concerning the sky' (traditional formula) and declare unfavourable omens therein. Such a declaration (*obnuntiatio*) made it illegal for a popular assembly to vote. Normally the mere announcement of intention to watch by a competent magistrate was in effect a ban – the unfavourable omens to follow could be presumed.

4 Metelli Metellus Nepos, Consul this year.

Publi Cicero often refers to Clodius by his praenomen (ironic familiarity).

summa sc. *contionum*. No notice would be taken of Milo's announcement unless he actually 'obnuntiated' in the Campus Martius, where the election would be held.

ante mediam noctem Strictly this should mean the night of the 19th, but Cicero was thinking of the following day and means 'before midnight prior to the 19th'.

fratrum The two Claudii should be regarded as half-brothers (not cousins) of Metellus Nepos. In classical usage *frater* and *soror* = 'first cousin' apply only to the children of brothers (*fratres patrueles*). *contentio* refers to the efforts of the three to have the elections held.

veniretur See on Letter 1.6 (*laboraretur*).

de nocte 'before daybreak'.

†prope† deviis *prope* seems meaningless. Perhaps read *properans*.

inter lucos The asylum of Romulus on the lower ground between the two heights of the Capitoline Hill was called *inter duos lucos*.

nundinae An annual market-day.

biduo On the 20th and 21st (there has been some controversy about the dates in this passage).

5 hora noctis nona Between 2.15 and 3.15 in the morning of the 22nd.

Marcellus Probably C. Claudius Marcellus, Cos. 50, standing for Curule Aedile. Evidently *he* did not expect any election that day.

vacuum sane Perhaps 'empty, really' (i.e. 'as good as empty') rather than 'quite empty' (= *sane vacuum*), which would be in literal contradiction to *pauci*.

pauci pannosi sc. *esse nuntiabantur*.

sine lanterna The ragamuffins did not even have a lantern among them in the dark.

illi Clodius and his followers.

heroë Milo. In Latin the loan-word *heros* has a Latinized genitive and ablative singular (*herois*, *heroë*).

nova quaedam divina 'certain recent brilliancies'.

iam i.e. 'after all that has happened'.

invidi et perfidi Hortensius is doubtless chiefly in mind.

nobilitati The manuscripts read *nobili*, but Cicero does not seem here to be thinking of an individual (such as L. Lucullus) but rather of the conservative aristocracy as a whole, which failed to rally energetically to his defence.

6   pro facultatibus nostris 'so far as my means allow (and no further)'. *ne...essem* explains why Quintus was not repaid the entire sum due.

respondemus *respondeo* is often used of paying a debt. *respondimus* (R. Klotz) would be easier, but the historic tense of *exhaustus essem* may be explained as due to an implied condition, 'if I had repaid in full and at once'.

LETTER 12 (*Q.fr.* 2.4)

Q. Cicero spent the first five months of 56 in Sardinia as Legate to Pompey, who had been put in supreme charge of Roman grain supplies with extensive powers.

1 Sestius noster As Tribune in 57 P. Sestius had fought valiantly on behalf of Cicero's recall, almost losing his life in a Forum *mêlée*. He had been charged *de vi* in this connexion and was defended by Cicero in an extant speech. Cicero considered him a tedious writer and speaker, but nothing is known of the personal differences alluded to in this letter.

a.d. II This alternative to *prid.* is found in inscriptions, but only rarely in Cicero's manuscripts. It is, however, not unlikely that copyists sometimes replaced it by *prid.*

quod...esse *quod* is relative. *nullam...esse* explains *how* the jury's unanimity was in the public interest; cf. *Att.* 12.21.5 *quod ipsum erat fortis aegroti, accipere medicinam.*

saepe With *intellexeram.*

humanissime 'with the best of grace'. Forbearance with others and willingness to forgive offence is an important element in Roman *humanitas*; see Letter 2.1.

moroso 'cantankerous'.

Vatinium P. Vatinius, Tr. pl. 59, an ally of Caesar. Cicero 'cut him up' while interrogating him as a witness; the published version, *In P. Vatinium testem interrogatio*, survives. Later Cicero and Vatinius were on excellent terms.

dis hominibusque plaudentibus A mock-heroic effect.

Paulus L. Aemilius Paul(l)us, Cos. 50.

nomen...delaturum 'lay charges against'. Properly the *nominis delatio* was the second stage of a prosecution, preceded by *postulatio*. But the procedures are not precisely known.

Macer Licinius C. Licinius Macer Calvus, distinguished orator and poet (often mentioned in association with Catullus). The inversion of cognomen and nomen seems to have been a rather colloquial usage at this period. It is rare in Cicero's literary works, common in his letters, though never or hardly ever occurring in the case of *nobiles*.

ab Sesti subselliis From the defence benches occupied by Sestius and his supporters.

illi Vatinius, *defuturum* being ironical.

quid quaeris? Often in the Letters to introduce an epigrammatic summing-up or conclusion, much like *quid multa?*

2 Tyrannio A nickname which replaced the original name of Theophrastus of Amisus in Pontus. He was a celebrated teacher and scholar who had settled in Rome. The geographer Strabo was one of his pupils. Besides holding classes in Cicero's house in Rome he helped in arranging the library in his house in Antium.

curavi sc. *ut solveretur*, as often.

contubernales 'under the same roof'; the houses adjoined.

Crassipede Tullia's second husband, Furius Crassipes (praenomen unknown), was a young patrician. The marriage soon ended in a divorce, but we do not know the circumstances.

sed...exiturus 'But it is the two days after the Latin Festival (this is now over), which are looked upon as holy days, and he is going out of town.' This explains why the betrothal ceremony (*sponsalia*) could not take place at once (it was actually held on 4 April). The annual festival called Latinae (feriae) or Latiar was held on a date fixed by the Consuls of the year.

LETTER 13 (*Att.* 4.5)

The conference held at Luca in April 56, at which Pompey and Caesar mended fences, opened a new political epoch for Cicero. Warned that further opposition to the dominant coalition might get

him into fresh trouble, he set a new course and for the next few
years became its obedient instrument, at least to the extent of defending henchmen of Pompey and Caesar in the courts, even when these
had been personal enemies of his own like Vatinius and Gabinius. In
late May or June he delivered a speech in the Senate (*De provinciis
consularibus*) lauding Caesar's victories in Gaul. This is probably the
'palinode' referred to in this letter, though some think that was a
private letter to Caesar or Pompey (which hardly fits in with the
statement in sec. 2 that he wanted to bind himself irrevocably to the
new alliance) or an earlier speech or speeches in favour of Caesar.

1 **ain tu?** i.e. *aisne tu?* 'Come now!'

mea sc. *scripta*, as often.

ab eo Probably Pompey.

exempla duo Written *exempla ii* this would easily become *exemplari*
(see critical note). Cicero never has *exemplar* literally of a copy of a
document.

iam dudum Cicero does not use *dudum* with a present tense except
in combination with *iam* or *tam* or *quam*.

παλινῳδία The term 'palinode' ('recanting ode') was invented by
Stesichorus, who took back what he had written about Helen of Troy.

sed...consilia 'But goodbye to principle, sincerity, and honour!'

principibus After his recall from exile Cicero was apt to complain
of the ill-will of the leading 'optimates', who actually made much
of the abominable Clodius – a demagogue, but one of their own
class. Atticus' friendship with Hortensius accounts for *istis*.

senseram This refers to what happened in 58. With *noram* understand *id*.

te auctore Atticus had advised Cicero to cultivate good relations
with Pompey and Caesar.

2 **ut scriberem** If the palinode was the *De provinciis*, Cicero is
thinking of the written version which he was about to publish.

ἀποθεώσει 'in my "apotheosis" of Caesar'. If this reading is right,
the word seems to be somewhat facetious, and may be quoted from
a previous letter.

ut scripseram 'as I told you I should'.

ille Caesar.

villam Cicero's villa at Tusculum.

Catuli Probably the elder (Cos. 102). Pliny (*Nat. hist.* 22.12) says it belonged to Sulla, who may have bought it from Catulus and passed it on to Vettius, a murky character who had profiteered in the proscriptions and died in gaol.

domum...oportere The rebuilding of Cicero's house on the Palatine may have been approaching completion (cf. Letter 12.2). The *principes*, who had criticized him for rebuilding it, were now criticizing him for not selling it (they thought Cicero should live somewhere less conspicuous), as though, if he had a right to sell the house, he had not an equal right to rebuild it.

sed quid ad hoc si 'But what is that compared to the fact that...?'

quibus sententiis i.e. *iis sententiis quibus.*

etiam ipsi Cicero does not use *et* (= *etiam*) before *ipse.*

laetati...dixisse Cicero develops this point in the lengthy political apologia which he addressed to Lentulus Spinther about eighteen months later (*Fam.* 1.9.10).

3 viaticam Crassipes praeripit 'Crassipes is forestalling your welcome-home dinner.' Atticus will have wanted Cicero to dine with him on the night of his return to Rome, but he had already accepted an invitation from his future son-in-law (see next letter). (*cena*) *viatica* = (*cena*) *adventicia*; cf. Plaut. *Bacch.* 94 *ego sorori meae cenam hodie dare volo viaticam.* The ellipse of the noun (as often with feminine adjectives such as *calida* (sc. *aqua*)) happens to be paralleled in Petron. 90.5 *adventicia.*

tu sqq. Atticus is supposed to protest: was Cicero going out to dinner in the suburbs straight after his journey? The term *horti* does not mean 'gardens', as commonly supposed and translated, but an estate near Rome (outside the old city boundary, *pomerium*) consisting of a house (*villa*) and grounds. It seems to have been at this period associated with fast living: cf. *Cael.* 27 *si fas est defendi a me eum qui nullum convivium renuerit, qui in hortis fuerit, qui unguenta sumpserit, qui Baias viderit* (Clodia's *horti* across the Tiber were a resort of Rome's 'smart set'). Actually Crassipes' property was on or near the Appian Way by which Cicero would re-enter Rome.

quid enim tua? sc. *interest.*

tui Two slave-clerks (*librarioli*) sent by Atticus. *structione* refers to the tiers of bookshelves (*pegmata*), *sittybae* = book-labels. The clerks also painted the walls and ceiling.

LETTER 14 (*Att.* 4.12)

This letter, probably the next in the series to Letter 13 chronologically, gives an idea of Cicero's private business and social activities at this period, after he had taken a back seat in politics, though still active in the courts.

Egnatius L. Egnatius Rufus, with whom Cicero and his brother had business dealings. The name 'Halimetus' can hardly be right, and we know nothing of his affair. Aquilius may be C. Aquilius Gallus, a celebrated jurist.

Macroni Nothing is known of Macro and of what he wanted from Cicero (perhaps his services in court).

esse In effect, *esse posse*. The force is: 'it doesn't look as though I am obliging' (i.e. 'going to oblige') 'Macro'.

Pilia Atticus' wife, married the previous February.

facio fraudem 'cheat'; cf. Plaut. *Mil.* 164 *ut ne legi fraudem faciant aleariae*. The senatorial decree presumably restricted expenditure on meals in public places and so would not apply to the *horti*. *deversorium* could be either public ('inn') or private ('lodge').

LETTER 15 (*Fam.* 5.12)

In a letter to Atticus (4.6.4) which used to be assigned to June 56 but, as shown by L. R. Taylor, was really written from Cumae about 19 April 55, Cicero tells him to get this letter from its addressee, L. Lucceius, and to thank him for promising to make haste in meeting Cicero's wishes. Thus it will have been written about 12 April. It is in Cicero's most ornate style, and he was proud of it (*Att.* l.c. *valde bella est*). On Lucceius see Letter 1.5. His historical work, which is here so warmly praised, is mentioned nowhere else, and Cicero himself says nothing about him in the excursus on Latin historiography in his *Laws* (1.6f.). It would therefore appear that his history remained unpublished, though he lived at least another ten years. Or it is just possible that it was written in Greek, like that of L. Lucullus.

1 coram Take with *agere*.

ostendis 'promise', a common sense of the verb in Cicero's letters.

opinionem 'expectation' (not 'opinion'). Cicero seems to have read the work only recently.

res i.e. *res gestas*, 'achievements', as often.

monumentis The word is used of any kind of record intended to preserve the past in memory.

commemoratio posteritatis '(the idea of) posterity talking about me'. The manuscript reading *ad spem quandam* makes poor sense, especially with *illa cupiditas* (sc. *me rapit*).

suavitate ingeni 'The charm of your talent' (not with reference to the 'sweetness which characterises the whole disposition of Lucceius', as Tyrrell and Purser).

2   Italici belli et civilis The Social War of 91–89 was followed almost immediately by the civil struggles which ended with Sulla's victory in 81, sometimes considered as three separate civil wars.

ut...Numantinum A brachylogy, *bellum* lacking a governing verb. More regularly this might have run: *Callisthenes, qui Phocicum bellum, Timaeus, qui Pyrrhi, Polybius, qui Numantinum conscripsit.* Alexander the Great's historiographer and victim Callisthenes wrote a history of Greece from 387 to 357 and a monograph on the Sacred War (*Phocicum bellum*) of 355–347. Timaeus' history of Sicily, or of the Greeks in the West, may have ended in 272 and appears from this passage to have been followed by an account of Pyrrhus' Italian campaigns (281–275). This too is the only evidence for Polybius' history of the Numantine War (143–133); his *Universal history* ended with the fall of Corinth and Carthage in 146. Two of the parallels are therefore inexact, since Callisthenes and Polybius in the two monographs were not dealing with periods covered by their general histories, whereas Lucceius was preparing to deal with 63–57 in his main work (*dum ad locum venias*). Nor can we be certain about Timaeus. Cicero may in fact have been unable to produce a complete analogue.

quiddam interest 'it makes a certain difference'.

3   bene et naviter Like English 'well and truly'; cf. Liv. 43.7.3 *si Cretenses bene ac naviter destinarent potiorem populi Romani quam regis Persei amicitiam habere.*

leges historiae To tell no untruth, to conceal no truth, to avoid any suspicion of fear or favour (*De orat.* 2.62); cf. Pliny the Younger's letter to Tacitus (7.33.10). This passage is generally taken at face value, as a specimen of Ciceronian vanity. It is really a parade of modesty and an exercise in flattery: how highly he must value Lucceius' praise to make such a request! Cicero did not seriously believe that the wine of his achievements needed any bush.

Herculem Xenophontium This famous allegory, 'the Choice of Hercules' (between Virtue and Pleasure, appearing to him in female form), was invented by Socrates' contemporary, Prodicus. Cicero read it in Xen. *Mem.* 2.1.21f. Cf. *Off.* 1.118.

eam Resumes *illam* after the two intervening clauses.

4 corpus Seldom used of a single 'book' (*liber*), which was probably all Cicero expected, despite *libris tuis* in sec. 9. He was thinking of the work as an artistic whole made up of several episodes (consulship, exile, recall).

illa...scientia 'that special knowledge of yours'.

multorum...proditionem Cicero persisted in the belief that some of his friends, notably Hortensius, deliberately gave him bad advice, leading him to leave Rome in face of Clodius' threats. That did not prevent him from publicly representing his withdrawal as an act of patriotic self-sacrifice, taken to save Rome from civil war; cf. Letter 10.2.

habet...delectationem The first appearance of this idea seems to be in a fragment of Euripides (Nauck 133: 'but it is sweet to remember troubles when safely over them'), translated by Cicero in *Fin.* 2.105. Its most famous expression is Virgil's *forsan et haec olim meminisse iuvabit* (*Aen.* 1.203). We should say 'gives pleasure'. So *habere dolorem* can mean "be grievous' as well as 'be grieved'.

5 casus...iucunda Lucretius' *suave mari magno* (5.1) comes to mind, but the pleasure there lies simply in the contemplation of other people's distress from a position of immunity. Here sympathy enters in. In the pagan world pity was regarded as a painful emotion; cf. Virgil's happy farmer (*Georg.* 2.498): *neque ille | aut doluit miserans inopem aut invidit habenti.*

Epaminondas The great Theban leader who died in battle against the Spartans (362); cf. *Fin.* 2.97. It was a dishonour for a soldier to lose or throw away his shield in battle; cf. Hor. *Od.* 2.7.10 *relicta non bene parmula.*

†redituque Themistocles never returned from his exile in Persia, and it is incredible that Cicero, who refers to Themistocles' death in exile more than once elsewhere, could have blundered on such a point in so carefully composed a letter, addressed moreover to a historian. The least unlikely solution is to read *interituque*. According to one account Themistocles took poison so that he would not have to attack his country in the service of the Persian king.

viri Hellenistic historians like Duris of Samos and Phylarchus were much given to the working up of dramatic episodes; see A. H. McDonald, *J.R.S.* 47 (1957) 163.

7 Apelle...Lysippo Horace (*Epist.* 2.1.239) refers to this story, for which Cicero is the earliest source.

nec...perhibendus The normal order would be *Spartiates ille Agesilaus*. Perhaps *ille* should be omitted or changed to *mihi*. If the text is otherwise sound, *perhibendus* seems to mean 'to be brought into the case (in support of my contention that great men are careful about whom they choose to celebrate them)'; cf. *Att.* 1.1.4 *sine eo quem Caecilius suo nomine perhiberet* ('brought in' as advocate). It cannot mean 'a man to be talked about'.

neque...esse cf. Xen. *Ages.* 2.7, Plut. *Ages.* 2. Apuleius (*Apol.* 15) unkindly says that Agesilaus was ashamed of his appearance (*diffidens forma sua*).

imagines...statuasque Perhaps an echo of a passage in the speech *Pro Archia* delivered some seven years earlier (30): *an statuas et imagines, non animorum simulacra sed corporum, studiose multi summi homines reliquerunt; consiliorum relinquere ac virtutum nostrarum effigiem nonne multo malle debemus, summis ingeniis expressam et politam?*

hoc Abl., taken up by *quod*.

Timoleonti The liberator of Sicily. Polybius (12.23.4) says that Timaeus 'makes him greater than the most glorious gods'.

praeconium Again cf. *Arch.* 24 *cum in Sigeo ad Achillis tumulum astitisset, 'o fortunate' inquit 'adulescens, qui tuae virtutis Homerum praeconem inveneris!'* Arrian and Plutarch have the story.

Hector The quotation, one of Cicero's favourites, came from Naevius' tragedy *Hector proficiscens*: *laetus sum laudari me abs te, pater, a laudato viro.*

8 scribam ipse de me In point of fact Cicero had written in 60 a prose account of his consulship in Greek and contemplated writing one in Latin (*Att.* 1.19.10). He also wrote a poem *De consulatu suo* in the same year and later one on his exile and return (*De temporibus suis*).

multorum Scaurus, Sulla, and others wrote their memoirs. Xenophon's *Anabasis* may be the prototype for this sort of composition.

praecones In 396 competitions were instituted at Olympia to pick heralds and trumpeters for the festival. The victors were probably crowned on its last day. But a passage of Suetonius (*Nero* 24.1) and another of Dio Chrysostom (*Orat.* 13.11) show that in Nero's time and later they *did* proclaim themselves. Presumably the practice had changed.

9 recipis causam The phrase is regular of an advocate accepting a case, as is *cavsam suscipere* (see tec. 10).

ac ne sqq. This paraphrases what has already been said in sec. 1. Such redundancies are quite characteristic of Cicero's more elaborate letter-writing.

gloriola Note the deprecatory diminutive.

10 commentarios Notes to be worked up into literary form (Greek ὑπομνήματα). Caesar so entitled his works on the Gallic and Civil Wars, eliciting Cicero's comment in the *Brutus* (262) that only fools would attempt to embellish *them*.

LETTER 16 (*Att.* 4.10)

1 Ptolomaeum Surnamed Auletes ('The Piper'). He had been driven out of Egypt in 58 and his restoration (i.e. who should conduct it) became a major political issue in 57–56. The job had now been done by the governor of Syria, Gabinius, at Pompey's instigation.

pascor Cf. *Att.* 4.11.2 *nos hic voramus littⁱras.*

Fausti Faustus Cornelius Sulla, son of the Dictator. His father owned a villa in the Cumae district which presumably contained the library he brought back from the East (Plut. *Vit. Sull.* 26). Faustus seems to have given Cicero the run of it; or the books may have been bought or borrowed.

rebus sc. *me pasci.* The sea-food for which the Bay of Naples was famous.

sedecula Probably in Atticus' house on the Quirinal.

istorum The Consuls, Pompey and Crassus. *iste* is used because they were normally in Rome.

ambulare Cicero often refers to conversational walks with his friends.

eo Pompey.

qui curet Atticus favoured Epicureanism, which held the contrary; cf. *Divin.* 2. 104 *Epicurusne? qui negat quicquam deos nec alieni curare nec sui.*

2 Laconicum A kind of sweat-bath. Cicero seems to be writing of some improvements now in progress at his house on the Palatine. The original rebuilding can hardly have been still going on.

circa sunt Editors used to read *Cyrea sint*, 'buildings in the style of Cyrus' (a contemporary architect).

quoad poteris See on Letter 1.7 and *Att.* 4.6.4 *fac ut...domum nostram quoad poteris invisas.*

Philotimum A trusted freedman of Cicero's wife, employed as his agent in various matters.

respondere 'repay' (see on Letter 11.6). The new walk and bath will enable Cicero to repay Atticus' hospitality in kind.

Parilibus The Parilia or Palilia, a festival in honour of the shepherd goddess Pales, took place on 21 April.

LETTER 17 (*Q.fr.* 2.9)

The date is uncertain. Cicero wrote from a villa, the building, or rather rebuilding, of which was not yet complete (secs. 2–3), therefore either Tusculanum or Formianum (the Cumanum was acquired after the exile, the references to Marius (see next letter) rule out the Pompeianum, and at Antium Cicero possessed a house, not a villa). Quintus and Marius seem to have been in Rome.

1 in isto i.e. *in ista re quam scribis* (literary work). Cicero composed his dialogue *De oratore* in 55.

essem 'were engaged'.

tu scis...otiantem This conjecture assumes a saying to the effect that to interrupt an idle man is to do him a favour. Private study or literary work came into the category of *otium*, as opposed to business (*negotium*).

qua quidem As usually after a relative pronoun, *quidem* shows that the relative clause is a statement valid in its own right, independently of the main clause.

colloquare *mecum* must be understood from *me*.

μουσοπάτακτος 'smitten by the Muses', 'moonstruck'. This expression is found nowhere else, but cf. μουσόληπτος (and νυμφόληπτος, μουσομανής).

ἀναντίλεκτον 'unanswerable'.

Ciceronis Quintus' son. Sons, at any rate only sons, are familiarly referred to by cognomen. So M. Cicero's son is 'Cicero' in the Letters, not 'Marcus', and the two cousins are 'Cicerones'.

2 nihil dicam aliud 'Well, I'll say no more than this, that...' Cf. *Q. fr.* 3.4.2 *me a se dissentientem non tulit (nihil dicam gravius)*. Cicero is *not* predicting what he will say in the future if he ever (again) has reason for the suspicion.

sic fit sqq. Cicero quotes from a verse of Sophocles, fr. 962 (Pearson) meaning 'If what you did was terrible, what you suffer must be terrible too.' But for ἔδρασας ('did') in the original he substitutes ἔφησας ('said').

Ptolomaei The chief of a delegation from Ptolemy the Piper's revolted subjects had been murdered in 57. A certain Asicius was accused of the crime, but defended by Cicero and acquitted.

hominem Marius. Concerning him see the next letter.

ad Baias Prepositions are normally thus used with *Baias* (*Baiis*), which was probably felt as equivalent to *Aquas*. Baiae was not a town in its own right but an apanage of Cumae.

Neapoli Movement from X (town or small island) to Y is generally expressed with the preposition *ab*, e.g. *Fam.* 4.5.4 *cum ab Aegina Megaram versus navigarem*, but exceptions occur.

machaerophoris Probably royal guards who came with the royal litter; but the details of the anecdote are obscure.

ne rudem quidem 'not even roughly finished'. Cf. Mart. 7.36.2 *et rudis hibernis villa nataret aquis*.

3 peculiare fuerit 'will be something quite special'.

Anicium Perhaps C. Anicius, a Senator and personal friend for whom Cicero wrote a letter of recommendation in 44 (*Fam.* 12.21). He may have been related to Atticus' cousin Anicia (Nep. *Att.* 2.1). Marius would stay with him.

ita...possimus 'Scholar as I am, I can live with workmen in the house'. *ita* has a qualifying force: 'I am a scholar but with the qualification that...'

Arce nostra A conjecture by Tunstall, *arce* Ὑμίᾳ, though impossible, pointed the way. The meaningless *araxira* or *araysira* came from *arcenra*. The reference is to a place called Arx ('citadel') near Arpinum, now Rocca d'Arce. Cicero did not need Greek philosophy from Hymettus, the famous mountain in Attica, to teach him how to put up with discomfort; early training in his native hills had done that.

4 de interpellatione 'as for interruption'.

Philoctetam Marooned by his comrades on the way to Troy, Philoctetes will have cursed his fellow-countrymen in one of the lost plays bearing his name (he does not do this in Sophocles' extant one).

amabo te 'I beg you', a common colloquial expression. Literally it means 'I shall love you (if you do what I ask)'.

hortus domi est *hortus* usually means 'kitchen garden'. What *domi est* means is doubtful. Possibly 'in good shape', opposite to *foris est* 'is done for'. Cicero seems to be saying that his guests won't starve, but may have to be content with simple vegetarian fare.

LETTER 18 (*Fam.* 7.1)

The recipient, M. Marius, may have been a family connexion of Cicero's, one of the Marii of Arpinum. He lived at leisure in a villa on the Bay of Naples, near, though not necessarily next door to, Cicero's Pompeianum. The letter is in the nature of an essay, reminiscent of the younger Pliny; Marius had asked Cicero to send him something which would stop him feeling sorry to have missed Pompey's magnificent games. These were held in mid August 55 after the dedication of Pompey's theatre (the first in Rome to be built of stone) and the temple of Venus Genetrix.

1 valetudinis Letter 50 nine years later shows Marius as a martyr to gout.

per valetudinem 'so far as your health was concerned'. Cf. sec. 2 *ut ei desinere per omnes homines liceret*.

constiterit Probably from *constare* rather than *consistere*; cf. *Fam.* 1.9.11 *ne si summa quidem eorum in me merita constarent* et sim.

Stabianum Constans thought Marius lived on the south side of the bay, opposite Pompeii. The reading *perforando* (sc. *pariete*) for *perforasti et* cannot be guaranteed, but at least makes sense.

communes Marius, reading in the privacy of his bedroom, is contrasted with his friends, drowsily watching a public show. But the contrast is not clearly brought out and *communes* ('shared in common'; it cannot mean 'vulgar') is odd. The text may be faulty, but Madvig's *comminus* is even less plausible. A close view in a theatre is not a disadvantage.

mimos Pantomimic performances, more sophisticated and also more indecent than the Atellan farces which they superseded in popularity.

semisomni According to Valerius Maximus (2.4.6) streams of water were channelled through the theatre to relieve the heat.

quae...probavisset Sp. Maecius Tarpa is mentioned twice by Horace as a judge in poetry competitions (*Sat.* 1.10.38, *A.P.* 387). He may have been Chairman (*magister*) of the Guild of Poets (*collegium poetarum*). He had chosen the plays for the afternoon performances. The subjunctive *probavisset* may be explained as generic or as expressing the thought in the spectators' minds.

2   omnino Concessive as often in Cicero, 'to be sure'.

honoris causa First = 'by way of compliment (to Pompey)'; second = 'for the sake of their repute'.

decessisse The codex Mediceus, which is virtually our only authority, has *decesse*; also *spectamus* (sec. 3, for *spectavimus*) and *praetermisse* (sec. 6). No reason is apparent why three colloquial contracted forms should be used in this letter. As Cicero thought, the actors had retired from the stage so as not to fall below their reputations. Pliny (*Nat. Hist.* 7.158) mentions an actress of 103 years old who was brought back to give a performance at the votive games in A.D. 9.

Aesopus Clodius Aesopus, the leading tragic actor of his day, was a personal friend of Cicero's. In his prime he had a magnificent voice (*Sest.* 123).

desinere 'retire'.

si sciens fallo With this formula the taker of an oath imprecates punishment upon himself should he be wittingly false to it. The oath seems to have been part of Aesopus' role. It is not likely that, as has been suggested, actors were sworn in before the performance.

reliquos ludos Comedies or mimes.

apparatus 'décor'.

quo quidem The usual function of *quidem* in a relative clause is to emphasize, giving such a clause the importance of a main statement.

sescenti Common for a large, undetermined number.

Clytaemestra The spelling without 'n' is ancient and classical. The play was by Accius. Livius Andronicus and Naevius are each credited with a fragment from a 'Trojan Horse'.

creterrarum Perhaps as part of the spoil after the sack of Troy. Elsewhere Cicero has the form *crater* or (once) *cratera*. Here the archaic form may come from the play.

habuerunt We should say 'caused'. Cf. on Letter 15.4 *habet... delectationem*.

3 Protogeni Presumably a slave whose job was to read to his master aloud (*anagnostes*).

ne tu The asseverative *ne* ('truly') is only used before a pronoun.

Graecos...ludos These seem to have been plays performed in Greek, as distinct from Latin adaptations like 'Clytaemestra'.

Oscos i.e. Campanian. The Atellan farce, called from the town of Atella in Campania, was a sort of ancient Punch and Judy show.

senatu vestro The local town council. Graffiti show a M. Marius as standing for Aedile in Pompeii, though if Constans is right about the whereabouts of Marius' villa he would have belonged to the district of Nuceria.

via Graeca Perhaps an old road bordering the mountains from Stabiae to Sorrentum, alternative to a newer road along the coast.

contempseris The tense indicates that Cicero refers to a particular gladiatorial show, or perhaps some incident in which Marius had been involved.

et operam et oleum A common phrase for a waste of effort. *oleum* is the midnight oil of the lamp, here applying to the athletes who oiled themselves at Pompey's expense: 'Pompey himself admits that they were a waste of time and midday oil.'

venationes Fights between men and wild beasts.

praeclara This quasi-aesthetic appreciation of the splendour of wild beasts is noteworthy; cf. Plin. *Nat. Hist.* 8.42 *leoni praecipua generositas tunc cum colla armosque vestiunt iubae.* Poets will speak of a lion as *nobilis* or *magnanimus*.

misericordia According to Pliny's evidently romanticized account the spectators rose in a body and cursed Pompey (*Nat. Hist.* 8.21).

4 ludis scaenicis i.e. during the earlier part of the games.

Galli Canini L. Caninius Gallus had been active in Pompey's interest as Tribune in 56. The charge against him is unknown, but he is likely to have been convicted and withdrawn to Athens.

vita nulla est 'life isn't worth living'.

non...meritos This perhaps includes Caninius Gallus (though since he was a friend of Marius this is not very likely) and L. Cornelius Balbus, whom Cicero defended in an extant speech in 56. Vatinius and Gabinius were yet to come.

5 villas Cicero had only two at this time on the Bay of Naples, Cumanum and Pompeianum. Marius would therefore seem to have lived at some distance from the latter, unless *nostras* means 'our'. He also may have had more than one villa in the area.

6 me...subinvitaras 'given me a sort of invitation'.

epistulis...meis 'because of any letters of mine'.

LETTER 19 (*Q.fr.* 2.10)

1 convicio 'clamorously'. Cf. Q. Cicero to Tiro (*Fam.* 16.26.1) *verberavi te cogitationis tacito dumtaxat convicio quod fasciculus alter ad me iam sine tuis litteris perlatus est.* The original meaning of the word seems to have been 'outcry'.

codicilli Waxed wooden tablets, used for sending short, informal notes.

2 Tenediorum Delegations from overseas were heard by the Senate in February. A petition from the island of Tenedos for the status of a free community had just been summarily rejected. The precise origin of the proverbial expression 'axe of Tenedos' was variously explained. It had to do with the eponymous hero Tenes and a drastic code of law which he was supposed to have introduced.

me...Favonium The persons are mentioned in order of debating precedence: M. Calidius, a noted orator, was *praetorius*, M. Favonius, a satellite of Cato (Mommsen called him 'Cato's Sancho'), *tribunicius* or *quaestorius*.

ab Sipylo Mt Sipylus in Lydia (*ab* = 'beside'). The other Magnesia, on the Maeander, was in Caria. Pansa may have been a tax-farmer, but nothing is known about him and his demand.

Pomponio i.e. Atticus.

3 Lucreti According to St Jerome, Cicero 'corrected' (*emendavit*) *De rerum natura* after the poet's death.

multis luminibus ingeni 'sparkling with natural genius'.

tamen Natural genius and art are often contrasted, as by Ovid of Callimachus (*Am.* 1.15.14 *quamvis ingenio non valet, arte valet*). The absence of one might be condoned for the sake of the other, but Lucretius had both. Cicero's judgement on another didactic poet is somewhat comparable: *poeta ineptus, et tamen scit nihil* (*Att.* 2.20.6) – a bad poet not redeemed by learning. Proposals to add *non* before *multis* or *multae* were misguided.

virum...hominem Of course nobody can in literal earnest be be both 'a stout fellow' and less (or more) than human, but the juxtaposition is mildly funny. The work was presumably a translation of the fifth-century philosopher-poet Empedocles, perhaps by Cicero's friend Cn. Sallustius (Letter 2.1).

LETTER 20 (*Fam.* 7.5)

C. Trebatius Testa of Velia in south Italy no doubt carried this letter with him when he left to join Caesar in Cisalpine Gaul, probably in late April 54. He was in his early or middle thirties, a friend of Cicero's, and already an eminent jurist. Horace makes him his partner in the dialogue of *Sat.* 2.1. Cicero's relations with Caesar were at this time better than ever before or after.

IMP. At this period the title of *imperator* was conferred upon a victorious general by his troops.

1 me...alterum 'my *alter ego*'.

exirem Cicero had been appointed Legate to Pompey (as controller of grain supplies) in 57, but apparently was not assigned any duties. In 55 Pompey was given a five-year command over the two Spanish provinces and there was talk of Cicero going out with him as Legate. His appointment as Legate for the second time was made in the following autumn, but neither Pompey nor Cicero left Italy.

dubitatio The reference is doubtful; perhaps to fears of more trouble with Clodius.

vide...sumpserim 'behold my presumption'.

promisi...polliceri There is no difference in meaning between the two verbs.

2 Balbo L. Cornelius Balbus came from Gades (Cadiz). After Pompey made him a Roman citizen he became Caesar's adjutant and political agent, later his adviser in financial matters. In 40 he became the first provincial to hold the consulship.

accuratius 'rather particularly'.

M. Curti filium i.e. M. Curtius, whom Cicero had recommended to Caesar for a Military Tribunate to be taken up the following year (*Q.fr.* 2.14.3). Caesar *ex hypothesi* knew his father (another Curtius, C. Curtius (Rabirius) Postumus, was a good friend of his) and referred to him in his reply as 'M. Curtius' son'. A later letter of recommendation to Caesar (*Fam.* 13.15) begins *Precilium tibi commendo unice, tui necessari, mei familiarissimi, viri optimi filium.*

vel...vel The first *vel*, mistakenly suspected or deleted by editors, means 'even', the second 'or'.

Leptae Q. Paconius Lepta of Cales, later Cicero's adjutant in Cilicia. We do not know why Caesar mentioned him here.

delega A term of business for transferring a claim or an obligation, or the person representing the same, to a third party.

si vis 'if you please'.

sustulimus manus A gesture of amazement; cf. *Acad.* 2.63 *admirans* (*quod quidem perpetuo Lucullo loquente fecerat, ut etiam manus saepe tolleret*).

mitto...duxerim 'I send you Trebatius accordingly. I thought it right to send him on my own initiative in the first instance, but at your invitation in the second.' *invitatus = invitatio* is unique in classical Latin.

3 vetere verbo 'old-fashioned word' or 'old saying' (the latter sense is common in Plautus). There is no knowing what it was.

Milone Apparently Cicero had asked a favour on Milo's behalf. But the name looks somewhat suspicious, since Caesar and Milo were normally political opponents.

more Romano i.e. in simple, straightforward language, without affectation or artifice.

6   C S T

probiorem...virum The choice between *vir* and *homo* with certain adjectives was largely a matter of convention. One normally said *vir bonus* rather than *bonus homo*.

familiam ducit 'is the best of the bunch'. The phrase probably derives from a band of gladiators; cf. *Phil.* 5.30 *frater eius, utpote qui peregre depugnarit, familiam ducit.* It is not likely to mean 'heads a school of law'.

singulari memoria A specially important gift in a jurist, as Cicero implies in *De orat.* 1.128.

tribunatum sc. *militarem.* There were six such posts to a legion, some filled by popular election, others by the commanding general.

praefecturam The function of *praefectus* could cover a variety of military and civil duties or could be merely honorary.

de manu, ut aiunt, in manum This phrase is not in fact found elsewhere, though Plautus has *e manibus dedit mi ipse in manus* (*Trin.* 902). It may come from grasping by the hand in token of ownership (*mancipium*).

tuam...praestantem Freely rendered 'the hand of a great conqueror and a great gentleman'. This correlation between the right hand in fighting and in pledging is found elsewhere, as in Virg. *Aen.* 7.234 *dextramque potentem,* | *sive fide seu quis bello est expertus et armis.*

putidiusculi 'just a trifle fulsome'. *putidus* can mean 'in bad taste', and fulsome flattery is one variety of that. So Cicero writes of his own speeches in praise of Pompey as *meis putidissimis orationibus* (*Att.* 2.9.1).

quamquam...licebit 'though that is scarcely allowable with you. But you *will* allow it, I see you will.' Caesar's good nature, evident in his letter, will tolerate even flattery of himself!

LETTER 21 (*Fam.* 7.6)

The first of a series of letters to Trebatius in Gaul. Nearly all of them are short and jocular. The jokes, as usual with Cicero, often turn on more or less elaborate word-play (*amphibolia, double entendre*) which is the despair of translators. Appropriately they deal largely in legal terminology and much fun is poked at Trebatius' alleged professional incompetence, cowardice, and the incongruous figure of a jurist in Caesar's camp.

Mention of a number of letters sent by Cicero to Caesar and Balbus indicates that some little time had passed since Trebatius left Rome.

1 Balbum Now again with Caesar.

accessio As a financial term, an 'extra' or 'bonus', as *decessio* = 'deduction'.

ineptias Cicero seems already to have heard from his friend, who at first found it hard to adjust to life in Gaul.

urbis et urbanitatis The word *urbanus* had come into fashion at this period to denote smartness and sophistication, such as distinguished the man of the metropolis from the rustic.

consilio To get rich.

Medeae The following passage turns upon quotations from Ennius' Latin version of Euripides' *Medea*. Besides the cited lines Cicero interweaves Ennius' words with his own.

quae...optimates A trochaic tetrameter acatalectic (i.e. the last foot has two syllables, not one). Probably an elaboration of Medea's speech in Euripides (214ff.) which begins 'Women of Corinth'. *habebant* will be Cicero's substitute for *habetis* in Ennius.

manibus gypsatissimis Generally taken as referring to the actor's make-up. But H. D. Jocelyn (*The tragedies of Ennius*, pp. 358ff.) seems right in following an old interpretation according to which the words 'must reflect Medea's description of herself or her report of someone else's description', contrasting the 'made-up' foreigner with the Corinthian dames. *gypsum* (γύψος), usually 'plaster', appears as a whitening cosmetic in a Greek epigram of uncertain date (*Anth. Pal.* 5.19). The Ethiopians painted their bodies with it (Herod. 7.69).

vitio...verterent 'turn to her reproach'. The expression is common in drama but not found elsewhere in Cicero (who uses *vitio dare*). *ne...patria* seems to paraphrase an Ennian line like *ne mihi vitio vos vertatis exul a patria quod absum* (O. Skutsch).

multi...improbati 'Helping self and helping country many a rover wide doth roam. | Naught accounted in his staying sitteth many a stay-at-home.' On the metrical problem see my edition. The lines seem to be formally related to Eur. *Med.* 215ff., but the sense has been changed.

2 cavere 'take precautions', hence in lawyers' language 'draft a legal document', since such documents are frequently designed to guard against various eventualities. Cicero likes to play on the two senses. *decipiaris* below also seems to have a legal flavour; cf. *Mur.* 22 *tu caves ne tui consultores...capiantur.*

Britannia Caesar's second British expedition was launched in July (official calendar) 54. Trebatius did not take part.

essedariis On the British war-chariot (*esseda*) see Caesar's account in *Bell. Gall.* 4.33.

agere 'act'.

qui...sapit 'He that cannot help his own case, be he wise, his wisdom's vain.' Cicero constantly in these letters plays on the special application of *sapere, sapientia* to legal learning. He quotes the line again in *Off.* 3.62. It has no equivalent in Euripides' text and looks like a rendering of a Greek line of uncertain origin quoted in *Fam.* 13.15.2.

LETTER 22 (*Att.* 4.15)

Atticus had left for Epirus on 10 May preceding.

1 Eutychide A recently manumitted slave of Atticus, otherwise unknown. On the naming see Appendix III. Evidently the normal practice in this respect could be modified by the manumissor if he chose. Atticus had been adopted under the will of his uncle Q. Caecilius four years previously, so that his name became officially Q. Caecilius Pomponianus Atticus (cf. *Att.* 3.20). But his former nomen and praenomen remained in ordinary use.

Dionysius A learned freedman of Atticus who became tutor to the two Cicero boys.

tua...benevolentia The manumission was evidently done as a favour to Cicero, who was grateful to Eutychides for his behaviour in his own 'distress' (i.e. exile).

συμπάθειαν Translatable by its English derivative, 'sympathy'. Literally 'fellow-feeling'.

2 praetor Clodius The governor of a province is often called *praetor* irrespective of his actual title. C. Claudius Pulcher, brother of Cicero's persecutor, had been Praetor in 56 and was at this time Proconsul in Asia. After his return to Rome he was convicted on a charge of extortion (*de repetundis*) and went into exile. On the form 'Clodius' see Letter 5.6.

Pituanius Presumably a member of Claudius' staff, who helped him in his financial malpractices. *Graecis litteris*, which would normally mean 'Greek literature', is here humorously applied to the documents with which Pituanius would have to deal. The reference to his learning, as to the Proconsul's charm, is of course ironical.

homo 'a decent fellow', with the usual human feelings; cf. *homines visi sumus* in Letter 63.2, where the implication is different.

3 dedi Perhaps the letter never reached Atticus. At any rate it has not survived.

ἡμερολεγδόν 'in the form of a diary'.

ut conicio Superfluous with *videris*; such redundancies, among other forms of inattentive writing, are found elsewhere in Cicero's familiar letters and even in his published works.

4 IIII For the date see Asconius' commentary on the *Pro Scauro* (18. 17 Clark).

Sufenas et Cato M. Nonius Sufenas and C. Porcius Cato (not to be confused with Cato Uticensis) had been Tribunes in 56 in the 'triumviral' interest. Their prosecutions will have been in connexion with the disturbances which prevented the holding of elections that year. Procilius may have been similarly involved, but in his case the charge was murder.

τρισαρεοπαγίτας Lit. 'triple Areopagites'. Cf. *Att.* 1.14.5 *senatus* Ἄρειος πάγος: *nihil constantius, nihil severius, nihil fortius.* The Areopagus, the ancient Athenian council of state, took its name, 'Ares' Hill', from its place of assembly.

patrem...abunde 'but when it comes to slaughtering a paterfamilias in his own house, they disapprove – not, however, overwhelmingly even then'.

XXVIII The normal number for a jury in murder cases seems to have been 51, so possibly the true figure here is *XXVIIII*. But one juror may have put in a blank vote.

Publius Clodius.

lacrimans The manuscript reading *criminans* would imply that Clodius was prosecuting Procilius. But Cicero seems to be explaining the size of the not-guilty vote. And since it is a prosecutor's business to incriminate, the word would be quite pointless. Madvig proposed *me criminans*, but Cicero does not appear to have been involved. In

56, after the Luca conference, he stayed out of trouble. Besides, if Clodius had attacked him, the complimentary *diserto* would be strange, and Cicero would hardly go on to explain that he kept silent because Tullia (*pusilla*) was afraid that Clodius might take offence. *lacrimans* puts all to rights. 'The part played by tears in the ancient oratory is somewhat at variance with our modern Northern tastes' (Wilkins on *De orat.* 2.190, with examples).

Hortalus Hortensius. The use of his cognomen is exceptional in Cicero.

verbum nullum sc. *fecimus*; cf. *Att.* 1.18.6 *Crassus verbum nullum contra gratiam.*

laborat 'is out of sorts'.

offenderet The subject is 'it', i.e. *si verba fecissem*. But *offenderem* may be right.

5 Reatini The dispute between the neighbouring towns of Reate and Interamna (Terni) in central Italy concerned a cutting through the mountains by which Lake Velinus was connected with the river Nar to the north. It was the work of M'. Curius Dentatus, Censor in 272 and builder of the second Roman aqueduct. The exceptionally fertile plain of Rosia or Rosea (Le Roscie), which belonged to Reate, was thereby relieved of flooding caused by the lake, while remaining moderately moist (*et umida tamen modice*). Interamna complained that its territory was being flooded instead, probably in consequence of some recent damage. Cicero seems to have won his case, for the cutting remained in operation seventy years later (cf. Tac. *Ann.* 1.79).

Τέμπη 'their Vale'. Tempe (indeclinable neuter plural), the famous valley in Thessaly, is used by the Augustan poets for 'valley(s)' in general.

consules i.e. *coss.*, becoming *cos.*, whence *consulem* in the manuscripts. The plural is demanded by *Scaur.* 27 (delivered about a month after this letter; see sec. 9): *ego nuper, cum Reatini, qui essent in fide mea, me suam publicam causam de Velini fluminibus et cuniculis apud hos consules agere voluissent, non existimavi me neque dignitati praefecturae gravissimae neque fidei meae satis esse facturum, nisi me causam illam non solum homines sed etiam locus ipse lacusque docuisset.* The case was clearly to be heard in Rome, and Cicero's visit to Axius' villa near Reate was to collect information. The Consuls of this year were Ap. Claudius Pulcher and L. Domitius Ahenobarbus. The visit to the same villa by the former, mentioned by Varro in *R. r.* 3.2.3 does not, as formerly supposed, relate to this occasion; see note in my edition.

qua with *sua* Τέμπη. Cicero could hardly say that he was called in *because* (*quod*) the lake was flowing into the Nar, which presumably had been going on ever since Curius made the cutting.

Narem Rivers are regularly masculine, and there is no support for a neuter form *Nar*.

modice cf. Colum. *R. r.* 3.63 *loco modice umido, non uliginoso*.

vixi cum 'I stayed with'.

Axio Q. Axius, a wealthy senator. Cicero's correspondence with him, in one 'book', was extant in antiquity. Varro describes the villa as *perpolita*.

quin etiam *qui* may be right but *quin* makes sense, implying that for Cicero such an excursion was something quite out of the common.

Septem Aquas A group of lakes lying to the north of the Plain of Rosia. It was probably on this occasion that Cicero noticed a phenomenon which he recorded in his lost work *De admirandis*, that the hooves of pack animals hardened in the marshes of Reate (Plin. *Nat. hist.* 31.12).

6   Fontei Cicero defended an ex-governor of Narbonese Gaul with this name about 69 in a partially extant speech. The reference here is probably to a different person, but why Cicero returned on his account is beyond our knowledge.

spectatum Supine; cf. *Sest.* 126 *via...qua spectatum ille veniebat*.

plausu Such demonstrations of popularity or the contrary were a regular feature of Roman theatrical or other shows. Cicero took them seriously and often refers to them.

Antiphonti An otherwise unknown actor. Arbuscula is mentioned in Horace's *Satires* (1.10.77). But there is no likelihood that Horace took this and other references from Cicero. He was ten years old at this time and will have moved from Venusia to Rome within the next few years.

operam sc. *dedi*.

manu missus Successful performers were sometimes given their freedom by popular demand. In this case success was anticipated.

palmam tulit 'took the prize', in the form of a wreath, which might be of gold.

nihil tam... Perhaps best left as an aposiopesis. Otherwise something has fallen out of the text (*ieiunum* and *sine arte* have been suggested).

verum...habeto From a letter of Horace Walpole: 'His acting I have seen, and may say to you, who will not tell it again here, I see nothing wonderful in it; but it is heresy to say so.'

Andromacha The role rather than the play ('as Andromache'); cf. Ov. *Rem. am.* 383 *quis ferat Andromaches peragentem Thaïda partes?| peccet, in Andromache Thaïda quisquis agat.* Besides the extant play by Euripides, others with the same title are known to have been composed by Sophocles and another Antiphon. Cicero indulges in his favourite kind of joke with a play on two senses of *maior*, '(physically) larger' and '(artistically) better': for the latter cf. Quint. *Inst.* 10.1.74 *in historia praedictis maior.* In both senses Antipho was the smallest thing on the stage, except for the young child Astyanax. *parem habuit neminem* would normally imply 'nobody else was so good (big)'; here facetiously 'nobody else was so small (bad)'. For once this piece of Ciceronian wit can be reproduced in English without strain: 'As Andromache at any rate he stood head and shoulders above Astyanax. In the other roles he didn't have his equal.'

ludi The *ludi Apollinares* were celebrated annually from 6 to 13 July.

venatio The beast-fight which ordinarily came after the games; see Letter 18.3.

7 campum The Campus Martius, where voting took place.

ardet So in a contemporary letter to Quintus (2.15.4) *ambitus redit immanis...res ardet invidia.* Pliny (*Nat. hist.* praef. 9) with reference to this passage writes *flagrantibus comitiis*; cf. Tac. *Ann.* 14.28.1 *comitia ...quod acriore ambitu exarserant.*

σῆμα sqq. 'a token I shall tell'. From *Il.* 23.326 = *Od.* 11.126.

ex triente...bessibus 'went up from ⅓ to ⅔%'. *bes* (gen. *bessis*) is held to derive from *duo as(sis)*, i.e. *duae assis partes*. Interest was commonly reckoned by the month.

non moleste fero As a wealthy man Atticus lent money at interest to individuals, a normal form of investment.

Memmium See Letter 24. Four candidates were standing for the consulship of 53: C. Memmius, Cn. Domitius Calvinus, M. Aemilius Scaurus, and M. Valerius Messalla Rufus. Disorders made it impossible to hold elections until July of the following year, when Calvinus and Messalla were successful. But all four were ultimately found guilty of *ambitus* and went into exile.

consules Those of the current year. The compact is revealed in *Att.* 4.17.2. It bound the Consuls to support the two candidates, who in return promised when in office to promote certain legislation in their interests. Memmius soon afterwards 'blew the gaff', causing much scandal.

Scauro Son of the great *princeps senatus* of the same name and one of Pompey's principal lieutenants in his eastern campaigns.

fronte an mente Similarly elsewhere, e.g. *Planc.* 16 *tabella, quae frontes aperit hominum, mentes tegit.* Pompey was often suspected of dissimulation, though according to Caelius Rufus he did not have the intelligence to conceal what he was really after (*Fam.* 8.1.3).

ἐξοχή 'prominence'. None of the four stood out.

pecunia...exaequat 'money levels standing all round'.

fore ut ducantur 'are likely to drag on' (= *ductum iri*).

HS quingena sc. *milia*, '500,000 each'.

ut...tribueretur The *ut* clause defines the terms on which the deposits were made.

8 comitia i.e. *tribunicia*.

   ut putantur i.e. *ut fore putantur*.

9 Messius C. Messius had been a supporter of Pompey, though he joined Caesar in the Civil War. Cicero was under a personal obligation to him for sponsoring a bill for his recall in 57.

legarat Messius had been nominated by the Consul, as presiding magistrate in the Senate, to the post of Legate to Caesar, doubtless at Caesar's request. At this period provincial governors in practice appointed their Legates, who were always or nearly always senators, but formally the power of appointment lay with the Senate.

tribus The lex Licinia *de sodaliciis*, passed by Crassus as Consul in 55, was another effort to curb electoral malpractices, directed against the misuse of clubs or societies. Under this law the prosecution chose four tribes from which the jury had to be selected, but the accused had the right to reject one of them. Messius was probably elected Curule Aedile for 55 early in that year. According to Dio (39.32.2) those elections led to bloodshed. He seems to have been acquitted in this and two other trials.

agitur tamen satis 'but we have our hands full'. *sat(is) agere* was no doubt a colloquial expression at this period. Except here it is found only in pre-Ciceronian and post-Augustan authors.

Drusum M. Livius Drusus Claudianus, adopted son of the famous Tribune and father of the future Livia Augusta. Scaurus was acquitted on a charge *de repetundis* concerning his governship of Sardinia, but subsequently convicted *de ambitu*. Cicero's speech defending him at the former trial is partially extant.

indices 'titles', i.e. labels to be attached to the speeches when published. *gloriosi* refers to the celebrity of the fathers of the two defendants.

in quibus...fuerit This would seem to imply that Consuls-Designate were immune from prosecution (except on charges relating to the elections themselves).

10 Britannia Caesar's second British expedition was now in progress.

quid agat 'how he is getting on'.

Dionysium...iubeas 'remember me to Dionysius'. *salve* was, of course, the regular Roman greeting.

venias Cicero assumes that Dionysius will accompany his *patronus* back to Italy.

LETTER 23 *(Att. 5.1)*

To fill a gap created by Pompey's law, passed in 52, requiring a five-year interval between office in Rome and a provincial governor-ship, former magistrates who had not proceeded to provinces were called upon to do so. Cicero was appointed for one year as Proconsul to Cilicia, which as a Roman province comprised the southern coast of Asia Minor and much of the interior as well as the island of Cyprus. He set out at the end of April 51. This letter was probably written at his villa near Formiae, close to Minturnae (cf. sec. 5). Sec. 2, a brief series of business items, is here omitted.

1 discessu At Tusculum (sec. 3).

meo The genitive would be usual, but cf. *Quinct.* 37 *quis huic rei testis est?*

3 transversum...versiculum A line of writing along the margin of the last page of the letter (*extremae epistulae*). 'Your last letter' would be *proximae*.

Arpinas Adjectival form from *Arpinum*, corresponding to *Tusculanum* from *Tusculum*. Such neuter adjectives used substantivally may mean either a district (= *Tusculanus ager*) or a property within the district (sc. *praedium*). Cicero's family estate at Arpinum lay in a broad river valley a few miles from the town.

frater Quintus accompanied his brother to Cilicia as Legate and their sons went with them. Under the republic wives did not go with their husbands on provincial assignments.

ille sic dies sc. *abiit*; cf. *Ad Brut.* 5.3 *itaque ille dies silentio.*

Arcano A villa belonging to Quintus, called from Arx (see Letter 17.3).

maneret 'stayed the night'. So regularly.

dies i.e. the holiday, *dies festus*, probably the feast of the Lares on 1 May. Quintus wished to spend it with his household.

Aquini sc. *mansi*.

mulieres...pueros Household slaves and farm-workers (*pueros* = *servos*), who were to take their lunch with the family, as at the Saturnalia.

Statius A much favoured slave, now freedman, of Quintus. M. Cicero himself disapproved of his influence with his master.

videret 'see to'.

4 discubuimus The old rule that women sat at table while men reclined seems to have no longer been in force at this period.

quid quaeris? See Letter 12.1.

humanitatem...defuisse 'her manners that day in my opinion left something to be desired'. One aspect of *humanitas* was polite and civilized behaviour.

5 Pomptinum C. Pomptinus, an experienced general, was another of Cicero's Legates.

A. Torquatum A. Manlius Torquatus was Praetor in 70. Cicero was friendly both with him and his younger (distant) relative Lucius.

aliquid i.e. something amicable.

LETTER 24 (*Fam.* 13.1)

Cicero stopped at Athens from 24 June to 6 July. C. Memmius, a politician with literary interests, was living there in exile, but had left for Mytilene the day before Cicero arrived. He is mentioned unfavourably by Catullus and is generally assumed to be the Memmius to whom Lucretius dedicated the *De rerum natura*. If so, Lucretius was sadly deceived in him. Cicero's tactful intervention in the matter of Epicurus' house was mainly to oblige Atticus, to whom he wrote enclosing a copy (*Att.* 5.11.6).

1 iniuria Memmius had been condemned *de ambitu* in 52 in connexion with the consular elections for 53, in which he had been a candidate. Cicero naturally affects to regard this as a miscarriage of justice.

plus fuisset 'would have been greater (than it is)'. But the writing here is a little confused. Cicero is thinking not only of the pleasure derived from Memmius' *sapientia* (in that case he would have written *quod potest*) but of the pleasure which the meeting itself might have given him.

commode 'conveniently' to Memmius as well as to himself.

2 id...persuaseris 'I hope you will grant me a favour which, as you will see, matters a good deal to me and not at all to you, but only if you have satisfied yourself beforehand that you will do it gladly.'

Patrone Head of the Epicurean school in Athens.

mihi omnia sunt 'I have all manner of ties'. Not to be confused with *mihi omnia est* 'he is all in all to me'.

coluit The perfect states the 'cultivation' as a single historic fact.

commodis et praemiis Possibly this refers to Patro's appointment as head of his school or to dues in Rome which Cicero helped him to recover.

Phaedro Patro's predecessor.

Philonem Of Larissa, head of the Academy. Cicero became his disciple when he came to Rome in 88 (*Brut.* 306).

3 placarem To Atticus (5.11.6) Cicero mentions that Memmius was annoyed (*iratus*) with Patro.

parietinarum Ruins of Epicurus' house in the Athenian deme Melite. In his will Epicurus, who died in 268, left the house to his heirs subject to the use of it by his school during the lifetime of his successor Hermarchus (Diog. Laert. 10.17). But the garden was to be at the disposal of the school in perpetuity. Evidently the site of the ruins was now in Memmius' possession. The reverence of the Epicureans for their founder, almost amounting to a religious cult, comes out conspicuously in Lucretius' poem.

commendatione mea 'by a vicarious request of mine'.

4 gentem cf. *Nat. deor.* 1.89 *gens vestra* (i.e. *Epicurei*) and *Fin.* 4.51 *magister eius et tota illa gens.*

honoris mei causa 'as a favour to me'.

nisi tamen 'except that, after all,...'; cf. Letter 25.3.

laborare sine causa 'make a fuss about nothing'.

honorem 'his office'.

obtestationem Probably a death-bed injunction.

5 non quo sit ex istis Atticus' sympathy with Epicureanism was not taken over-seriously. Cicero often jokes with him on the subject in a way which would have been grossly offensive to a true believer like Lucretius.

politissimus The Epicureans professed to despise literary culture, something for which Cicero could never forgive them.

ambitiosus 'self-seeking', as of one who obliges another person in order to curry favour with him.

illiberalem 'unhandsome'.

decretum This decree of the Areopagus (see on Letter 22.4) presumably had empowered Memmius to pull down the ruins and build on the site. The Greek word generally means 'written record, memorandum'; see Liddell–Scott–Jones.

6 prius...ut facias 'Before you decide to comply with my request I want you to be satisfied that you will do so gladly for my sake.' *tibi persuadeas* has to be understood with *ut facias*. But perhaps we should read *quam facias*, 'I want you to be satisfied that you will do this gladly for my sake before you do it.'

LETTER 25 (*Att.* 5.14)

Cicero arrived at Ephesus on 22 July and travelled on by land through the province of Asia. This letter was despatched from Tralles, but may have been written during a halt on the road.

1 dederam...dedi The tenses are 'epistolary' (see on Letter 1.3) and *pridie* = 'yesterday'. *dedi* could amount to 'I shall despatch from Tralles (after I get there)'.

παράπηγμα ἐνιαύσιον 'annual peg'; cf. *Att.* 5.15.1 *ex hoc die clavum anni movebis*. Cicero is thinking of a calendar with movable pegs to mark the dates. A specimen has been discovered at Pozzuoli.

Parthicum After the destruction of the Roman army at Carrhae in 53 the Parthians were a continual threat to Rome's eastern provinces. They invaded Syria in 52 and again in 51.

pactiones New contracts were made every five years between the Roman tax-farmers (*publicani*) and the provincial communities paying taxes to Rome.

Appio Ap. Claudius Pulcher, the outgoing governor. On the use of his praenomen see on Letter 11.3.

2 nemini ne minimo quidem Normally in Latin two negatives cancel one another, but when a negative is followed by *ne...quidem* or *non modo* emphasizing a particular word or phrase this does not happen.

magno timore Cicero often omits *in* in expressions of this sort, e.g. *Att.* 6.1.23 *nec nulla nec magna spe sumus*.

Tullium L. Tullius, another Legate. He does not seem to have been related to Cicero.

recta sc. *via*, as often.

3 illud ἐνδόμυχον 'that domesticity'. The Greek word means 'in the inner recess'. It refers to selection of a third husband for Tullia.

subtiliores 'more detailed'; cf. *Att.* 1.13.4 *sed haec ad te scribam alias subtilius*.

LETTER 26 (*Fam.* 15.1)

Cicero duly entered his province on 31 July. He continued eastward, pausing to hold assizes at the principal towns along his route, until he joined his army at Iconium in Lycaonia on 24 August. On 3

September he set out for Cilicia proper and wrote this despatch to the home authorities shortly before pitching camp at Cybistra in the south-western corner of Cappadocia.

1 s....v. *si vos valetis benest. ego exercitusque valemus.* See on Letters 4.1 and 5.1.

M. Bibulo Newly appointed governor of Syria.

2 regis Antiochus I of Commagene, the little kingdom lying between Syria and Cappadocia, had been reigning since 69 or earlier.

Tarcondimoto A chieftain, later king, in the Amanus mountains.

Tybae This place has now been identified with Dabiq, a town north of Aleppo.

Iamblicho Son of Sampsiceramus (Letter 7.1), phylarch (emir) of Emesa.

3 socios 'the provincials'.

Cilicum The 'Free Cilicians' (Eleutherocilices) inhabiting the highlands of the Taurus and Amanus were chronically hostile to the Roman government. Cicero mounted a successful campaign against them later in the year.

4 paene cerno Cicero was the man on the spot, or at any rate relatively close to it.

opinionem 'expectation', i.e. prospect; cf. Letter 15.1.

5 dilectu Levy of Roman citizens.

nam 'for as to the allied auxiliaries...'. This 'occupatory' use of *nam*, prefacing an explanation of why an item was not mentioned sooner or is not worth mentioning at all, is very common.

sociorum Unlike *socios* above, this refers to 'free communities' and allied rulers, not including ordinary provincials.

acerbitatem An obvious reflection on the misgovernment of Cicero's predecessor, Ap. Claudius Pulcher, with whom his relations were temporarily strained.

6 Deiotari Originally tetrarch of one of the three Galatian tribes, he had by now become king of almost the entire region. In 45 Cicero spoke on his behalf before Caesar, whom he was accused of having plotted to assassinate.

inanis The new king of Cappadocia, Ariobarzanes III, was impoverished and insecure. Two or three days later Cicero wrote another despatch (*Fam.* 15.2) describing how a plot against the king's life was revealed in his presence.

tyrannique 'despots' – autocratic rulers who had not been recognized as kings.

LETTER 27 (*Fam.* 2.12)

In late June 50 Cicero's term as governor had little more than a month to run. He was in camp on the river Pyramus, in the south-east corner of Asia Minor. M. Caelius Rufus, Curule Aedile this year, shone as politican, orator, man of fashion, and correspondent. Book VIII of *Ad familiares* consists entirely of letters from him to Cicero, mostly written during the proconsulate.

IMP. See on Letter 20. Cicero had been saluted *imperator* after successful fighting in the Cilician highlands.

1   Quinquatrus The festival of Minerva from 19 to 23 March. Another friend and correspondent of Cicero, C. Scribonius Curio, now Tribune, was agitating on Caesar's behalf.

ridere Caelius was accustomed to laugh his way through the crazy world; cf. *Fam.* 8.7.1 *hunc risum meum,* 8.14.4 *quam primum haec risum veni* and, on Cicero's side, 2.13.3 *quam ego risum nostrum desidero!*

nihil...litterarum See on Letter 3.1.

hospes plane 'as a complete stranger'.

2   Diogenes A Greek who had come out along with a freedman of Caelius called Philo the previous autumn with a letter and messages for Cicero. Their mission to Pessinus in Galatia seems to have been on some business of Caelius. Adiatorix was the son of one of the Galatian tetrarchs subordinate to Deiotarus.

ista luce Cf. *Leg. agr.* 2.71 *nisi forte mavultis relictis his rebus atque hac luce rei publicae in Sipontina siccitate...collocari.*

peregrinatio 'sojourn abroad'.

iudicavi In his speech *Pro Plancio* (64ff.) Cicero tells how on his way back to Rome after his quaestorship in Sicily (where his record was, as he considered, rather distinguished) an acquaintance asked him for the latest city news. This deflation taught him that for a man of his stamp reputation was not be be gained in the provinces. Military glory was, of course, another matter.

sententia 'intention' (to decline provincial office).

3 triumpharem The idea is: 'triumph enough for me to be with my own folk'.

contemnenda...conservata The gerundive expresses what might have been, the participle what had actually taken place. The sentiment is not to be taken too seriously; Cicero had already declined provinces in 63.

LETTER 28 (*Fam.* 9.25)

L. Papirius Paetus was a wealthy resident of Naples, a contemporary and old friend of Cicero. Like Atticus, he had Epicurean leanings and took an active interest in his own finances. The twelve extant letters addressed to him are familiar and mostly jocular.

1 summum...ducem Cicero was fully alive to the humorous aspect of his metamorphosis into a victorious general.

Pyrrhi...Cineae King Pyrrhus of Epirus, who fought against Rome in 281–275, was the author of a treatise on tactics. His minister Cineas wrote an abridgement of a work on strategy by one Aeneas.

hoc amplius 'and this in addition'.

navicularum For purposes of escape, of course.

negotium 'to have someone to deal with', especially as an opponent, is expressed by *negotium* or *res* with *esse* (*habere*) *cum aliquo*.

Παιδείαν Κύρου 'The education of Cyrus', Xenophon's interminable account of the Ideal Ruler, seems to have been a favourite with the Romans. Scipio Aemilianus is said to have always had a copy by him, and Cicero paraphrases a passage from it in his *De senectute* (79–81). It is much concerned with the Ruler in war.

2 ad imperandum 'for orders'. Sallust and Fronto, both archaizers, use this expression. The gerund gives the idea of the verb without indication of subject; cf. Virg. *Georg.* 3.206 *namque ante domandum | ingentes tollent animos* (sc. *equi*).

M. Fabio M. Fabius Gallus, art connoisseur and another of Cicero's correspondents (cf. Letter 51). Editors have called him 'Fadius' contrary to the manuscript tradition and for no good reason.

controversiis Perhaps with reference to the recently composed *De re publica*. But Cicero may also be thinking of oral arguments. Fabius was an Epicurean himself.

combibonibus = συμπόταις ('fellow-drinkers'). Lucilius is the only other author to use this word.

3 iudiciis turpibus Cases involving disgrace (*infamia*), including cases of theft (*furtum*). Q. Fabius' action in putting up for sale a property owned jointly with his brother came within that category.

Matonem et Pollionem Unknowns, unless Pollio is the famous C. Asinius Pollio, soldier and author.

quid multa? sc. *dicam*, 'in short', 'in a word'.

mehercule This exclamation, standing for *ita me, Hercule, iuva*, lends only mild emphasis: 'I really cannot fully express on paper...'.

tam...quam We should expect *non mehercule perscribere possum quam mihi gratum facturus sis* (or *fueris*). Perhaps *tam* should be *tantum*; cf. Ter. *Hec.* 416 *non...dici potest | tantum quam re ipsa navigare incommodumst* et sim.

LETTER 29 (*Fam.* 15.6)

Cicero's relations with M. Porcius Cato, austere moralist and leading conservative, were nominally cordial, but there seems to have been little love lost on either side. When Cicero wrote to ask the Senate to decree a public thanksgiving (*supplicatio*) for his victories in Cilicia (such requests were almost invariably granted), Cato refused to vote for it, though congratulating Cicero on the excellence of his administration. He explained his action in a stiff and insincere letter (*Fam.* 15.5), to which this is a reply. In fact, Cicero keenly resented Cato's behaviour, as a later letter to Atticus makes plain (*Att.* 7.2.7).

1 laetus sum Cicero uses the quotation twice elsewhere (cf. Letter 15.7), and of course knew that it came from Naevius' *Hector proficiscens*. *opinor* is simply to avoid the appearance of giving instruction; cf. *Att.* 1.20.3 *ut ait Rhinton, ut opinor*.

ego vero *vero* is often used in answers. Here Cicero is answering the whole purport of Cato's letter ('you must not resent my conduct'), and especially its last paragraph.

te...dares 'that you were glad to accord to friendship what you would have had no hesitation in according to truth'. *liquido* means 'unreservedly', as with *confirmare* and *negare*. Cicero tactfully conveys that Cato could not in honesty have said *less* than he did.

currum...lauream Cicero hoped for a Triumph when he returned to Rome, and would have got one but for the outbreak of the Civil War.

illud...iudicium The judgement of the philosopher, as opposed to the common herd. *illud* administers a sort of verbal nudge, to show that the other person knows what is implied.

2   superioribus litteris *Fam.* 15.4, an account of Cicero's military and other activities in the province, with an elaborate appeal for support in the matter of the *supplicatio.*

honos A Triumph.

quod si...gaudeas 'If it so turns out, all I ask of you is that (to use your own kind expressions), having accorded to me what in your judgement is most complimentary to myself, you should be glad if what *I* prefer comes to pass.' This relates to sec. 3 of Cato's letter: *atque haec ego idcirco...pluribus scripsi ut...existimes me laborare ut tibi persuadeam me et voluisse de tua maiestate quod amplissimum sim arbitratus et quod tu maluisti factum esse gaudere.*

sic Looks forward, not back to *gaudeas.* But the construction, which would normally have continued *ut manifestum esset tibi illum honorem* sqq., is modified by *resque ipsa declarat.*

scribendo adfuisti Decrees of the Senate were witnessed by selected senators, whose names were recorded, before being deposited with the City Quaestors in the temple of Saturn. For specimens see *Fam.* 8.4.

LETTER 30 (*Att.* 6.6)

Contrary to his original intention Cicero made his return journey by sea, taking ship from Tarsus to Side in Pamphylia, where he landed on 3 August. There he received letters informing him of Tullia's engagement to another young patrician, P. Cornelius Dolabella, whose past and reputation left much to be desired. Dolabella had just brought a charge of lèse-majesté (*maiestas*) against Cicero's predecessor in Cilicia, Ap. Claudius Pulcher, with whom he was now on excellent terms.

1 socer i.e. 'father-in-law-to-be'. So a Consul-Designate can be referred to as 'Consul'.

crede mihi Cicero usually writes *mihi crede*. Exceptions are found only in letters and all but one are in letters to Atticus.

Ti. Nerone Ti. Claudius Nero, also a young patrician, future father of the emperor Tiberius, had visited Cicero in Cilicia.

comitate Dolabella's moral failings were offset by his personal charm. He later became a favourite with Julius Caesar.

ἐξακανθίζειν 'cover with thorns' (cf. ἐξανθίζειν 'deck with flowers'), i.e. 'paint in dark colours'.

2 πυροὺς εἰς δῆμον lit. 'wheat for the people'. *largiris* vel sim. has to be understood. Atticus had evidently made a gift of grain to the city of Athens, where he had lived for twenty years.

libri *De re publica*. The discussion of public benefactions must have come in one of its lost portions. The subject is treated in *Off.* 2.55ff.

προπύλῳ 'porch'; Cicero wanted to build one in the Academy at Athens at his own expense, but Atticus had advised him to 'think about it'.

iam...non cogitet 'no longer thinking about it' (but doing it); cf. Cato, *R. r.* 3.1 *aedificare diu cogitare oportet; conserere cogitare non oportet, sed facere oportet*.

de Eleusine Ap. Pulcher's project to build a porch at Eleusis was completed after his death by his adopted son, as a surviving inscription records.

de Hortensio Cicero had received a letter from Caelius (*Fam.* 8.13) informing him that Hortensius was at death's door. The personal relations between the two orators through the years had been very variable.

3 Coelium The newly arrived Quaestor, C. Coelius Caldus. The question, whom to leave as his deputy in the province pending the arrival of a successor, had been exercising Cicero's mind for some time.

puerum Properly a Roman ceased to be *puer* when he put on the white toga at sixteen or seventeen years of age and became *adulescens*. Coelius will have been over thirty.

ἐπέχειν 'that you are suspending judgement'; a philosophical term.

traderem 'was I to hand over'. Cf. sec. 4 *ego sorte datum offenderem?*

nam 'occupatory' (see on Letter 26.5). Pomptinus had already left for home. As for Quintus, Cicero sometimes writes that he would have refused to stay on as deputy, but from what follows here it is evident that he might have been persuaded. The other two Legates will have been *quaestorii*. To appoint either of them in preference to the Quaestor would be a reflection on the latter, more especially when, as in this case, he was *nobilis* and they were not.

tamen Referring back to *illud non utile nobis*.

felicitate The Parthian attack on Cilicia which Cicero was afraid of in 50 never took place. Instead they withdrew across the Euphrates.

num est...provinciam? A challenging question demanding the answer 'no'. The transmitted reading (*non est*) is less forcible.

hic triennium Q. Cicero had governed Asia from 62 to 59, an exceptionally long term.

4　**iracundius** sc. *faceret* (*Quintus*), 'in case he might do something ...'. Quintus is taken to task for his irritability and verbal intemperance in letters which his brother wrote to him as governor (*Q.fr.* 1.1.37ff., 1.2.4ff.).

quae...hominum cf. *Att.* 13.22.4 *sed vita fert*. The implied criticism of Quintus is thus softened.

non dimittebat i.e. *dimittere nolebat* – in the event of his staying himself.

quod egerit Something like *id actum habebo* is to be understood in this expression, which Cicero uses several times elsewhere. 'I couldn't care less' in modern vernacular.

eo...radicibus 'Metaphora desumpta a quercu', as Boot says. Even potentates like Pompey and Caesar were not above attaching young nobles by choosing them as their Quaestors (under a special dispensation; the choice was usually made by lot).

Q. Cassium He seems to have broken with Pompey this year, and as Tribunes in 49 he and Mark Antony started the Civil War by fleeing to Caesar's camp.

ut...inquireret 'with the result that he would be spying...'.

senectuti Old men should seek a quiet life and avoid making enemies.

librari tui Atticus may have dictated a special letter to Cicero for Coelius to see. The statement that it was his secretary's composition may be a guess on Cicero's part.

παλιγγενεσίαν Cicero considered his return from exile as a kind of second birth; he had to start all over again, as it were. In his long letter to Cato (*Fam.* 15.4.13f.) he says that since his exile he had sought honours to which he had previously been indifferent as balm for his wounds.

LETTER 31 (*Fam.* 16.5)

Cicero travelled homewards by way of Athens and Patrae. In the latter, on 2 November, his much-loved freedman and secretary Tiro had to be left behind, too ill to continue the journey. A string of letters followed the parting.

QQ. *Quinti (pater et filius).*
S. P. D. *salutem plurimam dicit.*

1 **Thyrrei** Thyrreum, an inland town in the north of Acarnania on the road from Actium to Athens, must have been one of Cicero's stopping places on his way out to Cilicia the previous year. Evidently Xenomenes had met Tiro there and had now come to Leucas to pay his respects to Cicero on his way to Patrae.

tam...quasi Cf. Plaut. *Curc.* 51 *tam a me pudica est quasi soror mea sit.* Some editors needlessly read *quam si.*

Curio M'. Curius, a Roman businessman resident in Patrae, where he had been Cicero's host. Cf. Letter 46.

Lysoni Also resident of Patrae. Tiro was staying in his house.

medico His name, Asclapo, is known from other letters.

Marionem A slave.

meliuscule Adverbs such as *bene* and *libenter* are often used with *esse* like adjectival predicates.

unas *litterae* being grammatically plural but singular in meaning produces the odd phenomenon of *unus* in the plural. With other numerals distributive forms are used, e.g. *binae litterae.*

2 **quod poteris** sc. *facies*; cf. *Att.* 7.20.2 *sed tamen quantum poteris.*

Acastus One of Cicero's letter-bearing slaves (*tabellarii*).

recte Virtually = 'safely' – the normal expression.

nihil...humanius In such expressions the neuter is often used instead of the masculine *nemo.*

LETTER 32 (*Att.* 7.4)

Cicero landed at Brundisium on 24 November and made his way across Italy to Campania, finally arriving outside Rome on 4 January.

1 Dionysium Tutor to the two young Ciceros; see Letter 22.1.

libertinum 'of freedman status'. *libertus* simply = 'freedman'. *frugi* is often applied to freedmen and slaves, though not confined to them. Since Dionysius actually was a freedman, the addition of *ut* after *ne* would be an improvement logically. Cicero soon had reason to change his opinion of this man.

2 Pompeium Recently recovered from an almost fatal illness. The interview probably took place at Capua.

monere This advice may be connected with the fact that Pompey did not share Cicero's overriding desire for a peaceful settlement with Caesar. Cicero did attend the Senate in January.

nihil ad spem concordiae 'nothing to suggest hope of agreement'; cf. Caes. *B.c.* 2.28.3 *huc pauca ad spem largitionis addidit*.

illum Caesar.

Hirtium A. Hirtius, Consul in 43, on Caesar's staff in Gaul and author of Book VIII of *De bello Gallico*. A friend and correspondent of Cicero's.

ille Hirtius, who is also meant by *eum* below.

Scipionem Q. Caecilius Metellus Pius Scipio, Pompey's father-in-law and colleague in the consulship in 52. Originally a Scipio Nasica, he had been adopted into the Metellus family, but was usually called by his original cognomen (see Appendix III). Balbus seems to have been on good terms with him.

de tota re 'to discuss the whole situation'. The talk had presumably been intended to lead up to a meeting between Hirtius and Pompey, who was apparently in or near Rome at the time (*ad se non accessisse*).

τεκμηριῶδες 'proof positive'. In Aristotelian logic τεκμήριον is 'demonstrated proof, opposed to the fallible εἰκός or σημεῖον' (Liddell–Scott–Jones).

3 alterum consulatum Caesar had been Consul in 59 and was now expected to stand for the consulship of 48.

dederit As often, the verb agrees in number with the nearer of two subjects (*inimici...fortuna*).

ne See Letter 18.3.

ad urbem cogito sc. *venire*, a common form of ellipse. Cicero could not go inside the old city boundary (*pomerium*) without giving up his *imperium* and so becoming ineligible to celebrate a Triumph.

LETTER 33 (*Att.* 7.10)

The news of Caesar's military activity in north Italy, following upon his crossing of the Rubicon on 11 January, produced panic in Rome. Pompey left for Campania on 17 January, followed next day by the Consuls and large numbers of more or less prominent persons (not including Atticus). Cicero got off before daybreak, heading for Formiae.

laureatis A retiring governor kept his lictors as long as he kept his *imperium*. Laurels on their *fasces* betokened that his troops had conferred on him the title of Imperator (see on Letter 20).

de reliquo 'as for what is to follow'.

consili The evacuation of Rome. There is reason to suppose that Pompey had at any rate considered abandoning the capital as part of his strategic plan (see my note on *Att.* 7.8.5 (131.5 of my edition)), though the actual evacuation was made in such panic that the contents of the state treasury were left for Caesar to take over.

nescio adhuc *adhuc* quite often follows a verb at the end of a sentence or clause. The old punctuation with which *adhuc* attaches to what follows is absurd since Pompey had only left the day before.

in oppidis...stupens 'cooped up there in the country towns in a daze'. This describes Pompey's situation from then on. A great man like him would feel cramped in these petty places; cf. *Att.* 8.8.1 *in Apuliam se compegerat*. This letter was written in the haste and agitation of departure, and Cicero was not thinking very logically.

omnes i.e. *nos omnes*, all republicans. Watt substitutes *omnino* 'to be sure', which makes good sense; but it seems unnecessary to alter the text.

omnia sc. *acta sunt* vel sim.

vel...venerit 'if only just what comes into your head', i.e. 'even if you have nothing special to say'.

LETTER 34 (*Fam.* 14.18)

Cicero took his son with him from Rome, but his wife and daughter stayed behind.

1 an aliquo tuto loco Probably = somewhere well away from the war; cf. *Att.* 7.17.4 (of 2 February) *pueros* ὑπεκθέμενος *in Graeciam.*

esse tuto *esse tutas* would also have been correct, but the adverb is often preferred.

Dolabellam Tullia's new husband had joined Caesar.

eamque rem...esse The meaning seems to be that the family property in Rome would be safer with Terentia and Tullia in residence under Dolabella's protection.

omnes...habere An exaggeration. A few lines further on Cicero asks the ladies to find out what other ladies of their station are doing.

nostrorum...oppidorum Towns in Cicero's *clientela* like Capua and Atella. He does not mean 'under my authority', though he had been charged by Pompey with the supervision of a coastal area south of Rome.

in nostris sc. *praediis.*

2 utrum To stay in Rome or to leave.

isto loco cf. *Verr.* 2.5.181 *humili atque obscuro loco natus* et sim.

Philotimo See Letter 16.2.

LETTER 35 (*Fam.* 7.27)

Doubtless addressed to T. Fadius, Cicero's Quaestor in 63. He had been exiled, almost certainly in 52, after condemnation in one of Pompey's bribery courts; Cicero's letter of condolence (*Fam.* 5.18) is extant. He was now hoping to be restored by Caesar. Apparently he had asked Cicero to stand surety for a debt, and on receiving a refusal (money was very tight at this period) wrote a letter of reproach which put Cicero in a fury. The tone of his reply is harsh and offensive, as nowhere else in the whole correspondence.

The heading *GALLO* in the manuscripts is due to a confusion which perhaps goes back to Tiro himself; the preceding letters were written to M. Fabius (not Fadius; see Letter 28.2) Gallus. Commentators have gone far astray both in the dating and the interpretation of the letter.

1 miror...debebas Even if Fadius had a genuine grievance, which Cicero of course does not admit, their respective ages and ranks made his complaint unseemly.

credit 'believe' and 'give (financial) credit'. Cicero plays on this double sense in other letters, as does Martial (3.15.1): *plus credit nemo tota quam Cordus in urbe.* | *'cum sit tam pauper, quo modo?' caecus amat.*

tribunatum plebi As Tribune in 57 Fadius had worked for Cicero's recall.

intercessorem Another *double entendre*: 'veto-caster' and 'surety'. *intercedere* does not mean 'intercede' in classical Latin.

negas...dicere Fadius may have reproached Cicero for not coming out openly in favour of peace.

2 haec...cognosceres 'The above is to let you see that even in the style in which you aspire to shine you are a total failure.'

propter quem ceteri liberi sunt cf. *Fam.* 9.16.3 *olim arbitrabar esse meum libere loqui, cuius opera esset in civitate libertas.* The reference is of course to the saving of Rome from Catiline. Cicero would not have referred to his fellow-countrymen as 'free' after Caesar's return to Rome at the end of March 49 until the end of his dictatorship.

liberum non visum *liberum non putare* = 'treat with contempt'; cf. e.g. Prop. 2.8.15 *ecquandone tibi liber sum visus?*

nam This refers to *propter quem ceteri liberi sunt.*

detulisti Fadius must have given Cicero information about Catiline's plot in 63.

LETTER 36 (*Att.* 8.1)

Probably written on the night of 15–16 February (note the complaint of insomnia at the end). Pompey had written summoning Cicero to join his headquarters at Luceria in Apulia. At first Cicero temporized, but on the 17th, after hearing of a communication from Pompey to the Consuls, he actually set out. But further intelligence received at Cales caused him to turn back.

1   **redditae** 'delivered'. So often. Pompey's letter is not extant.

cetera i.e. all but the words in Pompey's handwriting (see below).

ad se Vibullius scripsisset Pompey will have written *ad me Vibullius scripsit*. L. Vibullius Rufus was *praefectus fabrum* (i.e. adjutant) to Pompey.

Domiti L. Domitius Ahenobarbus had raised a large army in central Italy. A few days after this letter was written he and Vibullius were trapped in Corfinium by Caesar and taken prisoner along with their entire force.

ipsam...epistulam i.e. a copy. There was not time to make one.

ipsius manu The rest of the letter was dictated.

id...accepi 'I took that to mean'.

pro relicto i.e. *pro relicta re*, 'as something abandoned', 'as a lost cause'.

caput ipsum Rome was the 'head', other areas the 'body'.

parcere has its usual meaning, 'spare' (not 'take thought for').

2   **rescripsi** The reply is extant (*Att.* 8.11B, a copy sent to Atticus eleven days later) and differs widely from Cicero's description. The most likely explanation is that he had not yet written it, *scripsi* and *misi* being epistolary tenses. When he did write to Pompey the following day his feelings had had time to subside.

hominemque certum 'a reliable man'. This was M. Tullius, who had been Cicero's official secretary (*scriba*) in Cilicia.

stabilis 'a firm point'; cf. Liv. 28.6.11 (*oppidum*) *fide praefectorum principumque...stabile atque inexpugnabile*.

3   **eundum.** Perhaps *sed* or *tamen* has dropped out; cf. sec. 4 *ibimus tamen Luceriam.*

ut...dissentire Both before and after the fact Cicero alleges his desire to stand well with conservative opinion (*boni*) and his feeling of personal obligation to Pompey (see below) as motivating his final reluctant decision to join Pompey overseas. But the true motive, as I believe, was basic political conviction or instinct; see my *Cicero*, pp. 153f.

M'. Lepidi sqq. Three Consulars. Ser. Sulpicius Rufus may have returned to Rome, L. Vulcatius (or Volcacius) Tullus may never have left, M'. Aemilius Lepidus, who had been at Formiae with Cicero, probably returned on 7 March.

4 unus The other *boni* did not count.

beneficio Pompey played a major role in bringing about Cicero's recall in 57. That he had done nothing to prevent the exile Cicero usually chose to forget. Since his own inclination was to remain in Italy, it suited him to put in the forefront of his reasons for leaving a reason which he knew was of no great force.

LETTER 37 (*Att.* 8.13)

After Caesar's capture of Corfinium Pompey fell back on Brundisium in order to sail overseas. Caesar pursued, laid siege to the town, and blockaded the harbour, but Pompey finally got away on 17 March. Cicero meanwhile remained in suspense at Formiae.

1 lippitudinis Cicero often complains of his eyes at this period. He normally wrote letters to close friends in his own hand.

nactus...esset...tramisisset The tenses are epistolary. Translate: 'if Caesar has found our Gnaeus there...'.

2 municipales...rusticani Country proprietors would be *municipes* of neighbouring towns. The distinction is between town-dwellers and land-owners living on their farms.

villulas...nummulos Contemptuous diminutives as in *Att.* 8.10 *dixit etiam alia quaedam de servulis suis qua re nobiscum esse non posset.*

quo *confidere* normally takes the dative of a personal object. Perhaps render 'who used to make them feel confident' rather than 'whom they used to trust'.

LETTER 38 (*Att.* 9.18)

On 28 March Cicero had an interview with Caesar, who was on his way from Brundisium to Rome. This letter will have been written immediately afterwards.

1 ne ad urbem sc. *veniremus*. Caesar was naturally desirous that leading men still in Italy should resume their normal public activities.

illa Anticipatory, as often: 'But we were mistaken in thinking him accommodating.' 'We', not 'I', because, as earlier letters show, Cicero had *not* expected Caesar to be 'easy'. But he politely associates himself in Atticus' error.

dicere Historic infinitive, appropriate in narrative.

Hispanias The Spanish provinces were governed by Pompey's Legates. Caesar invaded and conquered them a few months later.

iri The impersonal passive construction with intransitive verbs is very common in Latin. It corresponds to the use of *on* in French and *man* in German; cf. on Letter 1.6.

ut deliberarem sc. *me rogaret*.

2   νέκυια 'summoning of the dead', Atticus' term for Caesar's disreputable entourage, taken from the title of the eleventh book of the *Odyssey*. Caesar had called his following out of the shadows of insolvency, disgrace, and exile as Odysseus summoned up the ghosts from the underworld.

in qua...Celer 'Celer was one of the heroes'. Odysseus talked with the spirits of Agamemnon, Achilles, and other Greek heroes. Q. Pilius Celer was a relative, probably brother, of Atticus' wife, who had joined Caesar. Cicero thought well of him as a speaker.

Servi filius Homonymous son of the great jurist Ser. Sulpicius Rufus, Consul in 51. His father sent him to join Caesar's army at Brundisium, but nothing further is heard of him in the war. The elder Sulpicius later joined Pompey in Greece. On the use of the praenomen see on Letter 11.3 (*Appio*).

Titini Q. Titinius was a wealthy senator, on friendly terms with Cicero and Atticus. His son, Pontius Titinianus (he must have been adopted by a Pontius), was also serving with Caesar, to Cicero's disgust.

sex legiones sc. *sunt*.

hoc fuerat extremum 'This was to have been the finish', i.e. Cicero and Atticus had agreed that the former should finally make up his mind what to do after the meeting with Caesar. Cf. sec. 4 *extremum fuit de congressu nostro*.

3   κατακλείς Instrument for shutting doors, hence 'final phrase' or 'clausula'.

vidisti igitur virum, ut scripseras? 'So have you seen the great man, as you put it?' Atticus may be supposed to have written something like *omnia mihi perscribas velim, ut virum non modo audiam sed etiam videam*. This seems on the whole the best interpretation. Otherwise: 'Have you seen Caesar as your letter pictured him?', an ironical allusion to Atticus' misjudgement. But the Latin is less naturally taken so.

ingemuisti certe 'at any rate you must have groaned (as you read)'. So elsewhere, as Letter 17.2 *verebor ne quando ego tibi, cum sum una, molestus sim. video te ingemuisse.*

cedo Old imperative form from *cĕ* (as in *ecce*) and *do* (= *da*): 'Let's hear the rest.'

quid? Not, as usually, calling attention to what follows (*quid?* in that use is always followed by a question or exclamation), but implying that there *was* nothing more.

†pelanum *Pedanum* ('the Pedum district' or 'his place near Pedum') cannot be right, for Pedum, which probably no longer existed as a town, was well away from Caesar's route to Rome, the via Appia. *Pedi Norbanum* (O. E. Schmidt), is a better guess. The town of Norba lay about six miles east of the road. Q. Pedius was Caesar's nephew or great-nephew and had been one of his Legates in Gaul.

λαλαγεῦσαν 'the twitterer', i.e. the spring swallow. Cicero alludes to a poem by Leonidas of Tarentum (*Anth. Pal.* 10.1) beginning: 'It is time to sail, for the twittering swallow has arrived and the delightful west wind.'

tu...agas 'let bygones be bygones' (cf. Letter 70.2 *negabam oportere praeterita*). Atticus may have told Cicero that having settled everything comfortably with Caesar he could then sit back and wait for the spring. Thus the allusion to the swallow would be a kind of reproach for his misguided optimism about the interview. He is supposed to expostulate: 'I wish you would let bygones be bygones. Pompey himself has been wrong about many things.' *ne* with the second person singular of the present subjunctive in prohibitions is used in common sayings.

4   sed Resumptive.

de congressu nostro Practically a noun: 'the interview business'.

amabo te sqq. 'do let me have a letter, a political letter'.

LETTER 39 (*Fam.* 14.7)

Written on board ship in the harbour of Caieta (Gaeta) close to Cicero's Formian villa just before his departure for Greece. Terentia and Tullia were at Cumae.

1 te miserrimam habui 'made you very miserable'. Similarly *sollicitum aliquem habere* = 'make somebody anxious'.

causae Dative (predicative).

χολὴν ἄκρατον 'pure bile'. Cicero often uses Greek in medical matters.

soles Religion was Terentia's department; cf. *Fam.* 14.4.1 *neque di, quos tu castissime coluisti, neque homines, quibus ego semper servivi.*

id est...Aesculapio Probably a marginal note which found its way into the text, but just possibly an afterthought of Cicero's defining *deus aliquis.*

2 nos Cicero and young Marcus (see end of letter). Quintus and his son may also have been on board.

quo = *ut*, as often, especially when followed by a comparative adjective or adverb.

me...cum similibus nostri...defensuros i.e. *me et similes nostri.* When this construction is used by a classical writer there is nearly always something to account for it. Here perhaps Cicero was unconsciously influenced by *nostri.* By *similes nostri* he means 'fellow-*principes*'; personally he had a poor opinion of most of the optimate leaders (cf. Letter 36.3) and wrote to Atticus in March *ut has pestes effugiam, cum dissimillimis nostri esse cupio (Att.* 9.11.4).

utere Future (*utĕre*) not imperative (*utĕre*), as parallel passages indicate, e.g. *Att.* 13.50.2 *eum servum, si tibi videbitur, ad me mittes.*

si...fuerit Pompey's fleet was expected to blockade Italy.

etiam atque etiam 'once more'. Cicero had already said goodbye in person.

LETTER 40 (*Att.* 11.4)

One of a very few surviving letters written from Pompey's camp or the neighbouring town of Dyrrachium in 48. Cicero had no military or other official employment, and Plutarch describes him as playing the part of a sarcastic grumbler.

praedia Cicero was trying to sell property in order to raise money to pay his daughter's dowry.

venisse From *vēneo*.

sustentetur sc. *Tullia*.

Frusinati *Frusinas* is the adjectival form from Frusinum, a place thirteen miles west of Arpinum (now Frosinone). It seems odd that Cicero should be thinking of buying real estate at the very time when he was unsuccessfully trying to sell it, but he can hardly be understood in any other way.

tecum sc. *deliberavissem*, vel sim. *olim* in effect = 'before I left Italy'.

cetera Celer sc. *narrabit*. This may be Pilius Celer in Caesar's camp, or perhaps the slave who carried the letter.

meis rebus 'my record'. The language is rather vague, but seems to mean that affairs on the Pompeian side were so badly managed that Cicero could take no active part without danger to his *dignitas*. The fact may well have been that he was offered nothing that he considered adequate.

LETTER 41 (*Att.* 11.5)

After the republican defeat at Pharsalia in August 48 Pompey's forces scattered. Cicero, who had been prevented by ill-health from appearing on the battle-field, made his way with his brother to Patrae. There a violent quarrel broke out between them. Its immediate cause is uncertain, but resentments seem to have been mounting over the years on Quintus' side against his overshadowing elder; see my *Cicero*, pp. 179–85. A reconciliation of sorts took place after Cicero returned to Rome in the autumn of 47, but (contrary to the traditional belief) it is plain from his letters to Atticus that the old relations were never really restored.

Following a message from Caesar received through Dolabella Cicero returned to Italy in October 48, and remained at Brundisium for a year, in discomfort of mind and body, unable to return to Rome without Caesar's authority. This dismal period ended with Caesar's return from the East in September 47. Caesar met and talked with Cicero on the road from Tarentum to Brundisium, and the desired permission was graciously granted.

1 moverint sc. *ut in Italiam venirem*. The adjectives suggest that Cicero was thinking of his quarrel with his brother.

meis rebus *meae res* can mean 'my circumstances' or 'my record (of achievement)' according to context.

cum aliis Perhaps Caesar's friends Balbus and Oppius.

2 deversoria 'lodges'. Rich Romans kept houses along the main routes in which they could stop overnight, avoiding the discomforts of an inn. See also on Letter 14.

id quod quaeris Secrecy. Cicero would have to do part of the travelling in the daytime, so that he would be recognized on the road even if he passed through the towns at night.

3 Basilo L. Minucius Basilus had been a Legate of Caesar's in Gaul. Later he became one of his assassins.

Servilio P. Servilius Isauricus, Consul with Caesar in 48.

4 Vatinio This old enemy had been a friend since Cicero defended him in 54.

deest The present indicative brings out the fact that these persons actually were doing their best. For the change of mood in *possent* cf. Mart. 2.63.3 *luxuria est si tanti dives amares*. But here the construction may be elliptical: 'they are doing everything they can (or rather they would) if...'.

LETTER 42 (*Fam.* 14.12)

Cicero's relations with his wife had been deteriorating for a long while. Even in 50 he believed that he had caught her freedman Philotimus in some fraudulent accounting and seems to have suspected her of complicity. They were divorced in 46.

meorum The Quinti. The addition seems necessary to define *iniuriis*; cf. *Att.* 11.21.3 *tantisque nostrorum iniuriis*.

in viam...est Thus Terentia stands exonerated from one of the charges which according to Plutarch (*Vit. Cic.* 41) Cicero made against her at the time of the divorce, failure to visit him at Brundisium.

D. See on Letter 9.

LETTER 43 *(Fam.* 14.20)

Cicero's last extant letter to his wife, written from the district of Venusia in south Italy on his way back to Rome.

ut sint...ut sit A form of command mainly found in Plautus and Cato.

labrum Contracted form of *lavabrum*, a round tub for washing or sluicing after the sweat-bath. Specimens have been found at Pompeii and elsewhere.

ad victum et ad valetudinem 'for subsistence and health'. An anonymous epigram in the *Latin Anthology* (ed. Riese, 179) has *hinc capitur victus, sumitur inde salus*, where *hinc* refers to a fruit and vegetable garden, *inde* to baths.

LETTER 44 *(Fam.* 9.1)

The great antiquarian and polymath M. Terentius Varro of Reate had been a lieutenant of Pompey in politics and war and had governed southern Spain (Baetica) as his Legate. He surrendered there to Caesar in 48 and subsequently made his way to Greece, for at the time of the battle of Pharsalia he was in Dyrrachium with Cicero and Cato (*Divin.* 1.68, 2.114). He was a friend of Atticus and Cicero, but the latter stood in some awe of him, quoting on one occasion from the *Iliad*, 'One to be feared. E'en blameless folk he'd blame.'

Apparently he had been pardoned by Caesar a second time and given permission to return to Italy, where he was expected in the near future.

2 me...demisissem In joining Pompey in 48.

sive ad te Varro too had villas in both areas. Cicero could not in common courtesy assume that Varro would be the host. Hence the. addition to the text.

perficiam...videatur i.e. 'what suits you best will suit me too'.

LETTER 45   *(Fam.* 9.18)

On Papirius Paetus see Letter 28.

1 discipulos Hirtius and Dolabella, who were taking lessons in declamation from Cicero.

obviam To meet Caesar on his return from the African campaign. He landed in Italy on 26 July 46. Cicero must be joking when he says he 'sent' the two Caesarians. They would have gone anyway, and it is not clear why he did not go himself.

eadem sc. *via* or *opera*. So in comedy.

Dionysius The legend that Dionysius II, after his final expulsion from Syracuse in 345, became a schoolmaster in Corinth (*usque eo imperio carere non poterat, Tusc.* 3.27) passed into a Greek proverb ('Dionysius at Corinth').

sublatis iudiciis The great standing courts *de vi, de ambitu* etc., in which Cicero used to plead his *causes célèbres*, were no longer active under Caesar.

regno forensi cf. Quint. *Inst.* 10.1.112 *regnare in iudiciis dictus est.* In the Verrines Cicero uses expressions like *dominatio regnumque iudiciorum* of Hortensius.

2 munio By keeping on good terms with leading Caesarians. Dolabella and Tullia were now divorced, but Cicero's relations with him remained cordial.

in lectulo The diminutive is regularly used in this expression (in *lectulo (suo) mori*).

Pompeius...Afranius Pompey and Lentulus Crus (Cos. 49) were separately murdered in Egypt. Metellus Scipio and L. Afranius (Cos. 60) perished in Africa, the former killing himself to avoid capture, the latter killed by Caesar's soldiery.

necesse According to Plutarch (*Vit. Cat. min.* 72) Caesar said he would have liked to spare Cato's life. Evidently Cicero did not know this or did not believe it.

3 valetudine 'The Romans at times practised declamation to supply the place of physical exercise' (Tyrrell and Purser, quoting *Phil.* 2.42 *vini exhalandi, non ingeni acuendi causa declamitas*).

nescio an 'I rather think that...'. See Letter 11.2.

pavones A fashionable dish, believed to have been first served by Hortensius at an Augurs' dinner. Horace thought it tasted like ordinary fowl (*Sat.* 2.2.29).

tu...Hirtiano 'While you are enjoying Haterius' legal gravity in Naples, I regale myself here with Hirtius' gravy.' Haterius was presumably a lawyer, and a neighbour or guest of Paetus. Hirtius, a noted epicure, prided himself on his sauces. For the pun cf. the famous *ius Verrinum* in *Verr.* 2.1.121.

προλεγομένας 'first principles' (sc. θέσεις). This is the usual explanation, but the expression does not occur elsewhere and its meaning is not certain.

sus Minervam sc. *docet.* A well-known proverb in Greek and Latin. Since Minerva was the goddess of wisdom and intellect and the pig was considered the most stupid of animals (Plin. *Nat. hist.* 8.207, Enn. *Ann.* 105 *nam vi depugnare sues stolidi soliti sunt*), there is no necessity to suppose that it originated in a lost fable. Cicero means that Paetus knew more about oratory than he did himself.

4 quo modo video 'as I see it'.

aestimationes Under Caesar's debt regulations creditors had been obliged to take over the property of their debtors at pre-war prices. Such properties were now a drug in the market.

neque...implere 'and you have not sixpences enough to fill a pot'. The denarius was a silver coin worth four sesterces or ten asses.

cruditate sc. *mori.*

idem istuc sc. *fecisse. spero* means 'I expect' rather than 'I hope'. Paetus had complained of his losses in his letter, hence *istuc.*

cantherium 'gelding', but sometimes colloquially for 'horse'; from κανθήλιος = 'donkey', a sense not found in the Latin. *comedere* often means 'spend' or 'squander', here perhaps 'spend (the proceeds of the sale) on food'; cf. Hor. *Epist.* 1.15.39 *'non hercule miror'* | *aiebat 'si qui comedunt bona, cum sit obeso* | *nil melius turdo, nil vulva pulchrius ampla.'*

eam pulvinus sequetur 'a cushion will accompany the chair'. Or perhaps the cushion was to follow later, if Paetus gave satisfaction.

LETTER 46 (*Fam.* 7.28)

On M'. Curius see Letter 31.1.

1 istis 'the people where you are', i.e. 'Greeks'.
cum...urbs sc. *erat.*

2 ubi nec Pelopidarum Pelops was the father of Atreus and Thyestes. This line from an unknown play may have run: *ubi nec*

Pelopidarum nomen nec facta aut famam audiam. Cicero quotes pieces of it elsewhere.

avem albam White was a lucky colour; cf. Juv. 13.141 *gallinae filius albae*, Ov. *Am.* 3.12.1–2 *tristia...| omina non albae concinuistis aves.* But Cicero also seems to have had the idea of rarity in mind, perhaps unconsciously mixing up *rara avis* and *corvus albus.*

opera After returning to Rome in 47 Cicero filled his now abundant leisure with literary composition. Earlier in 46 he had produced his *Brutus, Paradoxa Stoicorum, Cato* (lost), and perhaps *Partitiones oratoriae.* He was now working on the *Orator.*

dicere As though *memini* (instead of *intellexi*) had preceded – careless writing, but tolerable in a familiar letter. The reference is probably to conversations at Patrae in 48.

te...desiderare 'You wondered what had become of the spirit you saw in my writings.' *ex* = 'using as criterion', as in phrases like *ex meo otio tuum specto. libris* refers to the *De re publica.*

3 haec 'things here', i.e. Rome.

LETTER 47 (*Fam.* 6.14)

Twenty-six letters of 46–45 are written to or from or concerning former republican partisans who were hoping for Caesar's pardon and permission to return to Italy. Friends in this situation knew that they could rely on all possible help from Cicero. One of them was Q̣. Ligarius, who had been taken prisoner after the battle of Thapsus. His life was spared, and after an extant speech delivered by Cicero before Caesar in October (true calendar) not long after this letter, he was allowed to come back. He repaid Caesar's clemency by joining the conspiracy against his life in 44.

2 a. d. V Kal. intercalares priores i.e. 24 September (true calendar); see Appendix I.

iacerent ad pedes As suppliants.

3 fac...sis *fac(ite)* with the subjunctive, with or without *ut*, emphasizes a command: 'be sure to...'.

ut difficillimis 'I shall give my support to your cause as though it were one of the utmost difficulty.'

amicissimos Cicero often refers to the friendly attitude towards himself of leading Caesarians like Balbus, Oppius, and Hirtius, with whom he had been on good terms before the war.

LETTER 48 (*Fam.* 9.26)

Written in early or mid November (true calendar) 46, soon after Caesar's departure for Spain, during a dinner-party at the house of P. Volumnius Eutrapelus, whose cognomen means 'witty'. He was one of Cicero's Caesarian friends and the recipient of two extant letters from Cicero, which pay compliments to his wit and learning. The famous actress (*mima*) Cytheris (sec. 2), Mark Antony's mistress and the 'Lycoris' of Cornelius Gallus' lost love-elegies, was Volumnius' freedwoman. By Roman social standards association with *mimae* was not fitting for respectable persons like Cicero.

1 hora nona About 2.30 p.m. The ninth hour (i.e. the end of it) was the usual dinner time in summer. For November it was rather early, as befitted a smart Roman dinner-party (*tempestivum convivium*).

harum exemplum sc. *litterarum. exemplum*, like 'text', can refer to an original or a copy, but usually means the latter.

codicillis Note that at a Roman dinner-party a guest apparently felt free to take out his tablets and write a longish letter (cf. Letters 68.4, 72.3). But it is possible that Cicero and others had been talking about Paetus and that this gave rise to the letter; see on sec. 3.

supra,. . .infra Three couches, with three diners to a couch, made up the usual Roman dinner-party (*triclinium*). If Cicero's was the middle couch, Verrius (of whom little otherwise is known) was in the place of honour, *imus in medio*, next the host, who reclined *summus in imo*.

servitutem Cicero had earlier thought that Caesar intended to 'restore the republic' in some shape or form, but had now become disillusioned.

qui philosophum audis 'who attend lectures in philosophy'; see below.

quem ad finem? 'for how long?' lit. 'up to what limit?'

minimum. . .cena 'I set very little store by my dinner' (Tyrrell–Purser).

ζήτημα 'problem'. This is explained in sec. 3. Dio, evidently an Epicurean, is otherwise unknown.

2 accubuit The two places 'below' the host on the *imus lectus* were generally occupied by members of his family or freedmen. According to earlier Roman custom women sat at dinner while men reclined, but this had probably been relaxed by Cicero's time; see Letter 23.4.

quem...sua The source is doubtful, but the preceding line is quoted in *Tusc.* 3.39 *hicine est ille Telamon modo quem gloria ad caelum extulit?*

Aristippus Of Cyrene, a pupil of Socrates and precursor of Epicurus in that he pronounced pleasure to be the highest good. Two of his books were dedicated to the famous Corinthian courtesan Lais.

Graece hoc melius The saying is quoted in Greek sources in slightly varying forms, one being ἔχω Λαΐδα, ἀλλ' οὐκ ἔχομαι, in which ἔχομαι (= *habeor*) has the double sense 'I am owned' and 'I cling to'. Hence the difficulty of translating into Latin. For the antithesis *habeo...habeor* cf. e.g. Sall. *Iug.* 2.3 *animus...habet cuncta neque ipse habetur. habeo* (ἔχω) also has an erotic sense, as in Plaut. *Bacch.* 1080 *duxi, habui scortum.*

istorum Relations with actresses and the like.

ne = *nedum*, 'much less'.

in solum sc. *venit. solum* probably means 'sole of the foot', not 'ground', but the origin of the expression is doubtful. *quidquid in buccam venit* is similarly used, as in Letter 33.1.

3 melius sc. *facis*, i.e. *rides*. 'Do *you* manage it better, actually making game of a philosopher? When he put his question whether anybody had anything to ask, you called out "Who's going to ask me to dinner?" The poor dunderhead thought you would be enquiring whether there is one sky or an infinite number. What business is that of yours? Well, but, confound it, is a dinner any business of yours, especially one in *this* house?' Following traditional sophistic practice Dio asked *num quis quid quaerit*, offering to hold forth on any given topic. Paetus called out *ego cenam a mane quaero*. A fragment of Pomponius, a writer of farces, runs: *cenam quaeritat: | si eum nemo vocat, revortit maestus ad maenam miser.* Cicero writes as though he had just heard the story. Clearly he did not get it from Paetus.

baro Cicero was fond of applying this term to the Epicureans, who made a boast of their indifference to literary culture. Cf. Letter 24.5 (*politissimus*).

unum Epicurus, like some earlier thinkers, held that there are innumerable worlds. After Aristotle 'world' (κόσμος, *mundus*) and 'sky' (οὐρανός, *caelum*) became confused.

ibi praesertim Paetus' ignorance of the art of dining and stinginess as a host is a stock joke in Cicero's letters to him. Luxurious banquets, such as this one doubtless was, were not his province.

4 scribitur Cicero was at this time working on his lost *Hortensius*, the book which drew St Augustine to philosophy.

si ulla nunc lex est Under Caesar's despotism; see on *servitutem* in sec. 1.

intra legem i.e. at a cost below the minimum fixed by Caesar's sumptuary law.

adventum Cicero was about to leave Rome on a brief tour of his villas; see the next letter.

LETTER 49 *(Fam. 9.23)*

On 17 November (true calendar) Cicero set out on his tour. He probably wrote this and the following letter at the same time, i.e. on 21 November, the day after his arrival at Cumae.

heri Both spellings, *heri* and *here*, seem to have been current in Cicero's time, but the former was the older. According to Quintilian (*Inst.* 1.4.8) the final vowel was pronounced indeterminately (*neque E plane neque I auditur*).

certum sciam 'know for certain'; see on Letter 5.7.

M. Caeparius Unknown. A Catilinarian conspirator of the same name came from Tarracina (Sall. *Cat.* 46.3).

silva Gallinaria Between Cumae and the river Vulturnus; described by Strabo as a dense, sandy wood, stretching for many stadia. It later became a haunt of brigands.

viserem Sometimes used of visiting the sick.

LETTER 50 *(Fam. 7.4)*

XIII Kal. sc. *Dec.*, 21 November by the true calendar.

Libone L. Scribonius Libo, a former intimate of Pompey, whose younger son Sextus married Libo's daughter. His sister Scribonia was Octavian's wife before he married Livia.

quanto post...simus 'after how long (lit. by how much) we shall be together', i.e. 'what a long time it is since we were last together'. *quanto post* is used as in Virg. *Georg.* 3.476 *nunc quoque post tanto* and elsewhere. Cicero and Marius had last met in the spring of 49.

hoc biduo aut triduo 'within two or three days'.

LETTER 51 (*Fam.* 7.26)

This letter has been variously dated, but doubtless belongs to the autumn or winter of 46–45, between the enactment of Caesar's sumptuary law in October (?) and Tullia's death the following February. On M. Fabius Gallus see Letter 28.2.

1 mea opera Cicero was no longer in forensic practice as before the war, but he may have taken some civil cases and might be called upon by his friends in other capacities, e.g. as supporter in court (*advocatus*), witness, or arbiter (*iudex* or *arbiter*) in civil suits.

male accipiunt 'handle roughly'.

στραγγουρικά...πάθη 'sufferings from strangury and dysentery'. The words come from a letter written by Epicurus on his deathbed.

alterum...alterum 'the latter...the former', as often.

2 quo modove commiserim 'what I did to deserve it'.

λιτότητα 'plain living'.

excepta 'exempted'.

cena augurali The College of Augurs, to which Cicero had been elected in 53 or 52, met periodically for sumptuous banquets.

Lentulum P. Lentulus Spinther, son of the Consul of 57, who had perished in the war. He entered the augural College in 57.

a beta et a malva The prepositions imply personification. Reid translates 'entrapped by Mr Beet and Mr Mallow'. But why 'Mr'?

Anicio See Letter 17.3.

visendi See Letter 49, *viserem*.

corpus 'flesh' or 'weight'.

si...depulero 'once I shake off the malady'. *si* with the future perfect sometimes has a temporal force, equivalent to *simul atque*.

LETTER 52 (*Fam.* 5.16)

Cicero's correspondence includes several letters of condolence upon bereavements or other misfortunes. Such letters had become a literary genre (*consolatio*, λόγος παραμυθητικός), with stock motifs (*loci communes*, τόποι); for a convenient résumé see W. C. Summers, *Select Letters of Seneca* (1910), pp. 243ff. This specimen was probably written during Caesar's régime and evidently before the death of Cicero's daughter in February 45. Titius, a common name, cannot be further identified. He had apparently lost sons in an epidemic.

1 nostrae necessitudinis esse 'that it was appropriate to our friendship'. *necessitudo*, as distinct from *amicitia*, usually implies some special connexion such as a family or official relationship.

tam diu sc. *quam iam tacui*. Cicero reproaches himself for having delayed writing so long.

2 tam graviter i.e. not so hardly as the misfortunes for which we are ourselves to blame. *neve* follows on from *ut meminerimus*.

eventisque i.e. *et ut eventis*.

4 sin illa...lugeas 'on the other hand, if the sting lies in your grief for the sad lot of the departed, a sentiment more in keeping with affection...'.

sin sit amissus Cicero's letters show no decided belief in personal survival after death. In some of his philosophical writings, composed after his daughter's death, he takes a more positive line.

deceptus 'cheated' of his expectation of life. So in grave-inscriptions this word sometimes means 'cut off (prematurely)', e.g. *fato deceptus, non ab homine*.

5 ne...contigisse Because (*a*) death is not an evil, whether the individual survives or no, and (*b*) life for the children was not worth living.

cura doloris tui 'the distress of your own grief'. *cura* here is practically equivalent to *dolor*.

casum incommodorum tuorum 'the troubles chance has brought upon you'. '*casus periculorum* corresponds to *cadunt* (= *accidunt*) *pericula* as *fuga Pompeii* to *Pompeius fugit*' (Housman, *Classical papers*, p. 520).

praecipere 'take beforehand'.

6 ante ferre 'apply in advance'.

repraesentare 'supply to hand'. The word is often used in business contexts of payment cash down.

LETTER 53 (*Fam.* 15.18)

C. Cassius Longinus, an intellectual nobleman with a distinguished military record, had fought on Pompey's side in the Civil War, but Caesar had pardoned and favoured him. Later he was to play a leading role in Caesar's assassination. At the end of 46 he was in Brundisium.

1 iretur See on Letter 38.1.

autem 'longer, that is, if. . .'; *autem* qualifies the foregoing statement.

φλύαρον **aliquem** 'some badinage'.

σπουδάζειν 'be serious', i.e. 'discuss politics'. Cf. Letter 63.2 (σπουδαῖον).

tua Cassius was an Epicurean convert.

in culina Epicurus' saying that 'the pleasure of the stomach is the beginning and root of all good' lent itself to malicious interpretation. When Cicero took up gastronomy he described himself as a deserter to Epicurus' camp (*Fam.* 9.20.1).

mea The Academic, founded by Plato.

molesta est 'is a scold'. The maxims of Plato were a reproach to Cicero's uneasy conscience.

alias res agere 'pay no attention'. We say 'my mind is on other things'.

Platonis In *Rep.* 387b Plato says that men should be free, fearing slavery more than death.

2 Hispania Where Caesar was fighting his last campaign against his own mutinous troops and other forces led by Pompey's sons.

LETTER 54 (*Fam.* 16.18)

The date is uncertain, except that it must have been subsequent to Cicero's return to Rome in 47.

1 non sic oportet? Apparently Tiro had deprecated 'Tullius' instead of 'Cicero' in the heading of Cicero's previous letter as too familiar (the only other persons so addressed by Cicero are his wife and children). Yet his earlier letters to Tiro are headed so in the manuscripts, and most of those written after Tiro's manumission add 'suo'. Perhaps the letter in question had to be shown to a third party.

quam quidem The commonest use of *quidem* after a relative pronoun is for emphasis, indicating that the clause contains an independent statement; so three times in this letter (see also on Letter 17.1). It can also be restrictive, e.g. *Att.* 7.2.3 *venio ad epistulas tuas... aliam alia iucundiorem, quae quidem erant tua manu.*

saepe *semper* may very well be what Cicero wrote (*sepe* and *sēper* or *sēp* are easily confused).

διαφόρησιν 'evaporation', i.e. 'perspiration'.

si... Tusculanum sc. *tibi profuit.*

in modum Literally 'rhythmically' (= *in numerum*), i.e. 'smoothly'. Tiro's pretence of affection, if that was what it was, worked as well as the real thing (of course Cicero is joking).

utut est 'however that may be'.

πέψιν sqq. 'Digestion, no fatigue, a short walk, massage, proper evacuation.' It is hard to say whether σύμμετρον means 'short' (cf. Philostr. *Vit. Ap.* 7.16 ξύμμετρος ἐς τὴν Ῥώμην ἀνάπλους) or 'duly regulated'.

bellus 'in good fettle'.

2 Parhedrum In Greek = 'neighbour', but here apparently a personal name. Cicero wanted to interest him in renting the garden in the Tusculanum, because the existing tenant-gardener (*holitor*) was behind with his rent.

Helico A previous tenant or would-be tenant, who paid, or offered to pay an (annual?) rent of 1,000 sesterces even prior to the carrying out of certain improvements at Cicero's expense. We do not know what he did to be called *nequissimus.*

aprico horto Presumably 'a spot in the garden especially laid out so as to catch as much sun as possible... used... for growing choice flowers' (Tyrrell-Purser).

tanta impensa A rather loose use of the ablative of accompaniment. *post tantam impensam* might have been expected.

derideat 'make fools of', by not paying his dues. Similarly in

Mart. 12.32.23 *quid quaeris aedes vilicosque derides?* of a house-hunter who could not afford to pay rent.

Mothonem Another tenant-gardener, probably at Cicero's house on the Palatine. Evidently he paid his rent, or part of it, in kind. After 'warming him up', Cicero now had more flowers than he knew what to do with. For 'wreaths' as a garden product cf. Mart. 11.18.7 *clusae cui folium rosae corona est* (generally misunderstood).

3   Crabra The Aqua Crabra, an aqueduct running into Rome, supplied water to the Tusculanum, for which Cicero paid.

etsi...aquae i.e. the weather was rainy. Perhaps there had been some flooding.

nullosne tecum libellos? sc. *habes*. Apparently a joke. The books were to be added to the library at the Tusculanum. We may suppose that Tiro had been sending frequent reminders about them.

Sophocleum The books may have consisted of Greek tragedies.

A. Ligurius A former officer of Caesar's in Gaul.

LETTER 55 (*Fam.* 9.10)

Dolabella was with Caesar in Spain.

1   Salvio Atticus had a *librarius* called Salvius, but this will refer to a freedman of Caesar's.

omnino 'to be sure'.

Niciam...Vidium Curtius Nicias of Cos was a savant and protégé of Dolabella, through whom probably he became a friend of Cicero. Vidius is unknown (Syme's proposed identification with P. Vedius Pollio, later a friend of Augustus, may be right but cannot be proved).

iudicem In a civil suit the City Praetor furnished names from among which a judge was selected by the parties.

profert...ὀβελίζει i.e. Vidius claimed that Nicias had borrowed money from him, which Nicias denied. *versiculis*, meaning either 'little lines (of writing)' or 'little verses', gives rise to some word-play: Nicias, who denies the authenticity of Vidius' document, is compared with the great Alexandrian critic Aristarchus, who standardized the use of critical signs. The ὀβελός was a horizontal stroke in the margin to indicate a spurious line; hence ὀβελίζει, 'obelizes'.

utrum sqq. 'whether they are the poet's or interpolated'.

2 quos apud Niciam sc. *comedisti*. The corrupt words no doubt refer to other delicacies, including perhaps *cochlearum*, 'snails'.

συμβιωτήν 'companion', lit. 'living-partner'.

nec committam sqq. Cicero playfully writes as though Nicias were facing a criminal charge, conviction on which would lead to exile. But if that happened, Dolabella would get Caesar to bring him back, for otherwise Plancus Bursa would have nobody to teach him his ABC. This T. Munatius Plancus Bursa had been exiled (Cicero prosecuting) because of his part as Tribune in the riots which followed Clodius' murder in January 52. Caesar had restored him. He was an uncultivated fellow, and Cicero detested him.

3 ut in bello 'being in a war, as you are'. In Greek the present participle of the verb 'to be', which Latin does not have, would be used: ὡς ἐν πολέμῳ ὤν.

labor longius 'I go rambling on', more literally 'I glide (*lābor*) further and further'.

P. Sullae See Letter 11.3. Both under the Dictator Sulla and under Caesar he had been a conspicuous purchaser of confiscated property.

quo modo perierit Writing to Cassius (*Fam.* 15.17.2), Cicero says it was doubtful whether Sulla had been killed by brigands or died of overeating.

hasta i.e. the auctioning of confiscated property; Caesar's victory in the Civil War, like Sulla's, produced a vast amount of this. A spear was stuck in the ground at public auctions.

LETTER 56 (*Att.* 12.15)

Tullia gave birth to a male child by her ex-husband Dolabella in January 45 (it lived only a few months) and died a month later. Cicero spent the first few weeks of bereavement in Atticus' house in Rome. On 6 March he left for his recently acquired villa at Astura, a lonely place in the Antium district, almost surrounded by the sea.

Appuleium A recently appointed Augur. Cicero, as a member of the College, was bound to present a sworn deposition of sickness to excuse his absence at the inauguration ceremonies. The Augurs were in charge of the traditional system of public divination from the flight of birds, derived from Etruria. Membership, especially for a non-*nobilis*, was a high distinction.

in dies ut excuser sc. *singulos*, 'from day to day'. It appears that this could be done through third parties, whereas an excuse *in perpetuum* would require Cicero's personal appearance.

Bruto M. Junius Brutus (by adoption Q. Servilius Caepio Brutus), Caesar's assassin. Like his brother-in-law and fellow-assassin Cassius, he had received Caesar's pardon and favour, and was at this time governing Cisalpine Gaul. He was a close friend of Atticus, and by now of Cicero also, to whom he had written a letter of condolence.

LETTER 57 (*Att.* 12.16)

nunc...ipsum 'at this very moment'.
domi sc. *me esse*.
Philippus L. Marcius Philippus, Cos. 56.

LETTER 58 (*Att.* 12.32)

After divorcing Terentia Cicero was remarried about the end of 46 to a ward of his own, a rich young girl called Publilia. The match quickly ended in another divorce. He mentions her directly only in this letter.

1   mea manu Apparently Cicero was using an amanuensis at this time for his daily letters to Atticus.

Publilio Presumably Publilia's uncle or brother, and probably another of her guardians.

illi (line 10) Publilius and Publilia's mother.

ut ego evolem Defining *una*. *me evolare* or *si evolaro* might have been written instead.

ut scribis Atticus could not have known about the circumstances which had just arisen, but may have written about the situation generally.

2   Ciceroni Young Marcus was about to go to Athens for a period of study and self-improvement (it did not work out quite like that) – a sort of university education. The poet Horace, who was about the same age, was there for the same purpose.

quibus...futurus erat Madvig's transposition of these words (see critical note) is certainly an improvement.

Argileti et Aventini Cicero owned rented property in these city areas.

Bibulum sqq. The three named were young men of high birth. Acidinus is probably identical with Horace's friend (Manlius) Torquatus, to whom he addressed an ode and a verse letter.

quanti sc. *conducant* (gen. of price).

LETTER 59 (*Fam.* 9.11)

Cicero spent April 45 in a villa belonging to Atticus in the Nomentum district, within ten miles or so of Rome. Since Dolabella was expected back from Spain in the near future, the letter must have been written after 20 April, when the news of Caesar's victory at Munda reached Rome.

1 casu Tullia's death.

ita...iuvari 'You will find me in a state which offers plenty of scope for your assistance.'

hilaritas Cicero says the same to Atticus about a fortnight later (*Att.* 12.40.3): *hilaritatem illam qua hanc tristitiam temporum condiebamus in perpetuum amisi, constantia et firmitas nec animi nec orationis requiretur.*

2 proelia Against the young Q. Cicero, who was in Spain talking against his uncle to anyone who would listen. Caesar seems to have been rather partial to him.

LETTER 60 (*Att.* 13.10)

1 Marcello M. Claudius Marcellus, Consul in 51, had been on Pompey's side in the Civil War (not neutral, as sometimes supposed), but after Pharsalia retired to Mytilene in the island of Lesbos. In September 56 he was pardoned by Caesar at the Senate's request (see Cicero's speech on the occasion, *Pro Marcello*), and was making his way back to Rome when a friend of his, Magius Cilo, murdered him at Piraeus. His former colleague in the consulship, Ser. Sulpicius Rufus, who was governor of Achaia at the time, sent Cicero a report of the circumstances (*Fam.* 4.12).

plura 'more' (than you had previously suspected).

quis...timeret 'who would have feared (was to fear)...?'

illud Anticipating *me reliquum consularem* (sc. *esse*). Atticus must be supposed to have written that after Marcellus' removal Cicero was the only one left of the Consulars who had been on the republican side in the war (there were several who had been neutral or semi-neutral). Cicero points out that this was contrary to fact, since it ignored Servius Sulpicius (whose neutrality in the war is a modern fiction).

παρὰ τὴν ἱστορίαν 'contrary to historical fact'. Cf. Mart. *Spect.* 21.8 as emended by Housman *haec tantum res est facta* παρ' ἱστορίαν ('contrary to the (mythological) story').

tu praesertim Atticus was a historian himself; see Introd. p. 14.

hoc sc. *consularem esse*.

qui...putem 'to whom the dead (*illis*) seem to have come out of it no less well (than the living)'.

domin an foris? sc. *possumus esse aliquid?*

ista 'those pieces (of mine)'. Cicero had just finished the first version of his *Academica* and the five books *De finibus*. Currently he was projecting a political dialogue located at Corinth in 146, but seems to have soon lost interest in the idea.

2   κοινότερα sqq. sc. *ut mittam*; 'some general subject with a political flavour'. Dolabella had asked Cicero to dedicate a literary work to himself.

3   si quid egerit Brutus had divorced his wife Claudia, daughter of Ap. Claudius Pulcher and sister-in-law to Pompey's elder son. Atticus and Cicero wanted him to marry Cato's daughter Porcia, as in fact he did.

sermunculum 'tittle-tattle', to the effect that the divorce was a move towards Caesar.

optime sc. *iudicabit*.

proficisci For Arpinum.

Spintherem P. Cornelius Lentulus Spinther the younger (Letter 51.2).

misit 'sent word' (that Spinther was coming). But there is something to be said for Boot's inversion *ad me. Brutus.*

insidiis 'by stealth', i.e. by an unknown assassin.

causam omnem sustinet 'sustains the whole case' amounts to 'accounts for the whole thing'.

quid sit i.e. *quid id* (*ea res*) *sit*, i.e. 'what he means'.

sponsor Cicero thinks as he goes along. The recollection that he himself had gone surety for Magius leads him to Magius' motive for the crime. According to Valerius Maximus (9.11.4) it was jealousy of Marcellus' other friends.

solvendo...non erat 'he was bankrupt' (lit. 'not for paying', i.e. not able to pay). The full form of the expression is found in Liv. 31.13.5 *nec tamen solvendo aere* (dat.) *alieno res publica esset*. For the construction cf. id. 2.9.6 *ut divites conferrent, qui oneri ferendo essent*.

ut erat 'as was his way'. Cf. *Fam.* 12.20 *quod si, ut es, cessabis*. The text has been suspected in both passages, probably without justification.

constantius 'rather firmly'. Cf. Plin. *Epist.* 6.34.2 *tanto consensu rogabaris ut negare non constans sed durum videretur*.

LETTER 61 (*Att.* 13.16)

Cicero's letters to Atticus at this period often concern his literary works. Besides a staff of copyists Atticus also had learned slaves or freedmen who could clear up historical points, and was a historian, or at least an antiquary, himself (see Introd. p.14).

1 pedem Usually explained 'a foot's distance', the accusative then being of 'space over which'. In reality *pedem egredi* = *pedem efferre* (cf. *Att.* 6.8.5 *pedem porta non...extulit*); similarly in a grave inscription (Buecheler, *Carm. epigr.* 215.2) *his parce tumulis ingredi pedem saepe*. Such accusatives are found in Greek, as in Eur. *Heracl.* 802 ἐκβάς...ἁρμάτων πόδα.

'Ακαδημικὴν σύνταξιν 'Treatise on the Academy'. The first of the two surviving Books of Cicero's *Academica* (*Academica posteriora*) is a dialogue between Cicero, Varro, and Atticus, part of the later edition. Our book II (*Academica priora* or *Lucullus*) belonged to the first edition, and the principal speakers are L. Lucullus and Cicero. σύνταξις is used of a work made up of more than one Book (σύνταγμα = *liber*).

παρὰ τὸ πρέπον '*inconvenant*'. In an English version the effect of Cicero's Greek can sometimes be reproduced by French or Latin.

non illa...ἀτριψία 'their – I won't say ignorance, but lack of *expertise* in such matters'. Cicero's statements in *Acad.* 2.4 about Lucullus' keen interest in philosophy must evidently be taken with more than one grain of salt.

Catonem Brutumque Both of these were really well versed in the subject, Cato as a Stoic, Brutus as a follower of Antiochus.

Antiochia ratio Antiochus of Ascalon, born *c.* 125 and personally acquainted with Cicero, had founded a new movement in the Academy; Cicero considered his doctrines to be practically indistinguishable from Stoicism.

2   ad illum sc. *mittere* ('dedicate').

quid Servilia? 'What of Servilia?' This great lady was Brutus' mother and a close friend of Atticus, allegedly also at one time Caesar's mistress.

ecquid agit? Brutus had recently divorced his wife in order to marry Cato's daughter Porcia; see on Letter 60.3.

ad Nonas 'by the Nones'. Understand *adero*.

cum Pisone sc. *age* or *colloquere*. This concerns an obscure financial matter. Piso's identity is uncertain.

LETTER 62   (*Att.* 13.33a)

1   Varrone See Letter 44. He had returned to Italy and was placed by Caesar in charge of Rome's first public library.

lupus in fabula 'talk of the devil'. Plautus and Terence have this saying. Its origin is doubtful.

id temporis = *eo tempore*. Similarly *id aetatis*, 'at that age'. Varro had arrived close on dinner-time and so had to be invited to stay.

sed...paenulam 'but I tried not to tear his coat'; i.e. did not press him too hard.

tuum 'that remark of yours', apparently referring to an occasion when Atticus had made excuses for having got rid of some unwanted visitors. Reid wished to take *tuum* with reference to *ut non scinderem paenulam*, in which case *et*, absent in one manuscript, should be omitted. The construction *et...-que* first occurs in Cicero, who has it in a number of passages.

quid refert? 'What's the difference?', i.e. 'he was going to stay anyhow'. With reference to the past one can say either *quid refert* (sc. *id factum esse* vel sim.) or *quid retulit* (sc. *id fieri* vel sim.).

C. Capito cum T. Carrinate C. Ateius Capito was on friendly terms with Caesar. *T.* should perhaps be *C*. C. Carrinas, son of a Marian leader, was Consul-Suffect in 43 and prominent thereafter.

de urbe augenda Caesar, now in Spain, had announced plans for new building in Rome.

ponte Mulvio The present Ponte Molle was built in 1805, partly from antique materials.

illum...Vaticanum 'the other Campus, the Vaticanus', on the west bank of the Tiber.

ad tabulam sc. *ibam*. Cicero had intended to go to an auction in order to bid for a property in the Campus Vaticanus to be sold by the heirs of one Scapula. His plan to acquire this or some other suburban property (*horti*) figures largely in his correspondence with Atticus in the spring and early summer following Tullia's death. It stemmed from his project to deify her by building her a temple.

audire...sum 'I was not sorry to hear it'. The news was unwelcome, but it was as well to hear of it in time to avoid a bad investment.

Camillo A legal expert. Cicero consulted him on business matters and knew him socially.

Idibus Cicero had proposed to return to Rome for the Scapula auction on 15 March. His other business there could wait for two or three days. But he did not want to put Atticus to the trouble of coming out to Tusculum, so he implies that he will stick to the original date if a meeting between them is called for.

2   de Bruto Cicero had wanted Brutus' assistance on the 15th, probably in connexion with the signing of a new will. But after hearing Capito's news he decided to postpone this business to a later date and wrote to Brutus cancelling his previous request.

LETTER 63 (*Att.* 13.52)

This celebrated letter was written from Cicero's villa near Cumae, or else from another near Puteoli which he had recently inherited from a wealthy banker there.

1   o...ἀμεταμέλητον! 'Strange that so onerous a guest should leave a memory not disagreeable.' But see critical note.

fuit...periucunde *fuit* may be used impersonally (cf. Petron. 46.2 *belle erit*) or the subject may be Caesar.

secundis Saturnalibus The Saturnalia began on 17 December.

ad Philippum 'to Philippus' place'. So *ad me* (*te*) often means 'to (at) my (your) house', as below.

a militibus The preposition could have been omitted; cf. 'thronged by the soldiers' and 'thronged with soldiers'.

CIƆ CIƆ 2,000.

commotus quid An indirect question often follows a verb expressing fear or surprise.

Barba Cassius Cassius Barba, a follower of Caesar and later of Antony. On the inverse order see Letter 12.1.

H. VII *horam septimam*, about 12.45 p.m.

rationes sc. *putabat*.

ambulavit Cicero says nothing about Caesar's arrival at his house. Omission of stages in narrative (κατὰ τὸ σιωπώμενον) belongs to epic technique; see E. Norden on Virg. *Aen.* 6.77.

Mamurra Caesar's adjutant (*praefectus fabrum*) in Gaul, lampooned by Catullus. The news was probably of his death; cf. *Verr.* 2.1.139 *sed recenti re de Mustio auditum est.*

ἐμετικὴν agebat 'he was on a course of emetics'. Understand δίαιταν and cf. *Deiot.* 21 *cum...vomere post cenam te velle dixisses.*

ἀδεῶς et iucunde 'with uninhibited enjoyment'.

bene cocto sqq. From Lucilius (1122, Marx). Perhaps *cibo* preceded, and perhaps *sermone bono* should be taken with *condito* ('seasoned with good talk').

2   οἱ περὶ αὐτόν 'his entourage'.

minus lautis...lautiores The three dining-rooms will have been occupied by guests of standing, including certain freedmen, while the inferior freedmen and slaves were accommodated in the servants' quarters.

homines *homo* may = 'a man like other men', not something less or more. Here almost 'man of the world', the opposite of rustic or recluse.

amabo te 'please'.

8   CST

eodem ad me sc. *veni. eodem* anticipates *ad me* ('to my house').

σπουδαῖον οὐδεν 'nothing serious', i.e. 'political'; cf. Letter 53.1.

φιλόλογα 'concerning literary matters'; but the word has a wide scope, covering philosophy, history, etc.

ad Baias See Letter 17.2.

ἐπισταθμείαν 'billeting'.

odiosam 'tiresome' ('a bore'). This does not refer to Caesar's company, but to the onus of entertaining such a guest. See beginning of letter.

dextra sinistra ad equum 'to the right and left of (Caesar's) horse' (*ad* = 'close beside'). A verb meaning 'rode' or 'marched' has to be supplied. This sounds like a precaution against a possible ambush. But Dolabella stood high in Caesar's favour, as indicated by his nomination to a consulship in the following year, so the gesture seems to have been a compliment.

LETTER 64 (*Att.* 13.42)

Although now on outwardly good terms with Quintus junior, Cicero considered him a scoundrel, unprincipled and unbalanced. Atticus seems to have been of much the same opinion.

1 καὶ μάλα sqq. Both these scraps of Greek ('right down in the mouth' and 'You there, why so pensive?') are in all probability from Menander.

bellum Caesar was preparing for a war against Parthia.

quae vis igitur? sc. *te cogit.*

et tamen i.e. 'in spite of all I have borrowed'.

avunculus Atticus.

tanti est sc. *ut mihi iratus sit.*

rem 'the thing itself' (marriage).

morem gesseris 'you will have pleased'.

2 diem meum sc. *natalem.*

3 Lepidus M. Aemilius Lepidus was Master of the Horse to the Dictator Caesar.

templum effandum The temple to be consecrated will have been that of Felicitas (Dio 44.5.2). *templum effari* is the technical term for the proclamation by Augurs of a piece of ground as an area from which auspices could be taken (*templum*).

μὴ σκόρδου sc. φάγω (partitive gen.); lit. 'so that I don't eat garlic'. There was a Greek proverb 'so that you don't eat garlic or beans', i.e. 'so that you don't sit on a jury or go to war'; for garlic, we are told, was eaten by soldiers going to battle as by cocks before a fight, and beans by jurors to keep themselves awake. The sense is: 'anything for a quiet life'.

LETTER 65 (*Fam.* 13.27)

Letter 20 shows how Cicero could write a letter of recommendation when he was really interested. Most of his *epistulae commendaticiae* are of a more routine character, written on behalf of persons of whom little or nothing else is known. This M. Aemilius Avianianus (an Avianius adopted by a M. Aemilius) was a resident of Sicyon, probably connected with the Avianii of Puteoli, with one of whom, the corn-factor M. Avianius Flaccus, Cicero had friendly relations of long standing.

After Pharsalia Ser. Sulpicius Rufus had retired to the island of Samos. But Caesar pardoned him, and in 46 made him governor of Achaia.

1 eodem exemplo 'with the same text' (see on Letter 48.1), i.e. 'duplicate'.

quod feci i.e. *gratias egi*.

vos 'you lawyers'.

de eadem re alio modo On this formula see A. H. J. Greenidge, *The legal procedure of Cicero's time* (1901; repr. New Jersey, 1971), p. 166: 'It was apparently a kind of introductory sentence...uttered by the parties for the purpose of safeguarding their future right of action by means of a new procedure, if the one adopted failed...the phrase seems to mean "by this, or whatever other mode of action is open to me, I assert my claim".'

2 unus est Clearly an exaggeration. If Aemilius had really been so intimate a friend, more would have been heard of him. Modern recommendations and testimonials are not always free from such overstatements.

plus prosis...mea In the Roman moral code a man of honour

8-2

(*vir bonus*) might do for his friends what he would scruple to do for himself; hence he might do for a friend's friends more than for his own.

3   quod commodo tuo fiat 'as far as you conveniently can'.

4   Servio See Letter 38.2. The son is called by his praenomen for the same reason as the father. Normally he would have been referred to by cognomen; see on Letter 17.1.

studio 'devotion to learning'. But *studium* is unusual in this sense, and *in me* could have dropped out after *singularique*.

LETTER 66 (*Att.* 14.1)

After Letter 63 there is a gap of more than three months in the correspondence with Atticus. It resumes with this letter nearly a month after Caesar's murder on 15 March 44. Cicero had taken leave of Atticus in Rome early on 7 April, when he set out for Campania. He spent the first night of his journey as the guest of C. Matius, a close friend of Caesar's and an old friend of his own.

1   tecum mane sc. *collocutus sum*.

nihil perditius sc. *illo* (i.e. *Matio*); cf. *Q.fr.* 3.7.1 *nihil est enim perditius his hominibus, his temporibus.* Matius prophesied doom, and with relish.

ille (line 2) Caesar.

tumultum Gallicum sc. *fore.* A native revolt was feared, also that the legions in Gaul might march on Rome. Neither happened.

non...abire 'it cannot all just pass quietly off'. Cf. Ter. *Andr.* 175 *mirabar hoc si sic abiret.*

Oppium C. Oppius, another of Caesar's intimates.

2   ne pigrere Best taken with *quaeso* rather than as = *noli pigrari.*

Sexto Pompey's younger son had survived Munda and was again at the head of an army in Spain.

magni refert Lit. 'it matters a great deal', here practically amounting to 'it's an important question' (*magna quaestio est*). Plutarch's Greek (*Vit. Brut.* 6) renders the sense well enough: 'I don't know what this young man wants, but whatever he wants, he wants badly.'

eum i.e. *Caesarem*. The same word below refers to Brutus, and then again to Caesar.

dixerit sc. *Brutus*. Cicero praises this speech in his *Brutus* (21), whereas in Tacitus' *Dialogue on orators* the spokesman for contemporary oratory disparages it as tedious and flat. Brutus favoured the plain, dry manner of Lysias, the so-called 'Atticizing' style. The speech seems to have been delivered in 47, when Caesar was returning to Rome after his victory at Zela. Deiotarus had supported Pompey in the Civil War.

Sesti rogatu The circumstances are unknown.

dubitem 'am I to doubt?' A so-called deliberative subjunctive used in questions.

facilis 'easy-going'.

ad propositum sc. *revertar*.

scribes In Latin the future indicative is often used in polite command, as sometimes in English, which, however, more often employs it for instructions from superior to inferior.

LETTER 67 *(Att.* 14.13B)

After Caesar's assassination his surviving colleague in the consulship, Mark Antony (M. Antonius), soon became the leading figure in Roman politics. Cicero was on nominally friendly terms with him, and remained so until the delivery of the First Philippic in September, though he increasingly disapproved of Antony's high-handed conduct. This letter concerns a former lieutenant of P. Clodius, who had been exiled in 52 for his part in the rioting which followed Clodius' murder. As such he was an enemy of Cicero, who had frequently vilified him in his speeches. His name was Sex. Cloelius (not Clodius, as it appears in editions etc. prior to 1961). Antony wanted to bring him back to Rome, but thought proper to ask Cicero's blessing in an extant letter *(Att.* 14.13A). Cicero's reply is unnecessarily fulsome, a tendency of his when writing to someone he disliked or distrusted but did not wish to offend. Later, after their quarrel, Antony read the letter out in the Senate, greatly to Cicero's embarrassment *(Phil.* 2.7ff.). Cicero's real sentiments are exposed in his letter to Atticus (14.13), to whom he sent copies of the correspondence: 'Mark Antony has written to me on the recall of Sex.

Cloelius, in how complimentary a style so far as concerns me personally you will see from his own letter, of which I enclose a copy; how unscrupulously, disgracefully, mischievously, so that one is sometimes tempted to wish Caesar back, you will readily appreciate...
As for me, I have shown myself all compliance to Antony. After all, having once made up his mind that he had a right to do what he pleased, he would have done it just the same if I had opposed.'

1   **fronte, ut aiunt** So in *Fam.* 1.9.17 *fronte atque vultu* and elsewhere.

  studio 'friendly disposition'. Antony later claimed to have been one of Cicero's disciples and a frequent visitor at his home, but Cicero denied it (*Phil.* 2.3).

  beneficio Antony, who was in charge of Italy during Caesar's absence in 48–47, claimed to have spared Cicero's life, and Cicero to some extent acknowledges the obligation in *Phil.* 2.5f.

2   **nullo negotio** 'without any trouble'.

3   **remitto** Of foregoing the right to punish at someone's intercession; cf. *Fam.* 5.10a.2 *meam animadversionem et supplicium...remitto tibi et condono*. Antony had placed the power to punish (i.e. continue punishing) Cloelius in Cicero's hands.

4   **puero Clodio** P. Clodius' son, also named P. Clodius Pulcher, was Antony's stepson.

  iis *is* is often used where English would use 'such'.

  si viveret...maneret Probably true. Cicero was generally ready to be friends with old enemies when circumstances changed.

5   **hoc a me dabis** 'You will give him this as coming from me.' *quoque* refers to Antony's letter, which had presented the matter in this light.

  aetas...aetate 'someone of my age from someone of his'.
  illud Anticipatory.

LETTER 68 (*Att.* 14.21)

Cicero arrived at his new property near Puteoli (inherited from the banker Cluvius) on 11 May.

1   **Lanuvii** Brutus and Cassius were now staying at Lanuvium. They

had been forced to leave Rome by the mob violence which broke out after Caesar's murder.

Eros A slave, perhaps of Philotimus, or freedman who was at this time looking after Cicero's financial affairs.

de re mea Dolabella owed Cicero money in respect of Tullia's dowry, which should have been returned after the divorce. *re = re familiari*, as often.

eas This was a fulsome letter of congratulation written by Cicero to Dolabella after the latter's suppression of some turbulent elements in Rome (Dolabella had succeeded Caesar as Consul). It is in both collections (*Att.* 14.17A = *Fam.* 9.14).

2   otium 'peace' (domestic) – according to Cicero, the Caesarians feared for the security of their gains unless they re-established their control by another war.

nosti...tectus The 'I know thee who thou art' construction is regular in Latin.

circumire Antony was touring Campania and the neighbourhood, whipping up support among Caesar's old soldiers who had been settled on the land there.

duumviri Magistrates of the Roman Colonies of Capua and Casilinum which Antony tried to refound (*Phil.* 2.102). Roman colonies were administered by two annually appointed magistrates corresponding to the Roman Consuls.

3   ad castra i.e. *ad bellum*.

illa res Caesar's assassination.

heredem Antony. I suspect that *regem sublatum* has fallen out of the text before *regni*; cf. *Att.* 14.14.2 *sublato enim tyranno tyrannida manere video*.

hoc...ponere A favourite quotation with Cicero, of unknown origin. The infinitives seem to be exclamatory.

ὑποσόλοικα 'somewhat incongruous'.

Ponti This Pontius will have been an otherwise unknown Pompeian, whose estate near Naples had been given or sold to Brutus' mother, Servilia. She had once, as generally believed, been Caesar's mistress.

'Cato maior' Otherwise known as *De senectute*.

ad te missus 'dedicated to you'.

βεβίωται 'I have had my time.' The Latin equivalent *victum est* seems not to have been used (perhaps because of possible confusion with *victum* from *vincere*), but *vivitur* occurs.

viderint iuvenes 'let the young men worry (look to it)', a common idiom; cf. *Fam.* 8.13.2 (Caelius) *quidnam rei publicae futurum sit...vos senes divites videritis.*

4 seu = *seu potius.*

apposita secunda mensa 'over dessert'; see Letter 48.1.

Vestorium A businessman of Puteoli with whom Cicero and Atticus had business and social dealings.

postridie Used instead of *cras* to suit the epistolary tenses. The writer's present and proximate future would be the reader's past.

cogitabam 'I am proposing (to dine)'.

Πεντέλοιπον This unintelligible nickname for Hirtius recurs in a neighbouring letter. It seems to have reference to his reputation as a gourmet or gourmand. The text may be corrupt in both places. παντόλειχον ('Lick-all') and πεντέλαιμον ('Five-gullet') have been suggested.

λῆρος πολύς 'A lot of nonsense!'

talaria The winged sandals of Mercury. *videre* = 'look to', hence 'get, procure', is mainly colloquial. Cicero was thinking of making a trip to Athens, where his son was being educated, and this would take him away from the new civil war which he saw brewing in Italy.

Octavi Under Caesar's will his great-nephew C. Octavius, the future emperor Augustus, was named as his adopted son and heir. Octavius was in Macedonia when Caesar died, and landed in Italy on 18 April to claim his inheritance.

tinniat 'chinks', i.e. is ready to pay his debt (the refund of Tullia's dowry).

an...fecerit 'or has declared a cancellation of debts in my particular case', with allusion to Dolabella's attempt to pass such legislation as Tribune in 47.

LETTER 69 (*Att.* 15.1*a*)

1 heri On *heri* in the manuscripts see on Letter 49.

Piliam Atticus' wife was staying at Cicero's villa near Cumae. He called on her there, and later they met again in the town.

Cn. Lucceius A friend of Brutus. A number of Lucceii appear in

Cumaean inscriptions as members of the local aristocracy. The corruption to *Lucullus* is found elsewhere, exemplifying the tendency of copyists to substitute a familiar name for one less familiar.

mansi 'I stayed the night.'

2 habitam in contione Capitolina On 16 March, the day after Caesar's murder. The speech in Appian (*B.c.* 2.137ff.) may be based on this published version. Note that *contio* can mean either a meeting or a speech delivered at a meeting.

ne ambitiose 'without currying favour', i.e. 'candidly'; cf. Cels. praef. 45 *sine ambitione verum scrutantibus* et sim. *ne* seems to be used carelessly for *non* because of *ut* preceding.

ὑπόθεσις 'theme'.

genere The 'Atticizing' style; see on Letter 66.2.

ὑπεραττικός ... Ἀττικώτατα 'too Attic ... impeccably Attic'; for the pun on Atticus' name see on Letter 6.5.

Δημοσθένους = *Demosthenis*.

fulmina So elsewhere of Demosthenes' oratory. Similarly a character in Aristophanes speaks of Pericles' 'thunder and lightning' (*Acharn.* 531).

et...dici Cicero makes the same point in *Orat.* 23.

Metrodorum The bearer. From the reference in *Fam.* 16.20 he seems to have been a physician, probably a freedman of Cicero's.

LETTER 70 (*Att.* 15.11)

The final section (4) is here omitted.

1 H. VI = *horam sextam* (noon).

Servilia, Tertulla, Porcia Respectively mother, half-sister, and wife of Brutus.

Favonius See on Letter 19.2.

curatione On 5 June the Senate at Antony's instigation charged Brutus and Cassius (both Praetors) with an extraordinary commission to procure grain overseas. Cicero considered it a petty, humiliating assignment, but none the less advised Brutus to accept it.

reliqui Take with *nihil* (= *reliquum*).

oculis Virtually = *vultu* ('expression').

Martem spirare So *Q.fr.* 3.4.6 Ἄρη πνέων; cf. Aesch. *Ag.* 375

Ἄρη πνεόντων (wrongly, perhaps, discredited by recent commentators) and Quint. Smyrn. 1.343 ἀναπνείοντες Ἄρηα.

egone...contumeliam? 'was I to take?' would normally be *acciperem*. The pluperfect may strengthen the objection: 'was it ever likely that I should take?'

atque 'to be sure, and what is more...'. This use of *atque* is found in comedy.

2 Decimumque D. Brutus, another leading conspirator. After Caesar's murder he left Rome to take over Cisalpine Gaul.

ad ea 'in reply'.

praeterita sc. *agere, ingerere* (cf. *Att.* 11.6.3 *sed ingero praeterita*). *actum ne agas* was a common phrase. Cicero went on to do exactly that.

locum 'topic, theme'.

quemquam Antony is meant. Cicero thought, or claimed to have thought (see Letter 74.1), that he should have been killed along with Caesar.

tua familiaris Servilia.

audivi sc. *dicentem*; cf. *Phil.* 2.17 *hoc vero ne P. quidem Clodius dixit umquam*. 'Well, upon my word! I never heard the like!'

pollicebatur This has often been noticed as an example of feminine influence on Roman public life. Servilia was probably relying on her contacts with Caesar's friends. As the decree seems to have already passed, some irregularity might be involved. Evidently it gave Brutus and Cassius other duties or status apart from the procurement of grain.

ludi The ludi Apollinares, running from 5 to 13 July, were Brutus' responsibility as City Praetor. Another Praetor, Antony's brother C. Antonius, actually presided in 43.

3 dempto = 'apart from'.

ἡ δεῦρ' ὁδὸς **sqq.** 'Prophet, what signifies your journey hither?' This line from an unknown play is quoted again in Letter 73.

evolare To Greece.

ubi...audiam See Letter 46.2.

LETTER 71 (*Att.* 15.16a)

Neither the place of origin (Astura or Arpinum? see below) nor the date is certain.

narro tibi 'Let me tell you.' Two other letters to Atticus begin in this way.

οἶκος φίλος From the proverb οἶκος φίλος, οἶκος ἄριστος (lit. 'Home is dear, home is best', i.e. 'East, west, home's best'). If the text is sound, the letter must have been written from Astura, the most secluded of Cicero's country houses; but why does he call the Tusculanum 'home'? The only answers seem to be that he had had it longer than his other villas (except the Arpinas, and perhaps the Formianum) and spent more time in it, or that it was near Rome. 'Home' for Cicero would naturally mean Arpinum. To make it mean that here we should need to read *et* for *sed* and transpose *itaque...Tusculanum* after the following sentence.

ῥωπογραφία Perhaps 'landscape-painting' with reference to wooded scenery (ῥῶψ = 'shrub'). There were dense woods at Astura. *ripulae* will refer to the coast, though Horace is the first writer to use *ripa* for *litus*. On the other hand, if Cicero wrote from Arpinum, he meant the bank of the river Fibrenus, which ran through his property.

Prognostica Cicero's verse translation of a section of Aratus' poem on astronomy concerning weather signs. The relevant lines are quoted in *Divin.* 1.15.

ῥητορεύουσιν 'are speechifying'.

LETTER 72 (*Att.* 15.27)

Cicero finally set out for Athens, though in the event he got no further than Syracuse. The letter, written at dinner (see the end) after receipt of a letter from Atticus, was probably dispatched the next morning.

1 pridie 'the day before (I received your letter)', i.e., in terms of the time of writing, 'yesterday'.

πάνυ φιλοστόργως 'in most affectionate terms'.

humane sc. *facit*. Sestius wanted to take leave of Cicero in person.

2 praeclare sc. *fecisti*.

congrediendi In Greece.

de gloria This lost work appeared in two books (*Off.* 2.31), but seems to have originally been written in one.

'Ηρακλείδειον 'à la Héraclide'. Heraclides of Pontus, a pupil of Plato, wrote tracts, often in dialogue form, on a wide variety of subjects. The work Cicero had in mind was a justification of Caesar's murder (*Att.* 15.4.3), cast in the form of a dialogue in which the author would take no part (*Att.* 13.19.4). Apparently it remained unwritten.

3 Planco L. Plotius Plancus, a former supporter of Caesar. Atticus had asked Cicero to use his influence with him in a matter affecting the town of Buthrotum near his own estate in Epirus.

Attica Atticus seems to have forgotten to give her Cicero's love.

quod...fecisti This cannot be elucidated.

Herode Herodes was an Athenian friend of Atticus, a man of letters and of good social standing, who was keeping an eye on young M. Cicero. Nothing is known of 'Metius' (Mettius or Maecius?).

turpem Atticus must have mentioned some new piece of misconduct on the part of Quintus junior.

αὐτῇ βουλύσει 'just as the shadows fall'. βούλυσις (βουλυτός is the usual form) lit. = 'the unyoking of the oxen'.

cenantibus See on Letter 48.1.

LETTER 73 (*Att.* 16.6)

By 25 July Cicero had reached Vibo Valentia in modern Calabria. Sicca, an old friend (see Letter 8) had property in the area.

1 prodromi 'forerunners', northerly winds supposed to blow for about seven days before the rising of the Dog Star, which was followed by the Etesians.

opportune sc. *accidit*.

pedibus Ropes attached to the sails in order to set them to the wind. When there was no wind (or when the ship was running straight before the wind) they would be drawn out at equal lengths.

Talnam Juventius Talna, a friend of Cicero's. Atticus had been interested in his son as a possible match for his own daughter. *Testam* (Préchac) would be C. Trebatius Testa, who had a house in Velia mentioned by Cicero in a contemporary letter to Trebatius himself (*Fam.* 7.20); but he does not say that he was staying in it.

obduxi Probably = *consumpsi*. Cf. *obducere* ('swallow') *potionem* et sim.

δολιχὸν sqq. 'pondering a lengthy voyage' (*Od.* 3.169).

corbita A large, slow cargo-ship.

actuariolis 'rowing-boats'. Leucopetra Tarentinorum is modern Capo S. Maria di Leuca at the end of the heel of Italy.

2 ἡ δεῦρ' ὁδὸς sqq. See Letter 70.3.

ocellos 'gems'. In *Nat. deor.* 3.91 Cicero calls Corinth and Carthage *duo illos oculos orae maritimae*; cf. Catull. 31.1 *paene insularum, Sirmio, insularumque | ocelle.*

ad ipsum sc. *periculum.*

in caelum ferri 'is enthusiastically approved' ('praised to the skies').

ita si 'with the proviso that'.

ista 'things in Rome'.

3 reliqua 'balances due'. These could be used to clear off the debts (*nomina*).

Cluviano 'the Cluvius property', at Puteoli. Cicero had bought out the other heirs.

Publilio See on Letter 58.1. Publilia's dowry had to be repaid to him.

iure non utimur 'we are not standing on our legal rights'.

Terentiae sc. *satis fieri me velle.* Her dowry too had to be repaid.

in Epirum sc. *ire cogitas.*

satis dato A legal term, denoting the giving of security for a loan. If it was not repaid, the security would be forfeit. The impersonal abl. abs. is like *sortito* ('by lot').

4 de gloria See on Letter 72.2.

tertio i.e. of the final edition of the *Academica* in four books.

σύγγραμμα 'treatise'.

desecabis...adglutinabis An ancient book was made up of sheets of papyrus glued together.

LETTER 74 (*Fam.* 12.3)

By early October M. Brutus and Cassius were on their way to the East, which they soon succeeded in taking over. But when this letter

was written, shortly after 2 October (sec. 2), Cassius may still have
been in south Italy. It reflects the situation after the delivery in the
Senate of Cicero's First Philippic on 2 September and Antony's
furious reply on the 19th.

1   **tuus amicus** Antony. Cassius had dined with him three days
after Caesar's murder.

   statua We do not hear elsewhere of this.

   inscripsit i.e., had it inscribed.

   molestus...esset Cicero often claims that, if the matter had
rested with him, Antony would have gone the same way as Caesar
(cf. Letters 68.3, 70.2). In fact, as a letter of 9 April (*Att.* 14.3.2)
goes to show, he seems at first to have been no more alive to Antony's
dangerous potentialities than were other people.

   vestrum 'your (i.e. yours and Brutus') affair'.

2   **illorum** Antony and his associates.

   Cannutio Ti. Cannutius, a Tribune hostile to Antony. According
to Varro (Gell. 13.12.6), Tribunes did not have the right to summon
anybody, but were commonly believed to have it and exercised it,
even to the extent of summoning a Consul to the Rostra. Antony may
of course have been willing to make the speech for his own reasons.

   turpissime...discessit 'came off most ignominiously', i.e.
spoke badly and was badly received.

   legato tuo Cassius had been appointed governor of Cyrene. The
names of his Legates are unknown.

   interpretari 'infer'.

LETTER 75 (*Att.* 16.9)

Cicero left Rome again some time after Antony departed for Brundisium on 9 October to meet Caesarian legions newly arrived from
Macedonia.

1   **binae** See on Letter 31.1 (*unas*).

   Octaviano Now in Campania, raising a force against Antony
from Caesar's veterans who had settled in the area.

   cui sc. *rescripsi.*

   non posse Dolabella had left for his province of Syria. If the remaining Consul, Antony, was in Rome, only he could convoke a meeting.

σκήπτομαι 'play for time'.

Pansa C. Vibius Pansa, former Caesarian and Consul-Elect.

ἀριστεία 'star performance'.

Brutum This must be D. Brutus in Cisalpine Gaul. The praenomen may have dropped out of the text. Cicero means that D. Brutus would join forces against Antony, if Octavian convinced him of his good faith.

centuriat 'is forming companies (*centuriae*)'.

dinumerat 'is paying out bounties'.

LETTER 76 (*Fam.* 12.22)

Q. Cornificius, poet and orator, was governor of the old Roman province of Africa (*Africa vetus*, part of modern Tunisia) by senatorial appointment. The exact date of this letter is doubtful, perhaps soon after 2 October (see below).

1   homine gladiatore 'gladiator-fellow'. *homo*, like ἀνήρ in Greek, added to nouns gives a contemptuous or pitying modulation.

collega Antony, Cicero, and Cornificius were all Augurs.

etiam Antony used words as well as weapons.

contionatur Perhaps with reference to Antony's speech on 2 October (see foregoing letter).

nunc *nunc* (abbreviated *n̄c̄*) is often confused with *non* (*n̄ō*). The change is necessary here because Cicero was not able to make any prediction at this time (sec. 2 *quid futurum sit, plane nescio*).

2   tyrannoctoni M. Brutus and Cassius.

longe gentium 'at the end of the world', an idiomatic expression.

illud profecto sc. *faciam*, if the text is sound. But I suspect that Cicero wrote something like *quid superest? illud profecto: quod potero* sqq.

LETTER 77 (*Fam.* 10.3)

L. Munatius Plancus was governor of northern Gaul (conquered by Caesar) with a large army under his command. His role in the coming war would necessarily be important. Cicero could write to him as an

old family friend, though one of Plancus' brothers, T. Munatius
Plancus Bursa (see Letter 55.2), was one of his pet aversions.

1 Furnium C. Furnius, Cicero's friend and supporter of long
standing, now Legate to Plancus. He had a long and distinguished
career ahead of him.

videre So to Cornificius (*Fam.* 12.30.3) *vultus mehercule tuos mihi
expressit omnes, non solum animum ac verba pertulit. audire* (the confusion
is found elsewhere) would mean that Furnius sounded like Plancus
talking about himself!

ignotam *ignarus* (see critical note) in a passive sense ('unknown')
occurs only once in classical Latin, Sall. *Iug.* 18.6.

quae...fuit 'all of which I heard with pleasure, the last item with
gratitude as well' – a good illustration of the difference between the
two adjectives.

2 studio...tuo 'by my desire and your choice'.

nemini...esse 'who does not allow that any man take priority
with you in virtue of old association'. *ut* would be easier than *qui*,
which seems due to a false analogy with such sentences as *Tusc.* 1.30
nemo omnium tam sit immanis cuius mentem non imbuerit deorum opinio.

3 sed...posses 'But, perceiving your sentiments as I did, I considered that you took a realistic view of your power to influence events.'

designatus Plancus and D. Brutus had been designated by Caesar
as Consuls in 42.

unus...gloriam 'To glory there is only one path...good states-
manship.'

4 fontibus Teachers and books; cf. *Arch.* 14 *illa quidem certe quae
summa sunt ex quo fonte hauriam sentio. nam nisi multorum praeceptis
multisque litteris mihi ab adulescentia suasissem nihil esse in vita magno opere
expetendum nisi laudem atque honestatem...numquam me pro salute vestra in
tot ac tantas dimicationes...abiecissem.*

tantum 'just so much'.

LETTER 78 (*Fam.* 9.24)

The west wind (Favonius = Zephyrus) was supposed to start
blowing about 8 February, so that this letter was probably written
in January (cf. sec. 2 fin.).

1 Rufum He cannot be identified. Rufus is perhaps the most common of Roman cognomina.

missis Paetus seems to have sent Cicero a letter from Rufus shortly before the journey mentioned below, in which Rufus expressed concern for Cicero's safety.

et Aquini et Fabrateriae The two towns, Aquinum and Fabrateria Nova, lay along the road between Puteoli and Arpinum. Which of Cicero's journeys between these places is referred to has not been made out with certainty. In *Phil.* 12.20 Cicero alludes to an abortive attempt on his life by Antony's brother Lucius.

inaudisse 'got some inkling'.

iis *is* or *ille* is sometimes used instead of a reflexive pronoun in a subordinate clause when the clause on which that clause depends is itself subordinate, with its verb in the subjunctive or in accusative and infinitive construction. So here *quam...futurus* depends on *quasi divinarent*, which in turn depends on *nihil aliud egerunt*.

2 Spurinna The *haruspex* who warned Caesar of the plot against his life. The name is Etruscan.

3 quam Graeci sc. *faciant* or *iudicent*. Cicero makes the same point in his *De senectute* (45), which he published in the previous year.

συμπόσια aut σύνδειπνα sc. *vocant*. The Latin explanations are likely to be a marginal note (gloss) which has found its way into the text. A resident of Greek-speaking Naples like Paetus would not have needed them.

4 praeclare...putem 'I should consider myself truly fortunate in my destiny'.

etiam atque etiam 'once again'; see above, *cura ut valeas*.

LETTER 79 *(Fam. 7.22)*

The date is uncertain, but the three preceding letters in the manuscript series, likewise to Trebatius, belong to the summer of 44.

antea i.e. prior to the heir's taking possession of the estate, but after the death of the testator. During this period the property was legally ownerless. A theft committed during the testator's lifetime was actionable.

furti...agere 'take action for theft'.

caput 'section', with reference to the eighteen books *De iure civili* by Q. Scaevola the Pontifex.

notavi Probably 'marked' (the copying would be done by a clerk).

sensisse 'held'. This use is common in the jurists, though not confined to them.

Sex. Aelium sqq. Sex. Aelius Paetus Catus (Cos. 198), M'. Manilius (Cos. 149), and his contemporary M. Junius Brutus were all eminent jurists.

Testae i.e. Trebatius himself (C. Trebatius Testa).

APPENDIXES

I ROMAN DATES

Until Julius Caesar reformed the calendar the Roman year consisted of 355 days divided into twelve months, all of which bore the Latin forms of their present names except Quintilis (= July) and Sextilis (= August). Each month had 29 days, except February with 28 and March, May, July, and October with 31. The first, fifth and thirteenth days of each month were called the Kalends (*Kalendae*), Nones (*Nonae*), and Ides (*Idus*) respectively, except that in March, May, July, and October the Nones fell on the seventh and the Ides on the fifteenth. Dates in classical Latin are expressed by the number of days before the next forthcoming Nones or Ides or Kalends, whichever is nearest, prefaced by *a. d. = ante diem*. Thus *a. d. IIII Non. Ian.* (*ante diem quartum Nonas Ianuarias*) is the fourth day before the Nones of January, i.e., by inclusive reckoning, 2 January. The accusative after *ante* seems to have arisen through misunderstanding; *die tertio ante Nonas* would be logical. A date immediately before one of the three pivotal days is usually expressed by *prid.* (= *pridie*), though *a. d. II* also occurs.

To convert into modern dates: (*a*) If the point of reference is the Nones or Ides, subtract the number in the Roman date from the modern date of these Nones or Ides and add 1, as in the example above. (*b*) If the point of reference is the Kalends, subtract the number in the Roman date from the number of days in the *current* Roman month (i.e. the month preceding the one in the Roman date) and add 2: e.g. *a. d. XIII Kal. Nov.* = 20 October ($31 - 13 + 2$).

The calendar was adjusted by means of 'intercalation'. At the discretion of the College of Pontiffs, usually every other year, an 'intercalary' month of 23 or 22 days was inserted after

24 or 23 February. But in the years immediately before the Civil War the College neglected this procedure, so that by 46 the calendar was well over two months in advance of the sun. Julius Caesar rectified the situation by inserting two 'intercalary' months totalling 67 days between November and December of that year in addition to the traditional one in February. He also gave the months their present numbers of days, thus almost obviating the need for future intercalations, though in 1582 a further discrepancy had to be met by the institution of a Leap-Year.

II ROMAN MONEY

The normal unit of reckoning was the sesterce (HS), though the denarius, equal to 4 sesterces, was the silver coin most generally in use. Differences of price structure make any transposition into modern currency misleading, but very roughly HS 20 may be taken as equivalent to the debased pound sterling of 1979. Sometimes sums are expressed in Athenian currency. The drachma was about equal to the denarius, the mina (100 drachmae) to HS 400, and the talent (60 minae) to HS 2,400. The Asiatic cistophorus was worth about 4 drachmae.

III ROMAN NAMES

A Roman bore the name of his clan (*gens*), the *nomen* or *nomen gentilicium*, usually ending in -*ius*, preceded by a personal name (*praenomen*) and often followed by a *cognomen*, which might distinguish different families in the same *gens*: e.g. Marcus Tullius Cicero. The *nomen* was always, and the *cognomen* usually, hereditary. Sometimes, as when a family split into branches, an additional *cognomen* was taken: e.g. Publius Licinius Crassus Dives. Other additional *cognomina* were honorific, sometimes taken from a conquered country as Africanus or Numidicus, or adoptive (see below). Women generally had only the one clan-name (e.g. Tullia), which they retained after marriage.

Only a few personal names were in use and they are generally abbreviated as follows: A. = Aulus; Ap(p). = Appius; C. = Gaius; Cn. = Gnaeus; D. = Decimus; L. = Lucius; M. = Marcus; M'. = Manius; N. = Numerius; P. = Publius; Q. = Quintus; Ser. = Servius; Sex. = Sextus; Sp. = Spurius; T. = Titus; Ti. = Tiberius (I omit one or two which do not occur in our text). The use of a *praenomen* by itself in address or reference is generally a sign of close intimacy, whether real or affected, but in the case of a rare or distinctive praenomen, as Appius and Servius, this is not so.

The practice of adoption, of males at any rate, was very common in Rome. According to traditional practice the adopted son took his new father's full name and added his old *nomen gentilicium* with the adjectival termination *-anus* instead of *-ius*: e.g. C. Octavius, adopted by C. Julius Caesar, became C. Julius Caesar Octavianus. But in Cicero's time the practice had become variable. Sometimes the original name remained in use. See my monograph, *Two studies in Roman nomenclature* (American classical studies 3 (1976)), part II.

A slave had only one name, and since many slaves came from the East, this was often Greek. If freed, he took his master's *praenomen* and *nomen*, adding his slave-name as a *cognomen*: e.g. Tiro, when freed by M. Tullius Cicero, became M. Tullius Tiro. Occasionally the *praenomen* might be some-body else's. Atticus' slave Dionysius became M. Pomponius Dionysius in compliment to Cicero (instead of Titus).

Much the same applied to Greek or other provincials on gaining Roman citizenship. Such a man retained his former name as a *cognomen* and acquired the *praenomen* and *nomen* of the person to whom he owed the grant: e.g. the philosopher Cratippus became M. Tullius Cratippus after Cicero had got Caesar to give him the citizenship.

CONCORDANCES

1	*Att.* 1.5	28	*Fam.* 9.25	54	*Fam.* 16.18
2	*Att.* 1.11	29	*Fam.* 15.6	55	*Fam.* 9.10
3	*Att.* 1.2	30	*Att.* 6.6	56	*Att.* 12.15
4	*Fam.* 5.1	31	*Fam.* 16.5	57	*Att.* 12.16
5	*Fam.* 5.2	32	*Att.* 7.4	58	*Att.* 12.32
6	*Att.* 1.13	33	*Att.* 7.10	59	*Fam.* 9.11
7	*Att.* 2.14	34	*Fam.* 14.18	60	*Att.* 13.10
8	*Att.* 3.3	35	*Fam.* 7.27	61	*Att.* 13.16
9	*Fam.* 14.2	36	*Att.* 8.1	62	*Att.* 13.33a
10	*Att.* 3.13	37	*Att.* 8.13	63	*Att.* 13.52
11	*Att.* 4.3	38	*Att.* 9.18	64	*Att.* 13.42
12	*Q.fr.* 2.4	39	*Fam.* 14.7	65	*Fam.* 13.27
13	*Att.* 4.5	40	*Att.* 11.4	66	*Att.* 14.1
14	*Att.* 4.12	41	*Att.* 11.5	67	*Att.* 14.13B
15	*Fam.* 5.12	42	*Fam.* 14.12	68	*Att.* 14.21
16	*Att.* 4.10	43	*Fam.* 14.20	69	*Att.* 15.1a
17	*Q.fr.* 2.9	44	*Fam.* 9.1	70	*Att.* 15.11
18	*Fam.* 7.1	45	*Fam.* 9.18	71	*Att.* 15.16a
19	*Q.fr.* 2.10	46	*Fam.* 7.28	72	*Att.* 15.27
20	*Fam.* 7.5	47	*Fam.* 6.14	73	*Att.* 16.6
21	*Fam.* 7.6	48	*Fam.* 9.26	74	*Fam.* 12.3
22	*Att.* 4.15	49	*Fam.* 9.23	75	*Att.* 16.9
23	*Att.* 5.1	50	*Fam.* 7.4	76	*Fam.* 12.22
24	*Fam.* 13.1	51	*Fam.* 7.26	77	*Fam.* 10.3
25	*Att.* 5.14	52	*Fam.* 5.16	78	*Fam.* 9.24
26	*Fam.* 15.1	53	*Fam.* 15.18	79	*Fam.* 7.22
27	*Fam.* 2.12				

EPISTULAE AD ATTICUM

1.2	3	3.3	8	4.12	14
1.5	1	3.13	10	4.15	22
1.11	2	4.3	11	5.1	23
1.13	6	4.5	13	5.14	25
2.14	7	4.10	16	6.6	30

7.4	32	12.16	57	14.13B	67
7.10	33	12.32	58	14.21	68
8.1	36	13.10	60	15.1a	69
8.13	37	13.16	61	15.11	70
9.18	38	13.33a	62	15.16a	71
11.4	40	13.42	64	15.27	72
11.5	41	13.52	63	16.6	73
12.15	56	14.1	66	16.9	75

EPISTULAE AD FAMILIARES

2.12	27	7.28	46	13.1	24
5.1	4	9.1	44	13.27	65
5.2	5	9.10	55	14.2	9
5.12	15	9.11	59	14.7	39
5.16	52	9.18	45	14.12	42
6.14	47	9.23	49	14.18	34
7.1	18	9.24	78	14.20	43
7.4	50	9.25	28	15.1	26
7.5	20	9.26	48	15.6	29
7.6	21	10.3	77	15.18	53
7.22	79	12.3	74	16.5	31
7.26	51	12.22	76	16.18	54
7.27	35				

EPISTULAE AD QUINTUM FRATREM

2.4	12	2.9	17	2.10	19

INDEXES TO THE COMMENTARY

References are by letter and section

I. *Proper names*

III. *General*

Printed in the United States
824100004B